THE ECUMENICAL MOMENT

Crisis and Opportunity for the Church

by

GEOFFREY WAINWRIGHT

Grand Rapids
WILLIAM B. EERDMANS PUBLISHING COMPANY

Library of Congress Cataloging in Publication Data
Wainwright, Geoffrey, 1939–
The ecumenical moment.

1. Christian union. I. Title.
BX8.2.W34   1983   270.8'2   83-8934
ISBN 0-8028-1979-6

CONTENTS

PREFACE

After an upbringing in English village Methodism, all my adult life as a Christian has been spent in ecumenical contexts. In this way I have studied, ministered, taught, and prayed, whether in Great Britain, continental Europe, equatorial Africa, or North America. The reflections gathered in this book stem from the second of two decades in active commitment to the cause of Christian unity. Their publication now corresponds to my increasing sense that the Church stands before a moment of critical opportunity, a *kairos* which includes a *krisis*.

My thanks are due to Jon Pott, Charles Van Hof, Milton Essenburg, and Sandra Nowlin for their technical help in bringing about this book. I dedicate the book in friendship to Raymond E. Brown, my colleague in Faith and Order and at Union Theological Seminary.

GEOFFREY WAINWRIGHT

New York, New York
Easter Eve 1983

vii

I
THE ECUMENICAL MOMENT

I. GLOBAL CRISIS

The state of global crisis can no longer be in doubt, and not only because the end of another millennium approaches. Along the East-West axis we are threatened by a totally destructive war. On the North-South axis we face the widening inequalities between the rich and the poor. As long as this world lasts, the Church must bear witness to it of the justice and peace which she knows from the deep, abiding, and definitive kingdom of God and which should find at least a provisional, fragmentary, and outward expression in the political realm.[1] "As long as this world lasts": respect for God's transcendent sovereignty over history should make believers wary of equating the results of human folly with "the End of the world"—as though humanity could, by continuing in sin, force grace to abound; as though the Parousia could, paradoxically, be compelled to occur. Yet any measure of responsible human cooperation claimed in the construction of God's kingdom must be matched by a corresponding assumption of responsibility for human works which may end in self-destruction.[2]

It was, I suggest, a presentiment, first, of this universalization of horizons, and then of this urgent confrontation with a destiny-deciding crisis—both marks of scriptural apocalyptic—which inspired the modern ecumenical movement. One of its pioneers, the American Methodist John R. Mott, spoke in 1900 with prophetic impatience of "the evangelization of the world in this generation."[3] It was a "world missionary conference" at Edinburgh in 1910 which became the conventional starting date of the ecumenical movement; and the

1

resultant International Missionary Council would eventually, in 1961, become part of the World Council of Churches. Meanwhile, any overly facile optimism had been immediately shaken by the "great war" between ostensibly Christian nations. After the first world war, Life and Work arose to bring the Churches together internationally in the area of "practical Christianity." The formation of the WCC having been delayed by the second world war, the political and economic concerns of Life and Work were then taken up on the Church and Society side of the new body that came into existence at Amsterdam in 1948. After Vatican II the Roman Catholic Church cooperated closely with the WCC in the areas of justice and peace. According to Romans 14:17, justice and peace are joined by "joy in the Holy Spirit" as characteristics of God's kingdom; and since the 1920s Faith and Order has been striving for unity in worship and in sacramental communion among the Churches, with Roman Catholics having more recently become full participants with the founding Protestants and Orthodox in that commission of the WCC. The Faith and Order Commission is in fact the principal instrument for implementing the constitutional aim of the World Council: to help the Churches advance to "visible unity in one faith and in one eucharistic fellowship." Only so will the Churches be able, as the membership basis of the WCC puts it, "to fulfil their common calling to the glory of the one God, Father, Son and Holy Spirit."[4]

One rejoices that otherwise divided Christians sometimes cooperate in political and social action intended as loving service to the neighbor in need. Indeed, liturgical, doctrinal, and constitutional unity would be a sham without an ethical counterpart. Yet the primary purpose of harmony among Christians remains doxology: "May the God of steadfastness and encouragement grant you to live in such harmony with one another, in accord with Christ Jesus, that with one mind you may with one voice glorify the God and Father of our Lord Jesus Christ. Welcome one another, therefore, as Christ has welcomed you, for the glory of God" (Rom. 15:5-7). Such unity among believers, grounded in the reconciliation between God and humanity proclaimed in the gospel, is the condition of people's coming to the faith. The ecumenical motto, *ut omnes unum sint*, picks up the Savior's prayer: "I do not pray for these only, but also for those who believe in me through their word, *that they all may be one*; even as thou, Father, art in me, and I in thee, that they also may be one in us, *so that the world may believe that thou hast sent me*" (John 17:21f.). As the word of faith is authentically spoken by a united company of believers, so "grace extends to more and more people" and the chorus of "thanksgiving may increase, to the glory of God" (2 Cor. 4:13-15). Then, at least, all are given the opportunity to arrive freely at the day when "at the name of Jesus, every knee will bow, and every tongue confess that Jesus Christ is Lord, to the glory of God the Father" (Phil. 2:11f.).

II. CHURCH AND SPIRIT

We can praise God together only *in truth*; and this doxological unity-in-truth must take *visible shape*. These two themes coalesce in the next chapter of this book, which is foundational to everything that then follows. It is no accident that the occasion of its writing was an Orthodox celebration of the sixteenth centennial of the Council of Constantinople (381). "Orthodoxy" allows a word-play on "right worship" and "right doctrine." A great contribution of the Eastern Orthodox Churches to the modern ecumenical movement has been their insistence on the "right doctrine" which is expressed in "right worship." With their strong awareness of a unified patristic heritage, they have sometimes enabled Roman Catholics and classical Protestants to go back behind the Western distortions and counter-distortions to join with themselves at a place where differing theological voices can be combined in a symphony without disrupting the unity of the faith. The presence of the Orthodox in the WCC and in National Councils of Churches has become particularly important in recent years as a counter to the liberal Protestant tendency which would minimize questions of doctrine. It is thanks in no small degree to the Orthodox participants that the next major project of the WCC Commission on Faith and Order aims "Towards the Common Expression of the Apostolic Faith Today," and that the ground-plan of this enter-

prise is provided by the Niceno-Constantinopolitan Creed.[5]
This theme has been incorporated into the program of the
Roman Catholic Bishops' Conferences and the Conference
of European Churches for the third European Ecumenical
Encounter in 1984. In theological discussions it is interesting, too, that many from the Churches of the third world, for
all their difficulty with the "Greek" terminology, find themselves closer *in faith* to the Churches which value the ancient creed than they are to Western liberals who, despite
their profession of solidarity with the poor, often sit lightly
to the creedal formulations.

The ancient creeds confess God as the maker of a world
for whose redemption the Son assumed human being and
died. The doctrines of creation, the incarnation, and the cross
are the ultimate basis for all Christian action on behalf of the
distressed. They also ground the nature of the Church's unity.
That unity properly takes costly, concrete form. It is sometimes argued that a kind of "spiritual" unity is sufficient
among Christians. It is true that verbal and institutional unity
would be a mere façade without unity of heart and mind.
But spiritual unity and visible unity are not truly alternatives: the alternative to visible unity is visible *dis*unity, and
that is a witness against the gospel. The Holy Spirit who
unites Christians in the bond of peace is the Spirit of the
Father who rests upon the Son; who is sent by the Father at
the prayer of the Son; and who with the Father and the Son
together is worshipped and glorified. As the Spirit of our
Maker and Redeemer, the Holy Spirit presses us to manifest
unity. So much needs to be said to charismatics who neglect
the institutional Church. With that proviso, the many signs
of pneumatic and pentecostal renewal in our century are to
be welcomed. For it is not by flesh and blood that people
are enabled to confess Jesus as the Christ, the Son of the
living God (see Matt. 16:16f.). The Father seeks those who
will worship him in Spirit and in truth (John 4:23f.): the
Spirit of truth reveals the truth as it is in Jesus; the life-giving
Spirit quickens the churchly body of Christ; the Spirit by
whom we live is the Spirit by whom we also walk in the
way of Christ. That is why the chapter "Church and Spirit"
precedes all our more detailed ecclesiological considerations.

III. THE LIMA TEXT

Questions of baptism, eucharist, and the ordained ministry
have occupied much of our attention in the Faith and Order
movement. In the nature of the case, rites by their symbolic
character bring to concentrated expression many issues in
the doctrine and self-understanding of the Churches. It is
here that divisions among Christians have arisen, sharpened,
and been perpetuated; it is from these points that healing
impulses may in turn spread throughout the Christian body.
From the first World Conference on Faith and Order at Lausanne in 1927, baptism, the Lord's Supper, and ministry have
figured on the ecumenical agenda. In January 1982, at Lima
in Peru, I was privileged to preside over the establishment
of the final text of *Baptism, Eucharist, and Ministry*, unan-
imously judged by the plenary Faith and Order Commission
to be ripe for transmission to the Churches which had called
for it.[6] The Churches now have before them a text on which
they are respectfully asked to decide "at the highest appropriate level of authority

> —the extent to which your church can recognize in this
> text the faith of the Church through the ages;
> —the consequences your church can draw from this text
> for its relations and dialogues with other churches, par-
> ticularly with those churches which also recognize the
> text as an expression of the apostolic faith;
> —the guidance your church can take from this text for its
> worship, educational, ethical, and spiritual life and
> witness."

The opportunity is unprecedented. Never has such a wide
range of Churches had the opportunity explicitly to own such
a broad measure of agreement on these matters. We stand
before a "significant theological convergence which Faith
and Order has discerned and formulated" (so the preface to
the Lima text). From many different points of departure, responsible Orthodox, Catholic, Lutheran, Reformed, Baptist,
Anglican, Methodist, Disciples, and Pentecostal theologians
have, over three generations and with increasing participation from Africa and Asia, elaborated a document which comes

as close as we are historically likely to come to substantial and practical agreement on the stated themes.

Compared with bilateral dialogues between confessions, the significant thing about this multilateral process and achievement is that it is impossible to avoid the "awkward" partner in favor of a more immediately congenial discussant. The Lima text does not state matters exactly as any one of us, as individuals or as denominations, would have done, had we been working on our own. That is precisely the point: people starting from a variety of traditions and marked by a series of different historical controversies have discovered a common reading of the Scriptures and of the early tradition which would allow a tolerably agreed understanding and practice in the present time.[7] The Lima text is a mature fruit of the biblical, patristic, liturgical, and ecumenical movements of the twentieth century that have provided the Churches with a vocabulary and concepts within the framework of which they can attain consensus: it is now the time to pass to the deeds of greater mutual recognition and ever increasing sacramental and structural unity. Who knows whether other forces may not break the understanding apart? Now is the time to solidify and deepen the agreement, for the sake of a united confession and practice before God and the world.

The road from Lausanne to Lima is described in chapter III of this book. There baptism, or in a more complex way Christian initiation, is the chosen example. It would have been possible to retrace a similar route for the Lord's Supper and for ministry. Instead, those themes are treated in a more synthetic manner in chapters IV and V (eucharist) and VI (orders), which themselves exemplify the same ecumenical milieu of reflection as that from which the Faith and Order texts have sprung.

IV. THE LORD'S SUPPER

With regard to the eucharist, the great breakthrough has been the recovery of the biblical and patristic notion of memorial (anamnesis). Thanks to the work of such various scholars as Odo Casel (Roman Catholic),[8] Joachim Jeremias (Lutheran),[9] and Max Thurian (Reformed),[10] the Western Churches are rediscovering the ancient and Eastern sense of the liturgy, and of the eucharist in particular, as that which—without repetition of the historically irreversible—puts succeeding generations of believers in mysterious touch with the original events of redemptive history on which our salvation depends; and that which—by means of symbolic participation— allows us already to join in the worship and life of heaven which is the goal of earthly existence.[11]

The Lima text locates the eucharist in that comprehensive panorama of reality which stretches, with the classical creeds, from "God the Father almighty, maker of heaven and earth" to "the resurrection of the dead and the life of the world to come." The Lord's Supper is there perceived, first, as "thanksgiving to the Father" ("the great sacrifice of praise by which the Church speaks on behalf of the whole creation"); second, as "anamnesis or memorial of Christ" ("the living and effective sign of his sacrifice, accomplished once and for all on the cross and still operative on behalf of all humankind"); third, as "invocation of the Spirit" ("The Church prays to the Father for the gift of the Holy Spirit in order that the eucharistic event may be a reality: the real presence of the crucified and risen Christ giving his life for all humanity"); fourth, as "communion of the faithful" ("The eucharistic communion with Christ who nourishes the life of the Church is at the same time communion within the body of Christ which is the Church"); and finally, fifth, as "meal of the kingdom" ("The eucharist opens up the vision of the divine rule which has been promised as the final renewal of all creation, and is a foretaste of it").

Yet all this is threatened as long as Christians, and indeed all humanity, remain disunited:

> Through the eucharist the all-renewing grace of God penetrates and restores human personality and dignity. The eucharist involves the believer in the central event of the world's history. As participants in the eucharist, therefore, we prove inconsistent if we are not actively participating in this ongoing restoration of the world's situation and the human condition. The eucharist shows us that our behavior is inconsistent in face of the re-

conciling presence of God in human history: we are placed under continual judgment by the persistence of unjust relationships of all kinds in our society, the manifold divisions on account of human pride, material interest and power politics and, above all, the obstinacy of unjustifiable confessional oppositions within the body of Christ. (§ 20)

As it becomes one people, sharing the meal of the one Lord, the eucharistic assembly must be concerned for gathering also those who are at present beyond its visible limits, because Christ invited to his feast all for whom he died. Insofar as Christians cannot unite in full fellowship around the same table to eat the same loaf and drink from the same cup, their missionary witness is weakened at both the individual and the corporate levels. (§ 26)

V. CONCILIARITY AND UNITY

The ability to share together at the Lord's table is the most concentrated sacramental test of Christian unity. But that cannot be separated from another aspect of visibility, which is the structures by which ecclesial life is ordered, by which pastoral and doctrinal decisions are taken, and by which Christian communities are networked together. That is why chapter V joins the themes of eucharist and conciliarity. Coming from their mixed histories, present-day confessions and denominations conceive the goal of Christian unity in rather different ways. In the early days of the WCC, it was necessary to state that no Church, in order to enter membership, had to renounce its own conception of the Church and its unity. This was formally expressed in the Toronto Declaration of 1950:

> There are room and space in the World Council for the ecclesiology of every Church which is ready to participate in the ecumenical conversation and which takes its stand on the Basis of the Council, which is "a fellowship of Churches which accept our Lord Jesus Christ as God and Saviour." The World Council exists in order that different Churches may face their differences, and therefore no Church is obliged to change its ecclesiol-

ogy as a consequence of membership in the World
Council. Membership in the World Council of Churches
does not imply that a Church treats its own conception
of the Church as merely relative. . . . Membership in
the World Council does not imply the acceptance of a
specific doctrine concerning the nature of the Church.
. . . The member Churches recognize that the membership of the Church of Christ is more inclusive than the
membership of their own Church body. They seek,
therefore, to enter into living contact with those outside
their own ranks who confess the Lordship of Christ.
. . . The member Churches of the World Council consider the relationship of other Churches to the Holy
Catholic Church which the Creeds profess as a subject
for mutual consideration. Nevertheless, membership
does not imply that each Church must regard the other
member Churches as Churches in the true and full sense
of the word. . . . The member Churches of the World
Council recognize in other Churches elements of the
true Church. They consider that this mutual recognition obliges them to enter into a serious conversation
with each other in the hope these elements of truth will
lead to the recognition of the full truth and to unity
based on the full truth. . . . The ecumenical movement
is based upon the conviction that these "traces" are to
be followed. The Churches should not despise them as
mere elements of truth but rejoice in them as hopeful
signs pointing toward real unity. For what are these
elements? Not dead remnants of the past but powerful
means by which God works. Questions may and must
be raised about the validity and purity of teaching and
sacramental life, but there can be no question that such
dynamic elements of Church life justify the hope that
the Churches which maintain them will be led into
fuller truth. It is through the ecumenical conversation
that this recognition of truth is facilitated.[12]

Fellowship within the WCC has in fact enabled the
Churches to draw rather more firmly the contours of the
unity envisioned. Our chapter V describes the progress from
New Delhi (1961) to Nairobi (1975). The local concentration
on the unity of "all in each place" needed taking up into a
pattern of "sustained and sustaining relationships" which

would link "local churches which are themselves truly united" into a "conciliar fellowship." At the present time, a few things need to be said about local unity and conciliarity and about the relation between the two ideas.

Conciliarity in the full sense cannot be taken as an easy alternative to the demands of unity. At best, our present "councils of churches" are steps on the way to true conciliarity. They are helping the denominational churches get used to taking decisions in common (and if their current bureaucratic administrators are resented by many in the churches, then the churches have it in their own hands to make their servants more accountable to the "sense of the faithful").[13] But as long as each separate denomination reserves to itself a final authority in matters of doctrine, discipline, and policy, full Christian unity will not have been attained. Full Christian unity includes a complete sharing of faith and life, and that ultimately entails a unified structure of order and governance. At each geographical level, Christian communities should regulate all that lies within their own competence (such is the principle of subsidiarity),[14] while an ever-widening network of relationships is needed to ensure catholicity.[15] It is hard to see how the aim can properly fall short of an "organic unity" in which those who have hitherto been Catholics, Methodists, Pentecostals, Baptists, and so on are henceforth all fully joined together in local ecclesial units which are themselves in communion with one another throughout the world.

Beginning where we are, that means that today in the United States we must rejoice with the Presbyterians in the union between the UPCUSA and the PCUS (1983), and with the Lutherans in the projected union between the LCA, the ALC, and the AELC (1986). Separate denominations within a single confessional family are thus entering into a full unity of worship, doctrine, and life. As between confessions, we must also rejoice in the "limited communion" newly established between those Lutheran denominations and the Episcopal Church in 1982: our hope must be that Lutheran hesitations concerning the faith of their partners and Episcopal hesitations concerning the ministerial order of theirs will soon be resolved in such a way as to allow the Lutherans and the Episcopalians to make a single ecclesial community, fully united.

In this connection, we recall the celebrated Chicago Quadrilateral of 1886, which has done so much to shape the modern ecumenical movement. Declaring that "in all things of human ordering or of human choice, relating to modes of worship and discipline, or to traditional customs, this Church is ready in the spirit of love and humility to forego all preferences of her own," the Bishops of the Protestant Episcopal Church in the United States of America went on:

> As inherent parts of [the] sacred deposit [of Christian Faith and Order committed by Christ and his apostles to the Church unto the end of the world], and therefore as essential to the restoration of unity among the divided branches of Christendom, we account the following, to wit:
> 1. The Holy Scriptures of the Old and New Testament as the revealed Word of God.
> 2. The Nicene Creed as the sufficient statement of the Christian Faith.
> 3. The two Sacraments—Baptism and the Supper of the Lord—ministered with unfailing use of Christ's words of institution and of the elements ordained by him.
> 4. The Historic Episcopate, locally adapted in the methods of its administration to the varying needs of the nations and peoples called of God into the unity of His Church.
>
> Furthermore, deeply grieved by the sad divisions which affect the Christian Church in our own land, we hereby declare our desire and readiness, as soon as there shall be any authorized response to this declaration, to enter into brotherly conference with all or any Christian Bodies seeking the restoration of the organic unity of the Church, with a view to the earnest study of the conditions under which so priceless a blessing might happily be brought to pass.

The new relationship between Episcopalians and Lutherans may help to draw the latter, hitherto only observers, closer to the deliberations of the Consultation on Church Union. This more complicated process, involving already ten

denominations, has for more than two decades been seeking
to bring its participants toward a Church of Christ Uniting.[16]
Present hopes center on a covenant of full mutual recognition which, by its own logic, should eventually produce
structural unity of an organic kind. This is surely the perspective in which to see the "interim eucharistic fellow-
ships" and "generating communities" which COCU has been
sponsoring. My own vision would run to a national web of
"dioceses" (probably much smaller than the dioceses, or
equivalents, of any single existing denomination), each containing "congregations" in various liturgical, spiritual, and
cultural styles with free interchange of affiliation among individual members, and each diocese being in conciliar communion with all other dioceses in the land and indeed in
every part of the world where unity among Christians had
progressed thus far. Where would that leave our present denominations and confessions?[17] A sample consideration of
that question will be offered in chapters X and XI.

VI. MINISTERIAL ORDER

The importance of the question concerning ministerial order
can be mistaken by no one who has taken part in unity negotiations between Churches, on the one hand, which have
a threefold ministry of bishop, presbyter, and deacon and
which claim an episcopal succession from the apostles, and
Churches, on the other hand, which shape their ministry
differently or make no such claim. Certainly, some subtheo-
logical factors, of a psychological and sociological kind, may
contribute to apparent difficulties: in this case each party
may feel that the others are threatening its communal identity, vocational integrity, or professional livelihood. But genuinely theological matters are at stake insofar as the structures
of an ecclesial community, the significance it attributes to its
ordained ministers, and the functions which such ministers
fulfill—all serve to express the community's life before God,
within itself, and toward the world, to locate the particular
community with regard to the wider Christian community
throughout time and space, and to demonstrate the community's response to the crises of Christian history and the

opportunities offered by a variety of surrounding cultures. Questions to do with the ordained ministry bring into focus the way God's grace is believed to work down the centuries and at any one moment.

The section on *Ministry* in the Lima Faith and Order text proposes a theological framework for the reconciliation of understandings and practices. Setting the ordained ministry firmly within "the calling of the whole people of God" (§§ 1-6), it declares that ordained ministers "serve to build up the community in Christ and to strengthen its witness" (§12). Since "these tasks are not exercised by the ordained ministry in an exclusive" but rather "in a representative way" (§13, commentary), the underlying thought appears to be what the United States Consultation on Church Union expresses thus: "Their ordination marks them as persons who represent to the Church its own identity and mission in Christ."[18] The function of "the priest," in the ministerial sense, it not to deny the priesthood of the whole people in Christ but rather to help it to expression (see *Ministry,* §17). Similarly, "deacons represent to the Church its calling as servant in the world" (§ 31). Churches without historic bishops are now invited to "appreciate the episcopal succession as a sign, though not a guarantee, of the continuity and unity of the Church" (§38): I suggest that it may be right to view the episcopal succession as a kind of sacrament which does not always produce its full fruits but is nevertheless not thereby rendered ineffective. Believing that the structure of the ordained ministry is in principle changeable (the New Testament provides no single blueprint, and the developments and crises of Christian history have in fact brought changes which were justifiable or even necessary), I join with the Lima text in holding that "the ministry of bishop, presbyter and deacon may serve today as an expression of the unity we seek and also as a means of achieving it" (§ 22), always supposing that Churches with and without this pattern should together seek "how its potential can be fully developed for the most effective witness of the Church in this world" (§ 25; see also § 35), and that the acceptance of the episcopal succession by those Churches without it should be "part of a wider process by which the episcopal churches themselves

also regain their lost unity" (§ 38).[19] The background in liturgical history for this way of thinking is supplied in chapter VI of the present book.

VII. SACRAMENTAL TIME, PLACE, AND ACTION

By now it will be obvious that my way of conceiving the
Church is broadly sacramental. Chapter VII, "Sacramental
Time," describes in greater detail the recovery of the an-
amnetic sense to which reference has already been made.
Those reflections on time provide also the theological and
spiritual framework in which to consider the crisis and opportunity confronting believers, the Church, and the world
at this ecumenical moment. Chapters VIII and IX might
equally well have been entitled "Sacramental Place" and
"Sacramental Action." The Church's place is at the hinge
between God and the world. In the theology which greatly
influenced the Second Vatican Council, the Church is viewed
as "the sacrament of the world's salvation."[20] The Church is
where people have come by faith to participate in the universal redemption won by Christ; it is where the kingdom
of God is enjoyed in a real, if still partly hidden, manner. As
such, the Church testifies, by its very existence and then by
its active proclamation, to the gospel promise of salvation for
each and all who will turn to the God who in Christ reconciled the world to himself. Therefore chapter VIII treats of
the worship of the Church before God and the mission of
the Church to the world, showing how worship and mission,
though distinct, are mutually involving. Inseparable from
both is ethics, as the chapter shows. That is why chapter IX,
where ethical questions come directly to the fore, could also
have gone under the rubric "Sacramental Action."

The chosen issue is that of social and political change in
face of injustice, with an examination of the alternative strat-
egies of revolution and quietism. In political terms, the attitude and practice I advocate could perhaps be read as a
compromising reformism; but that would be to miss the radical shift in perspective brought by the Christian faith, a shift
which calls forth in worldly terms the apparent paradoxes of
"revolutionary quiet" and "quiet revolution." When life is

viewed *sub specie aeternitatis*, this world both receives its true value and is relativized by the world to come. Christians are called to pray and work for the best possible approximation to the values of the divine kingdom, allowing God to act through their instrumentality. Their presence and behavior thus takes on a sacramental quality. It offers the world a chance to anticipate the age to come, but it cannot compel belief. That is why witness sometimes takes its strongest form as martyrdom.[21]

VIII. CONFESSIONS AND DENOMINATIONS

Christians may and do differ over the ways in which, in a particular situation, the values of God's kingdom are to find an ethical translation; but such differences need not be church-dividing, unless one version or another appears to depart so radically from an acceptably Christian position as virtually to unchurch its supporters. Structural divisions have usually taken place rather over doctrine, though disciplinary and cultural factors have sometimes entered in. "Heresy" quickly became a doctrinal rather than a sociological term, while the more polite modern usage of "confessions" (and the plural already reflects the problem) shows that the separate communities are divided from one another on doctrinal grounds (the *confessio fidei* in its primary sense is a singular, however many formally different expressions the *substantially identical* faith might take).[22] The doctrinal divisions among those who claim to be Christians need to be overcome so that the one faith may be confessed by a singly ordered body, the Church.

It is highly problematic, theologically, to call the denominations Churches. Yet the historical facts of separation cannot be made to unhappen. The need, at a first stage, is for the different confessions, denominations, or "Churches" to be reconciled into "the Church"; it is when that hard step has been taken, in repentance and faith, that it will be more appropriate to ask what abiding values might be retained, now more widely shared, from the life of the traditions during their separation. There is a spiritual logic to that sequence; but fears for our identity combine with the more positive factor of an awareness of God's grace toward us even in the times of schism to make us instead face *simultaneously* the questions of reconciliation and the confessional traditions.

That has clearly been the case in the bilateral dialogues which have flourished particularly since the official entry of the Roman Catholic Church into the modern ecumenical movement at the time of Pope John XXIII and Vatican II. Earlier bilaterals had sometimes been in principle worldwide in scope (as between Anglicans and Old Catholics, for instance), but it was above all the need to deal with the universally present Roman Catholic Church which suddenly gave fresh ecumenical life to the "family" groupings of Anglicans, Lutherans, Methodists, Reformed, and so on. In some cases, a heightened confessional awareness has made Churches more reluctant to enter into local and national union schemes. I consider this regrettable, since that is the level at which divisions are most obviously scandalous; but the price of local delay may be worth paying if the various series of bilaterals at the world level lead before long to massive reconciliations of the confessions in such a way that local unity then becomes a matter for rapid implementation by the Churches.

In this general context, I take my own Methodism to exemplify some issues which arise between the confessions on their way to churchly unity. Chapter X deals with a question which is bound to figure in conversations between any Protestant body and the Roman Catholic Church: the place of Mary, the Mother of the Lord, in the Christian faith. After a brief period in which, to go by many Roman Catholic intellectuals and ecumenists, it appeared that a deemphasis in Catholicism might ease the ecumenical situation, the strong Marian devotion of Pope John Paul II has recalled a pattern deeply rooted in popular Catholicism which retained institutional expression even after Vatican II.[23] It might be that Protestants could, by a superficial acceptance of J. M. R. Tillard's perceptive dictum that "the non-essential is also necessary," bring themselves to "tolerate" Marian devotion among Catholics while dispensing themselves from sharing in it.[24] I consider it more honest to tackle, by an oblique but promising route, the question of truth in the matter of Mary. We can ask what doctrinal and spiritual assumptions underlie the particular case of attitudes toward Mary and predications about her.

At this level, I judge that there is a high degree of compatibility between the soteriological accents of Methodism and Catholicism. If such a fundamental sympathy can be recognized, the climate becomes more favorable for approaching the concrete question of Mary's proper place in the Christian faith. To examine together the *meaning* of the Marian dogmas in Roman Catholicism is already to start on the substantive question of truth in connection with Mary. As Scripture and tradition are reread on all sides and in an ecumenical endeavor, it might be that apparent excesses on the part of Roman Catholicism would be trimmed, while certain gaps left by Protestant overreaction would be filled. Eastern Orthodox Churches demonstrate that a reverent devotion to the woman who bore the Savior may in no way infringe on the cardinal doctrines of christology, redemption, and the Trinity. There *is* an authentic Christian truth about St. Mary, and we are obliged to pursue it.

Chapter XI offers a reading, at once grateful and critical, of his own ecclesiastical tradition by an insider. I try to perceive the past, the present, and the possible future of Methodism, all within the broader tradition of Christianity with its sad divisions and its imperative to unity. As Thomas A. Langford has kindly written of my work, "Methodism has been his channel into catholic Christianity."[25] It has been my experience that the circumstances and character of Methodism have the capacity to lead people in that direction. My invitation to Christians of other confessions is that they should examine their own traditions for those features which can best move them toward that unity which is the Lord's will for his Church and a condition of the effective proclamation of the gospel in a desperate world.[26]

IX. THE WORLD'S SALVATION

All this occupation with matters of faith and order is far from being a case of fiddling while Rome, and Geneva, burn. It

is more clearly a case of preparing the Church to become
like the young martyr of second-century Lyons, Blandina:
Conformed at the stake to the Christ she had put on in baptism, Blandina went forth to the beasts "like one bidden to
a marriage supper."[27] It is a question of bringing the Church
to "glorify with one heart and one voice the God and Father
of our Lord Jesus Christ" (Rom. 15:6); for we are persuaded
that "neither death, nor life, nor angels, nor principalities,
nor things present, nor things to come, nor powers, nor height,
nor depth, nor anything else in all creation, will be able to
separate us from the love of God in Christ Jesus our Lord"
(8:38f.). At this critical moment in human history, feverish
panic may give way for Christian believers to a responsible
urgency undergirded by a confidence in the eternal God who
is Lord of history. We must do what we can to "save the
world"; but even if the folly of some or all should destroy
the present generation of humanity and therewith any future
for the human race on this earth, God would still have gathered to himself a considerable company of saints with whom
to enjoy eternity.

II
CHURCH AND SPIRIT

It might be argued that the early creeds had a five-part structure: God, Christ, Spirit, Church, last things. Pneumatology,
ecclesiology, and eschatology were, however, so closely in-
terrelated that together they came to compose the so-called
"third article."[1] Thus the Niceno-Constantinopolitan Creed
places the Church under the divine sovereignty of the Holy
Spirit—now, and always, and unto the ages of ages. In ad-
dressing the theme of the Holy Spirit in the life of the Church,
it will therefore be appropriate to draw the elements of my
systematic outline from the "third article" of that ecumenical
creed.

After the several stages of the Arian controversy, the primary concern of the Council of Constantinople was to affirm
the full deity of the Holy Spirit, the third hypostasis of the
Trinity. At stake, soteriologically, was the sanctification or
divinization of Christian believers.[2] Unless the third person
they had confessed and received at their baptism were fully
God, their own full salvation was compromised; for only God
can give participation in God.[3] In the order of knowledge
and experience, soteriological considerations may come first;
but soteriological considerations themselves require that, in
the order of being, the God of the economy be identical with
God in himself.[4] At the very beginning of the Constantinopolitan confession concerning the Holy Spirit, therefore, there
stands the divine name "Lord": "We believe in the Holy
Spirit, *the Lord. . . .*" It is as such that, together with the
Father and the Son, he is worshipped and glorified, as the
creed will soon declare. But meanwhile the economic role
of the Holy Spirit is introduced into the headlines, immediately after the statement of his personal divinity: "We believe in the Holy Spirit, the Lord, *the Giver of Life. . . .*" It
is because he is "heavenly king" that he can be "the treasury

19

of all good gifts" for us. It is because we receive from his bounty that we are enabled to recognize his divine sovereignty: *basileú ouránie . . . ho thēsaurós tôn agathôn.*[5] Our doxology springs from the divine economy and matches the divine being. That is why, as St. Basil argued, it is appropriate to praise the Father through (*diá*) the Son in (*en*) the Holy Spirit in *thanksgiving,* and to praise the Father with (*metá*) the Son together with (*sýn*) the Holy Spirit in *contemplation.*[6]

My subject—the Holy Spirit in the life of the Church— obliges me to speak largely in economic terms. It was therefore important to state at the outset the ontological grounding and the ultimate doxological direction of all that I shall now say, soteriologically, about the Holy Spirit in the life of the Church.

I. THE CONSTITUTION OF THE CHURCH

Let us look, first of all, at the part played by the Holy Spirit in the very constitution of the Church. The Constantinopolitan Creed declares that the Holy Spirit "spake by the prophets." It matters little for our purposes whether the reference is to the prophets of the Old Covenant or to the prophets of the New Covenant or to both.[7] According to the apostle Paul, the letter by itself is deadly, but the Spirit makes alive (2 Cor. 3:6). According to the evangelist John, the flesh on its own is of no avail, but the Spirit makes alive (John 6:63). These things are true even in the case of the Word incarnate. In St. Luke's account, it is by the overshadowing of the Holy Spirit that Mary conceives the Son of God, and the creed confesses that the Lord Jesus Christ was "made flesh from the Holy Spirit and the Virgin Mary." Again, at the baptism of Jesus, the Holy Spirit is seen to descend on him like a dove and, in Johannine terms, to rest upon him. It is by the Spirit of the Lord that the Christ is anointed to preach the good news (Luke 4:18f.). It is by the eternal Spirit that Christ offered himself to God as an unblemished sacrifice for our redemption (Heb. 9:11-14). When Jesus has been lifted up in glory, the Holy Spirit is then given to his followers (John 7:39; 19:30; 20:22). It is when "the Father's promise," "the power from on high," in short "the Holy Spirit," descends upon them that they are able to "tell the mighty works of God" (Acts 2:11), becoming witnesses to Jesus first in Jerusalem, and then in all Judea and Samaria, and finally to the ends of the earth (Acts 1:8; see also Luke 24:45-49). And, to revert to the Fourth Gospel: it is the Spirit of truth who brings to remembrance all that Jesus has said (14:26), who takes the things of Christ and declares them (16:14). Thus the New Testament makes it clear that the same Spirit who rested upon the incarnate Word empowers the proclamation of the gospel concerning him and still vivifies the words of life which he brought.

The Holy Spirit, then, plays an active part in the original foundation and continuing establishment of the Church. His constitutive role, however, is not limited to the *offer* of the gospel in the proclamation of the Word: the Holy Spirit also enables the human *response*. As the apostle declares: "No one can say 'Jesus is Lord' except by the Holy Spirit" (1 Cor. 12:3). In opposition to Pelagianism and semi-Pelagianism, St. Augustine helped the Church to see that even the first motions toward faith were a divine work in us.[8] In the Western tradition, there are diverse views as to whether or how humans cooperate with God in the work of faith. Lutherans stress the entire passivity of the human believer; but my own Methodist tradition views the matter more synergistically, along with the dominant Roman tradition; and our sense of "active receptivity" is perhaps not too far removed from the Orthodox understanding.[9]

It is, of course, in baptism that the divine offer and the divinely enabled human response come to focal expression. The Constantinopolitan Creed confesses "one baptism for the forgiveness of sins." It was clear from apostolic times that the Holy Spirit and the forgiveness of sins belonged together. St. Paul wrote: "You were washed, you were sanctified, you were justified in the name of the Lord Jesus Christ and the Spirit of our God" (1 Cor. 6:11). According to Acts, Peter had preached: "Repent, and be baptized every one of you in the name of Jesus Christ for the forgiveness of your sins; and you shall receive the gift of the Holy Spirit" (Acts 2:38). And the Fourth Evangelist made the link in his own

way: the risen Lord breathed on the apostles and said to
them, "Receive the Holy Spirit. If you forgive the sins of
any, they are forgiven; if you retain the sins of any, they are
retained" (John 20:22f.).[10]

The more serious your view of sin, the more important
will you consider the forgiveness of sins as an expression of
salvation. In the Byzantine liturgy, the invocation upon the
baptismal font certainly presents this aspect:

> Thou didst sanctify the waves of Jordan, thou didst
> send down thy Holy Spirit from heaven and crush the
> heads of the serpents that lurked there. Therefore do
> thou, our loving king, be present now in the visitation
> of thy Holy Spirit and sanctify this water. . . . Do thou,
> maker of all things, declare this water to be a water of
> rest, water of redemption, water of sanctification, a
> cleansing of the pollution of body and soul, a loosening
> of chains, forgiveness of sins, enlightenment of souls,
> washing of rebirth, grace of adoption, raiment of im-
> mortality, renewal of spirit, fount of life. . . .[11]

If forgiveness of sins has a negative sound in some ears, it
will be noted that the list of benefits assumes a more positive
note toward the end. And the same invocation later prays
"that the baptized, guarding the gift of thy Holy Spirit and
increasing the store of grace, may receive the gift of the high
calling and be numbered among the first-born who are written in heaven." To this eschatologically oriented salvation
we shall return in the final section of this chapter.

Meanwhile, most of what we have said so far concerning
the Holy Spirit's part in the constitution of the Church through
both divine gift and human acceptance may be summed up
in a Methodist hymn from the pen of Charles Wesley:[12]

> Spirit of faith, come down,
> Reveal the things of God;
> And make to us the Godhead known,
> And witness with the blood.
> 'Tis Thine the blood to apply,
> And give us eyes to see
> Who did for every sinner die
> Hath surely died for me.

No man can truly say
That Jesus is the Lord,
Unless Thou take the veil away,
And breathe the living word;
Then, only then, we feel
Our interest in His blood,
And cry, with joy unspeakable:
Thou art my Lord, my God!

Having spoken first of the constitution of the Church, we may now speak of its cult. Indeed, *The Apostolic Tradition* of Hippolytus declares that the Church as liturgical assembly is the place "where the Spirit abounds."[13]

II. THE CULT OF THE CHURCH

I have already mentioned the Constantinopolitan Creed's confession of the Holy Spirit as a proper recipient of the Church's doxology: "With the Father and the Son together he is worshipped and glorified." Here I want to describe the role of the Holy Spirit in the economy of the liturgy. Just as the Father's gifts descend through Christ to us in the Holy Spirit, so our thanksgiving in the Holy Spirit mounts through Christ to the Father.

According to Ephesians 2:18, it is in the one Spirit that we have access through Christ to the Father. The apostle Paul himself teaches that it is in the Holy Spirit that we are able, with and through Christ, to address God as "Abba" (Rom. 8:15f.; Gal. 4:6). If our worship is the requital of God's love—"We love him who first loved us" (1 John 4)—then the most intimate role of the Holy Spirit in enabling our worship is clear, for "the love of God has been poured into our hearts by the Holy Spirit which has been given to us" (Rom. 5:5). God's love for us, made manifest by Christ's dying for us while we were yet sinners, now arouses our love for God from within. The Anglican liturgy begins with a beautiful prayer:

Almighty God, unto whom all hearts be open, all desires known, and from whom no secrets are hid: cleanse the thoughts of our hearts by the inspiration of thy *Holy*

Spirit, that we may *perfectly love thee* and *worthily magnify* thy holy name, through Christ our Lord. Amen.[14]

The eucharistic epiclesis in the Byzantine liturgy sharpens the christological focus: without the sacrifice of Christ there is no Christian worship, and so God is prayed to send his Holy Spirit in order to make, or show, the bread and wine to be the body and blood of Christ; and it is through our participation in these that we sacramentally receive the blessings of salvation.[15]

Thanks to the contribution of the Orthodox Churches and also, in part, of such Calvinist theologians as Jean-Jacques von Allmen and Max Thurian,[16] the World Council of Churches Faith and Order texts on the eucharist are now making abundantly clear the entire dependence of the Church's worship on the Holy Spirit.[17] As a Methodist, I note from their *Hymns on the Lord's Supper* (1745) that the Wesley brothers appreciated the need for a eucharistic epiclesis. One hymn reads:

Come, Holy Ghost, Thine influence shed,
And realize the sign;
Thy life infuse into the bread,
Thy power into the wine.

Effectual let the tokens prove
And made, by heavenly art,
Fit channels to convey Thy love
To every faithful heart.

And, borrowing an image from *The Apostolic Constitutions,* another hymn makes the following invocation:

Come, Thou everlasting Spirit,
Bring to every thankful mind
All the Saviour's dying merit,
All His sufferings for mankind.

True Recorder of His passion,
Now the living faith impart,
Now reveal His great salvation,
Preach His gospel to our heart.

Come, Thou Witness of His dying;
Come, Remembrancer divine,
Let us feel Thy power, applying
Christ to every soul, and mine.[18]

After the constitution and the cult of the Church, I want now to treat the character of the Church.

III. THE CHARACTER OF THE CHURCH

By this I mean those four marks of the Church confessed by the Constantinopolitan Creed: one, holy, catholic, and apostolic. In indicating how the Holy Spirit is the divine source of these ecclesial characteristics, I shall—for reasons of time and space—be even more schematic than before. Given the facts of Christian history, it is also inevitable that this will be the most controversial section of the chapter.

1. Unity

In Ephesians 4, the appeal to the Church to maintain "the unity of the Spirit in the bond of peace" is grounded in the fact that there is one body and one Spirit, just as there is one Lord, one faith, one baptism, one God and Father, one hope to which we are called. The apostle Paul reminds the fractious Corinthians that "by one Spirit we were all baptized into one body—Jews or Greeks, slaves or free—and all were made to drink of one Spirit" (1 Cor. 12:13). The varieties of gifts are inspired by one and the same Spirit, whose diverse manifestations are all intended for the common good (vv. 4-11). The first chapter of that letter suggests that the divisions among the Corinthians are not so very different from what we would call "denominational": "I belong to Paul" ("I'm a Protestant"), "I belong to Cephas" ("I'm a Roman Catholic"), "I belong to Christ" ("I'm simply, well, . . ."). St. Paul's constant response is to show the sheer absurdity of division among Christians in light of the one crucified Lord, whose churchly body is animated by the one Spirit.

It would be hard to deny that the modern ecumenical movement was born of the Spirit. Yet it is important to be clear about the nature of the unity we seek. There is a liberal Protestant exaltation of pluralism which seems to hold that the many become one by the effortless aggregation of separate units, regardless of the inconsistencies and contradictions which characterize them.[19] Granted a serious Christian concern for truth, however, there is no bypassing the hard work of doctrinal and institutional dialogue concerning the gospel and its historical embodiment. But if unity remains a gift of the Spirit, then we should also open ourselves in common prayer for his healing and restorative grace.

2. Holiness

It might appear almost too obvious to mention that the Holy Spirit is the source of the Church's holiness. St. Paul teaches that the body of the individual Christian "is a temple of the Holy Spirit within you, which you have from God" (1 Cor. 6:19). Since individual Christians are members of the body of Christ (as v. 15 has already declared), it is fairly natural to conclude from this passage that the Church as a whole, being the body of Christ, is indwelt by the Holy Spirit—and hence "holy." Yet problems arise.

Insofar as sins remain in individual Christians, Protestants in particular have found themselves obliged to admit that the Church as a community and an institution is also disfigured by sin. But Catholics, and Orthodox even more strongly, have refused to speak of a sinful or even a sinning Church: how could the mother of holiness be thought to sin? Protestants, in turn, detect in such a position the erection of the Church as an artificial hypostasis in abstraction from the evident reality of the Christian community's historical existence. For my part, I should seek a solution along the lines of the *simul justus et peccator*. This, however, is not to be understood as an extreme and unremitting paradox—as though the believer, and the Church, remained totally in sin while having been made totally holy. Rather, the sanctification or divinization of the believer and the Church is to be conceived as a dynamic process in which the absurdity of sin is being overcome and a salutary eschatological transformation is taking place. Saints are being made.[20] The divine agent of holiness in the Christian and in the Church is precisely the Holy Spirit.[21]

Exposing myself to the charge of moralism, I should hold that becoming a partaker of the divine nature includes an inescapably ethical component, which requires also a cooperative effort from the human side. Throughout the Pauline epistles, declarations of divinely bestowed change are followed by exhortations to think and behave accordingly. The indicative implies the imperative: "If we live by the Spirit, let us also walk by the Spirit" (Gal. 5:25).

3. Catholicity

Here, by way of indication, I will simply mention a notion dear to my former teacher, Professor Nikos Nissiotis: "the qualitative meaning of catholicity."[22] Nissiotis distinguishes between "universal," which is merely a quantitative word (katá pantós), and "catholic," which is also a qualitative word katá + hólon). The deepest meaning of catholicity, its inner heart, is the *fullness (plérōma)* of God's saving act as it is achieved in Church and world. We remember the teaching of the Cappadocian Fathers, whereby the trinitarian operations of God come to completion precisely *in the Holy Spirit.*[23]

4. Apostolicity

Last to be listed among the characteristics of the Church is its apostolicity. The apostles in fact head the list of the official or ministerial charisms given to the Church: "And God has appointed in the Church first apostles, second prophets, third teachers . . ." (1 Cor. 12:28). "And his gifts were that some should be apostles, some prophets, some evangelists, some pastors and teachers . . ." (Eph. 4:11).

Next to Christ himself, the Church is built on the foundation of the apostles; and its faith is properly apostolic. As is well known, however, this has been and remains a controversial matter in Christian history. First, there is the problem among the episcopal churches, which all consider the successive generations of bishops to be the special guardians of the apostolic faith but which are not all in doctrinal agreement and living communion with one another. Second, there

is the difference between the episcopal churches and the
churches which do not claim to have bishops in personal
succession from the apostles. These latter churches usually
claim to be true to the faith of the apostolic Church and
sometimes deny that title to the episcopal churches. The
WCC Faith and Order text on Ministry seeks an irenical
approach.[24] In speaking of "succession in the apostolic tradition," it distinguishes between "apostolic tradition in the
Church" and "succession of the apostolic ministry." It calls
upon the episcopal churches to recognize "apostolic content" even in bishopless churches; and, in turn, the churches
without episcopal succession are summoned to "recover the
sign of the episcopal succession" as a "profound expression"
of "continuity with the Church of the apostles." It further
notes that "their acceptance of the episcopal succession will
best further the unity of the whole Church if it is part of a
wider process by which the episcopal churches themselves
also regain their lost unity." At stake, of course, in all this is
the understanding of Christ's promise that the Holy Spirit
would guide the Church into all the truth (John 16:13).

The four creedal themes of the Church's unity, holiness,
catholicity, and apostolicity are interwoven in the eschatological prayer of such a Wesleyan hymn as the following:

Head of Thy Church, whose Spirit fills
And flows through every faithful soul,
Unites in mystic love, and seals
Them one, and sanctifies the whole:

Come Lord! Thy glorious Spirit cries,
And souls beneath the altar groan;
Come, Lord! The bride on earth replies,
And perfect all our souls in one.

Pour out the promised gift on all,
Answer the universal: Come!
The fulness of the Gentiles call,
And take Thine ancient people home.[25]

After the constitution of the Church, its cult, and its characteristics, we now arrive at the fourth, final, and very brief
part of this chapter: the consummation of the Church.

IV. THE CONSUMMATION OF THE CHURCH

St. Irenaeus spoke of the Son and the Spirit as the two "hands" of God in creation.[26] The most direct scriptural support for this combination occurs in the verse of the Psalmist:

> By the word of the Lord the heavens were made,
> and all their host by the breath of his mouth. (33:6)

In the Old Testament, the work of God's Spirit in creation is characteristically prolonged into re-creation. The Psalmist says:

> When thou sendest forth thy Spirit,
>   [thy works] are created;
> and thou renewest the face of the earth. (104:30)

When, in Ezekiel's vision, the Lord breathes his Spirit into the dry bones, dead Israel is re-created after the manner of Adam's first creation (Ezek. 37; Gen. 2:7). The theme of new creation characterizes the work of the Holy Spirit in the New Testament: believers are born again of water and the Spirit (John 3:5), they undergo "the washing of regeneration and renewal in the Holy Spirit" (Tit. 3:5).

In this perspective of re-creation, it becomes appropriate to treat pneumatologically also the last two clauses of the Constantinopolitan Creed: "We look for the resurrection of the dead and the life of the world to come."

We have Pauline authority for attributing the work of resurrection to the Holy Spirit. The apostle writes in Romans 8:11: "If the Spirit of him who raised Jesus from the dead dwells in you, he who raised Christ Jesus from the dead will give life to your mortal bodies also through his Spirit which dwells in you." Sealed by the Spirit for the day of redemption (Eph. 4:30), Christians have already received the Holy Spirit as the "first installment" (*arrabón*) of their inheritance (2 Cor. 1:22; Eph. 1:13f.). And it is the Spirit who is even now changing them from glory into glory (2 Cor. 3:18).

The life of the world to come may also be spoken of in pneumatological terms. According to St. Paul, the kingdom of God is justice and peace and joy in the Holy Spirit (Rom. 14:17). To concentrate only on the joy: the Church at

Ephesus was counselled not to get drunk with wine but to
be filled with the Spirit, always and for everything giving
thanks in the name of our Lord Jesus Christ to God the Father (Eph. 5:18-20). Christ filled the eucharistic cup, say some
Eastern rites, with the Holy Spirit;[27] and eucharistic communion brings that "sober inebriation" in which the enjoyment of God consists.[28]

But we are not quite there yet. According to Romans
8:18-27, the Spirit-inspired groanings of our prayers join the
groanings of the whole creation as it waits eagerly for the
revealing of the children of God.[29] "We ourselves, who have
the first fruits of the Spirit, groan inwardly as we wait for
adoption as sons, the redemption of our bodies"—and then
"the creation itself will be set free from its bondage to decay
and obtain the glorious liberty of the children of God." In
that hope, we may properly conclude with Charles Wesley's
invocation to the divine Love:[30]

Finish then Thy new creation,
Pure and spotless let us be;
Let us see Thy great salvation,
Perfectly restored in Thee;
Changed from glory into glory,
Till in heaven we take our place,
Till we cast our crowns before Thee,
Lost in wonder, love, and praise.[31]

III
BAPTISM AND UNITY

I. FROM LAUSANNE TO MONTREAL

Since its beginnings the Faith and Order Movement has been concerned with questions of Christian initiation. In two short sentences the final report of the 1927 Lausanne Conference already indicates the tension that persists to this day between "the one baptism" and the variety of understandings and practices:

> We believe that in Baptism administered with water in the name of the Father, the Son and the Holy Spirit, for the remission of sins, we are baptised by one Spirit into one body. By this statement it is not meant to ignore the differences in conception, interpretation, and mode which exist among us. (§ 53)[1]

From the start also, the very nature of the Faith and Order Movement has meant that the debate on Christian initiation has not been limited to scholarly discussion among scriptural, systematic, and practical theologians: the question of the recognition of initiation across the boundaries of the divided Christian community lies close to the heart of the search for unity. If recognition is withheld from the initiation practiced by others, all the problems of a Cyprianic exclusivism in ecclesiology arise. If recognition of initiation is granted, the refusal of eucharistic communion becomes unjustifiable; yet sacramental communion between groups which remain confessionally, existentially, and practically separated is also a contradiction. It has been the general judgment of the Faith and Order Movement that the achievement of a tolerably agreed understanding and practice of initiation would contribute to mutual recognition as itself a vital component in the fuller visible unity which is being sought.

31

In the final report of the 1937 Edinburgh Conference, the statement on baptism is slightly expanded in comparison with Lausanne:

> Baptism is a gift of God's redeeming love to the Church; and administered with water, in the name of the Father, the Son, and the Holy Spirit, is a sign and seal of Christian discipleship in obedience to our Lord's command. It is generally agreed that the united Church will observe the rule that all members of the visible Church are admitted by baptism.
>
> In the course of the discussion it appeared that there were further elements of faith and practice in relation to Baptism about which disagreement existed. Since the time available precluded the extended discussion of such points as baptismal regeneration, the admission of unbaptised persons to Holy Communion, and the relation of Confirmation to Baptism, we are unable to express our opinion as to how far they would constitute obstacles to proposals for a united Church. (§§ 87f.)[2]

The Orthodox had already preceded these two paragraphs by a restrictive note on the conditions for sacramental validity (§ 86).[3] The Baptists added a restrictive footnote to the first sentence of paragraph 87: "As regards the above statement which has been passed by their brethren who practise infant Baptism, the Baptists could accept it as applying to the baptism of believers, i.e. of those who are capable of making a personal confession of faith."

A world war intervened. But then time again became available. In the 1950s, which were the heyday of "biblical theology" and of "christocentrism," Faith and Order produced a 25-page report entitled *The Meaning of Baptism.* The movement of the 1950s from optimism through pessimism to the regained optimism occasioned by the final report is described by J. E. Skoglund and J. R. Nelson in their *Fifty Years of Faith and Order.* Their description is worth quoting, both because it reflects a typical fluctuation of moods on the baptismal question and because *The Meaning of Baptism* already expresses fairly well the basic theology underlying the final Lima text of 1982. Skoglund and Nelson wrote thus of the 1950s:

Shortly after Evanston it was agreed that the subject of Baptism needed clarification as a bond of unity amongst the churches. When the subject was opened up for discussion at the 1957 New Haven meeting of the Faith and Order Commission, however, the participants were quickly disillusioned as to the unifying role of Baptism. What had seemed at the outset as the one thing held in common by all churches was subject to diverse and contrary interpretations and understandings. Yet the Commission on Christ and the Church would not give up study of the "one baptism *into Christ*". The questions raised at New Haven which seemed so disturbing were due to a lack of Christological depth in the understanding of Baptism. Once the mind could penetrate beneath the surface of the mere form of the ritual, important as that may be, the original biblical teaching on Baptism as the Church's unifying factor became evident. To be baptised into Christ by the Spirit means to be baptised into his one Body, and thus to share with all baptised Christians the unity of the Church. This fact cannot be concealed by even the most radical difference of interpretation and mode of Baptism.[4]

The authors immediately direct the reader to *One Lord, One Baptism,* in which the report *The Meaning of Baptism* was published.[5] The Fourth World Conference on Faith and Order (at Montreal, 1963) welcomed *One Lord, One Baptism* as showing "how wide is the agreement amongst the churches with regard to baptism." *The Meaning of Baptism* had seen baptism as "the expression of the whole *Heilsgeschichte.*" Montreal provided its own summary in the following terms:

Attention is focused upon the baptism with which Jesus himself was baptised (Mark 10:38). This began with his acceptance of solidarity with sinners in his baptism in the Jordan and continued as he followed the path of the Suffering Servant through passion, death and resurrection. The Spirit that came upon Jesus comes also on the Church and unites his people with him in death and resurrection, in and through the baptismal action. Participation in Christ is the central meaning of baptism. Though disagreement remains between those who practise infant baptism and those who practise believer-baptism, all would insist that personal commitment is necessary for responsible membership in the body of Christ. For all, moreover, baptism is related not only to the individual but also to the Church, not only to momentary experience but to life-long growth of participation in Christ. Those who have been raised by the Holy Spirit to new life in Christ are led from baptism to confirmation (or its equivalent) and to Holy Communion. The life is necessarily one of continuing struggle but also of continuing experience of grace. In faith and obedience the baptised live for the sake of Christ, of his Church, and of the world which he loves.[6]

Montreal thereupon takes a new step in Faith and Order discussion of initiation—a step which will be important in the future debate. It spells out in some detail the *ritual expression* of such a doctrine of initiation:

We have found general agreement that the following elements should find a place within any comprehensive order of baptism:
(a) an acknowledgment of God's initiative in salvation, of his continuing faithfulness, and of our total dependence on his grace,
(b) a declaration of the forgiveness of sin in and through Christ,
(c) an invocation of the Holy Spirit,
(d) a renunciation of evil,
(e) a profession of faith in Christ,
(f) an affirmation that the person baptised is a child of God and is incorporated into the body of Christ, whereby he becomes a witness to the Gospel.
    These will precede or follow baptism with water in the name of the Father, and of the Son and of the Holy Spirit.[7]

The Montreal report finally makes a number of practical recommendations: baptism "should normally be administered during a public service of worship" in order to make clear its situation within the corporate life of the community of the baptised; the sacrament might well be administered on great festival occasions, especially Easter (dying/rising); "instruction in the meaning of baptism should be provided regularly and systematically for the whole worshipping congregation"; the churches must always remind their members that baptism "brings to an end all human estrangements in both Church and world based on differences of race or class."

II. THE ACCRA STATEMENT: PREPARATION, RESPONSES, AND REVISION

The study of baptism was resumed, with the participation now of Roman Catholic theologians in Faith and Order, at the meeting of the Faith and Order Commission in Bristol, England (1967). In this new phase the aim would be to draw from "common perspectives of understanding ... conclusions for the churches' liturgy and practice"; the possibilities of mutual recognition were to be more directly examined. Consultations and comments produced a report entitled *Baptism, Confirmation and Eucharist*, which was presented to the Louvain meeting of the Faith and Order Commission in 1971.[8] Furthermore, the Commission discussed a draft statement entitled *Ecumenical Agreement on Baptism*, which was soon sent by the Executive Committee of the WCC to all Churches for reaction and comment.[9] The text was amended and approved by the Faith and Order Commission meeting at Accra, Ghana, in 1974. Together with statements on the eucharist and on the ministry, the statement on baptism received the attention of the Fifth Assembly of the WCC at Nairobi in December 1975; and *One Baptism, One Eucharist, and A Mutually Recognized Ministry* was sent upon the authority of the Assembly for consideration by the member Churches. "These statements," said the Assembly, "indicate a growing convergence in these three areas. We ask that the churches study these texts and transmit their responses to the Faith and Order Commission by December 31, 1976. In responding, the churches should not only examine whether the agreed statements reflect their present teaching and practice, but indicate the ways in which they are prepared to contribute to the common advance towards unity. On the basis of the replies, the study on baptism, the eucharist and the ministry should be continued and deepened."

The methods by which Churches composed and approved their replies varied greatly; consequently the replies carry

varying degrees of official authority. The replies received by
April 1977 were summarized and collated in a typescript
document indexed FO/77:3 (April 1977) and entitled
Churches on the Way to Consensus. This was considered by
a meeting of forty experts convened by Faith and Order in
June at Crêt-Bérard, Switzerland. This meeting drafted a
document entitled *Towards an Ecumenical Consensus on
Baptism, Eucharist and Ministry* for submission to the
standing commission of the Faith and Order Commission
later in the summer of 1977 and, after revision, to the Central
Committee of the WCC.[10]

Guided by the Crêt-Bérard report and by the responses
which the Churches continued to send in, the Faith and
Order Secretariat in Geneva—with Brother Max Thurian
seconded from Taizé—supervised the revision of the Accra
statement. I belonged to a small working group which assembled about twice a year for this purpose. We attempted
to give the text a firmer systematic structure, and we appealed to biblical scholars over points of exegesis raised by
the Churches. The plenary Commission of Faith and Order
confirmed the direction of the revisions at its meeting in
Bangalore, India, in 1978.[11] In 1979 two consultations were
called with special parts of Faith and Order's constituency,
the Orthodox Churches and those Churches which practice
only believers' baptism. The latter consultation, held at the
Southern Baptist Theological Seminary in Louisville, was
particularly important for our theme. Its five chief recommendations, coming from a meeting which had for the first
time drawn together believer-baptists and paedobaptists in
roughly equal numbers, all affected the final Lima text of
1982. The "five significant points of agreement within the
consultation" were recorded as follows:

1. The acceptance that believers' baptism is the most
clearly attested practice of baptism in the New Testament, together with the recognition that infant baptism
has developed within the Christian tradition and witnesses to valid Christian insights.

2. The statement that the personal faith of the recipient and continuous participation in the life of the church
are essential for the full fruit of baptism. In believers'

baptism the believing community has played its part in the nurture of that personal faith, whilst in infant baptism, the supportive believing community surrounding the infant will nurture the child's personal faith as it moves toward discipleship.

3. The recognition in all the group reports that both forms of baptism require a similar and responsible attitude towards Christian nurture and a serious development of the concept of the Christian catechumenate.

4. The reminder that the pressures of contextuality have always borne in on the understanding and practice of baptism and that in these present days contextuality requires rethinking by both groups as to what form of baptism they practice and why.

5. The conviction that indiscriminate baptism is seen as an abuse to be eliminated.[12]

Further draft revisions of the Accra statement were circulated among members of the Faith and Order Commission. At the Commission's 1982 meeting in Lima, Peru, a final opportunity was afforded for change. As at Bangalore, I was asked to chair work on the text. Discussion early in plenary session led to 192 written proposals for detailed emendations in the complete text, which was given the simplified title *Baptism, Eucharist, and Ministry.* Our working group sifted these, together with eleventh-hour suggestions from the Churches. A revised text was again presented to the full Commission, with one last chance for comment on the way proposed changes had been handled. Jean-Marie Tillard (Roman Catholic), John Zizioulas (Orthodox), and I (as a Protestant) were charged with instant decisions as to whether to accept each of the last-minute comments. Finally, in a rare and moving display of strict unanimity, the entire Faith and Order Commission voted the definitively revised text *Baptism, Eucharist, and Ministry* ripe for transmission to the Churches in accordance with the mandate given at the Fifth Assembly of the WCC in Nairobi 1975.[13]

The decisions and actions expected of the Churches were set out earlier, in our first chapter. The baptismal section of the Lima text is printed in full at the conclusion of the present chapter. Meanwhile, some far-from-exhaustive com-

ments may be offered on that section. The aim is simply to
pick out a few matters which the earlier series of responses
from the Churches suggest will be delicate. Fuller theological commentary will be found in a volume of essays edited
by Max Thurian and entitled *Ecumenical Perspectives on
Baptism, Eucharist and Ministry* (1983), while he and I have
compiled some comparative liturgical materials under the
title *Baptism and Eucharist: Ecumenical Convergence in
Celebration* (1983).[14]

III. COMMENTARY ON THE LIMA TEXT

The opening paragraph deals with "the institution of baptism." Here we had to tread a narrow line between the
Churches which requested a clear statement of institution
by the Lord himself and those which, influenced by modern
critical scholarship, viewed Matthew 28:19f. with historical
suspicion. The solution is found in the expression
"St. Matthew records," while attention is called to the fact—
surely remarkable when the question of dominical origin is
raised—that baptism was universally practiced by the apostolic Church from its earliest days.

Paragraphs 2-7 constitute a section headed "The Meaning
of Baptism." The cognitive and operative qualities of baptism are not to be opposed: paragraph 14 will rather say that
"baptism in its full meaning *signifies* and *effects*. . . ." I suspect that some of the deepest divisions in the area of Christian initiation concern the anthropology and theology of *signs*.
How far does the performance of signs *produce* the reality
which they signify? How far is any such production instan-
taneous, and how far is it spread over a future time span?
How far, on the other hand, does the performance of signs
presuppose already the existence of the reality signified? In
what measure must the reality be present before the signs
are allowed to express it? Psychological, aesthetic, and cultural factors in general enter so much into consideration of
these questions that it must be doubtful whether a single
unified answer will ever be given by theology. What this
diversity in anthropological-theological perspectives of
understanding means for the mutual recognition of initiation

rites is a question to which we shall return. It is, however, my hope that the general notions of "performative language" and "effective signification"—to which contemporary sacramental theology has been helped by linguistic philosophy and cultural anthropology—will provide an enabling conceptual framework in which the Churches can accept the Lima formulations. Here we should be rejoining a healthy Hebrew *and* Greek tradition.[15] While baptism serves as a *focus* of meaning and effect, it is clearly stated in the Lima text that "the Holy Spirit is at work in the lives of people before, in and after their baptism" (§ 5).

Paragraph 3 offers a broader and deeper christological grounding for baptism than the mere fact of historical institution is able to provide. It takes "baptism" as a unifying soteriological category stretching from Jesus' baptism in the Jordan through his passion, death, and resurrection to the first Christian Pentecost (explicit in §§ 5 and 14) and then Christian baptism. This unifying category had been hinted at by the Methodist scholar W. F. Flemington in his book *The New Testament Doctrine of Baptism* (1948); it was taken up by J. A. T. Robinson in an article "The One Baptism as a Category of New Testament Soteriology" (*Scottish Journal of Theology* 6 [1953], 275-84); it was heavily exploited in the Church of Scotland's baptismal studies in the 1950s (see *The Biblical Doctrine of Baptism* [1958]); thanks perhaps to the Scots member, T. F. Torrance, it strongly marked the WCC Faith and Order Report of 1960, *The Meaning of Baptism* (see especially chap. II, "Baptism and the Heilsgeschichte"). Torrance again made powerful use of the category in a 1970 lecture, "The One Baptism Common to Christ and His Church."[16] It is to be hoped that this idea is now more familiar to the Churches. Some had argued that the Accra text had not made "the forgiveness of sins" sufficiently explicit in its soteriology; but that point is now elaborated in § 4.

By its statement that the baptized are "confident that they will also ultimately be one with Jesus Christ in a resurrection like his," paragraph 3 introduces an eschatological note which many Churches had missed in the Accra text. That note is struck again by the "final deliverance" and the "entrance into full possession" in paragraph 5. A special paragraph

(§ 7) is devoted to baptism as "the sign of the kingdom," with the prospect of the day when every tongue will confess (see also § 9).

When paragraph 6 speaks of "our common baptism," "a basic bond of unity," "baptismal unity," and "our one baptism into Christ," it touches on what is probably the most difficult question of all: it is the very reason for the baptismal exercise in Faith and Order, and a positively agreed response would take the Churches a long way toward full mutual recognition. In its reply to the Accra statement, the Baptist Union of Great Britain and Ireland warned: "We must beware of shouting baptismal unity, baptismal unity, where honestly there is no more than a common use of words and language." Is it in fact "the one baptism," when understandings and practices vary as widely as they do? As to understandings: it may be said that the Churches are in fairly full agreement both about the basic theological referent of baptism, namely the saving acts of God in Jesus Christ, and about the broader existential referent of baptism, namely the human salvation which may be described as forgiveness of sin, rebirth, new life in the Spirit, membership in the Church, and so on; they differ, however, on the precise place and function of baptism in the process by which God's saving acts take effect in the salvation of particular human beings. In other words, they differ on *how* baptism "refers" to God's saving activity, and on *how* baptism "refers" to the human appropriation of that activity. There is, moreover, a close connection—probably with two-way traffic—between understanding and practice. There is obviously a relation between the understanding of initiation on the one hand, and on the other hand the stage or stages in the individual's life at which it is deemed appropriate for the rite or rites to take place. If it is maintained that there is nevertheless "one baptism" common to all, the implication is that baptism itself is somehow greater than even the major circumstances of its performance (i.e. the understanding on which it is performed, and the point at which it is performed). This is an extremely far-reaching claim, and at this juncture it is important to mention—first as a warning and then as an encouragement—the principle of "intention." The warning is that some notion of intention, however minimal, is required if the Christian sacraments are not to degenerate into magic. The hope is that some general intention—such as the promotion of human salvation in Christ—may be accepted by all the Churches as sufficiently covering what each does when it baptizes, without requiring that all agree on the precise way in which baptism contributes to this end.

The reply of the believer-baptist Churches of Christ in Great Britain and Ireland to the Accra statement rightly recalled attention to the fact that whole ecclesiologies are at stake in the matter of Christian initiation. It sharpened this point about different concepts of the Church in the following way: "We note that no reference is made to those persons who have been baptised as infants but have not made a personal commitment to Christ: we believe that the main problems involved in a mutual recognition of each other's baptism relate to the status to be accorded to such persons."[17]

Paragraphs 8-10 of the Lima text are headed "Baptism and Faith." An attempt is made to reassure Baptists: "The necessity of faith for the reception of the salvation embodied and set forth in baptism is acknowledged by all churches. Personal commitment is necessary for responsible membership in the body of Christ" (§ 8). In its objection to similar statements in the Accra version, the Evangelical Lutheran Church in Bavaria commented that baptism and the gospel were being turned into a "law": "That the gospel includes 'demands' is not, according to the doctrine of our Church, the teaching of the New Testament." And more precisely: "To speak of the 'necessity' for faith on the part of the baptized is possible only with difficulty in face of I Corinthians 7:14 and 15:29 and of the fact that mentally handicapped people receive baptism." Leaving aside the question of whether it is proper to draw norms from the case of those who are disadvantaged on the plane of nature ("the baptism of the mentally handicapped"), we may note with astonishment that the two New Testament texts which the Bavarian Church quotes in an apparently straightforward way as "scriptural proof" are in fact two of the most exegetically controversial texts in the whole New Testament.

In general it may be said that once the difficulty of the
exegetical and hermeneutical task in respect of baptism is
recognized there ought to be far less exclusive insistence on
one's own position and far more readiness to acknowledge
positively the inevitability of a diversified pattern of understanding and practice among the Churches. Many features
in the divergent understandings and practices can be seen
as bearing valuable testimony to particular Christian truths.
To hold them together in tension is probably the best form
of witness.[18]

Although the Accra text already declared, in rather Lutheran phraseology, that "the life of the Christian is necessarily one of continuing struggle and also of continuing
experience of grace," some Lutheran Churches balked at the
language of "growth," fearing that it would be taken in a
"moralistic" way. Since a wide range of other Churches welcomed the emphasis on "growth," it has been retained in the
Lima text (§§ 8-10), with an attempt to state things in genuinely ethical as distinct from legalistic terms. That Christian
initiation, though it has its "punctiliar" moments, is also a
process, represents an increasingly widespread view: it finds
ritual expression in the popularity of the "renewal of baptismal vows" to which point (c) of the commentary on paragraph 14 refers (see also § 23).

Paragraphs 11-12 face head-on the question of infant baptism and believers' baptism. The trend of the argument is to
justify a diversity of understanding and practice within a
coherent ecclesial totality. On the question of infant baptism
and believers' baptism, one may expect that the acceptance
of a diversified pattern will come easier to those Churches
which baptize *also* infants (or even make of infant baptism
a theological as well as a practical norm)—for these latter
Churches do of course themselves baptize upon profession
of faith in the case of a responsible convert. To assuage paedobaptists, it is insisted that the personal decision of faith in
the case of believers' baptism is rooted in God's faithfulness
to humanity and is set within the life and faith of the Church.
To assuage believer-baptists, the case for infant baptism insists upon "corporate faith," upon an "environment" of faith,
and upon the eliciting of a later confession of faith. Under

the governing rubric that "baptism is both God's gift and our human response to that gift" (§ 8), it is strongly stressed that both the paedobaptist and the believer-baptist patterns imply grace and faith, though of course the modalities differ.

The commentary to paragraph 12 mentions "some Churches, which unite both infant-baptist and believer-baptist traditions." No doubt the Church of North India, to be mentioned in a moment, is in mind; but a similar policy is practiced in the United Presbyterian Church in the USA. In such Churches, "it has been possible to regard as *equivalent alternatives* for entry into the Church both a pattern whereby baptism in infancy is followed by later profession of faith and a pattern whereby believers' baptism follows upon a presentation and blessing in infancy. This example invites other churches to decide whether they, too, could not recognize equivalent alternatives in their reciprocal relationships and in church union negotiations."

Paragraph 13 and its commentary face the thorny issue of "rebaptism." Certainly the Roman Catholic Church has largely abandoned its practice of giving "conditional baptism" to those who come to Catholicism from other denominations. But the issue of "second baptism" is a live one between paedobaptists and believer-baptists when persons who received infant baptism later come to believe that they should receive baptism upon profession of faith. This question held up for many years the inauguration of the Church of North India, which was to unite paedobaptist and believer-baptist denominations. In the united Church, the two patterns of initiation were to be practiced as equivalent *alternatives*: but what was to happen in the case of a request for "second baptism"? The question was eventually shelved for resolution within the context of an already united Church. The Church of North India came into being in 1970. It may just be worth stating, in an anecdotal way, that when, five years on, I asked a bishop of the new Church whether progress had now been made on this question, he replied that as a matter of fact not a single case had yet presented itself in his diocese. Nevertheless, the question remains awkward, theologically and pastorally. In Britain, it caused headaches in the negotiations for union between the paedobaptist

United Reformed Church and the believer-baptist Churches of Christ. It is a recurrent problem in pastoral practice in the United States.[19]

Paragraph 14 addresses "Baptism—Chrismation—Confirmation." The question of the relation between baptism and "confirmation" is perhaps the most embroiled question of all in the matter of Christian initiation, and it cannot be claimed that the Lima text succeeds in settling it. There is the split between those who hold "sacramental initiation complete in baptism" (to borrow the title of a pamphlet by E. C. Whitaker) and those who hold sacramental confirmation necessary to initiation. There is the split between those who administer both baptism *and* confirmation (chrismation) to infants and those who, while baptizing infants, administer confirmation, whether sacramental or nonsacramental, only at an age of responsibility. There is the question of the point at which a person becomes "qualified" to share in eucharistic communion. There is the question of the relation between the *rites* (whether baptism or confirmation) and the *experience* of faith and of the Spirit. Again it must be said that there is no realistically foreseeable solution apart from the recognition of legitimate diversity. The ritual differences which this entails are acknowledged in paragraphs 19-20. The recognition of the processive aspect of initiation may be a means of containing such differences within tolerable bounds that allow for mutual recognition.

Paragraph 17 makes the simple statement: "Baptism is administered with water in the name of the Father, the Son and the Holy Spirit." One North American response to the Accra statement raised the question of sexist language in the baptismal name. The whole prospect of interconfessional agreement would be set back, if not ruined, by the use of any other than a clearly trinitarian baptismal formula. There is ample opportunity for the use of varied imagery from Scripture and tradition in the prayers that surround the sacrament of rebirth.[20]

Finally it must be mentioned that the Lima text at several points develops the importance of baptism and baptismal unity as a basis and paradigm for Christian witness and conduct in the world. That matches well a recurrent theme in this book.[21]

THE LIMA TEXT ON BAPTISM

I. THE INSTITUTION OF BAPTISM

1. Christian baptism is rooted in the ministry of Jesus of Nazareth, in his death and in his resurrection. It is incorporation into Christ, who is the crucified and risen Lord; it is entry into the New Covenant between God and God's people. Baptism is a gift of God, and is administered in the name of the Father, the Son and the Holy Spirit. St. Matthew records that the risen Lord, when sending his disciples into the world, commanded them to baptize (Matt. 28:18-20). The universal practice of baptism by the apostolic Church from its earliest days is attested in letters of the New Testament, the Acts of the Apostles, and the writings of the Fathers. The churches today continue this practice as a rite of commitment to the Lord who bestows his grace upon his people.

II. THE MEANING OF BAPTISM

2. Baptism is the sign of new life through Jesus Christ. It unites the one baptized with Christ and with his people. The New Testament scriptures and the liturgy of the Church unfold the meaning of baptism in various images which express the riches of Christ and the gifts of his salvation. These images are sometimes linked with the symbolic uses of water in the Old Testament. Baptism is participation in Christ's death and resurrection (Rom. 6:3-5; Col. 2:12); a washing away of sin (I Cor. 6:11); a new birth (John 3:5); an enlightenment by Christ (Eph. 5:14); a reclothing in Christ (Gal. 3:27); a renewal by the Spirit (Titus 3:5); the experience of salvation from the flood (I Peter 3:20-21); an exodus from bondage (I Cor. 10:1-2) and a liberation into a new humanity in which barriers of division whether of sex or race or social status are transcended (Gal. 3:27-28; I Cor. 12:13). The images are many but the reality is one.

A. Participation in Christ's Death and Resurrection

3. Baptism means participating in the life, death and resurrection of Jesus Christ. Jesus went down into the river Jordan and was baptized in solidarity with sinners in order to fulfil all righteousness (Matt. 3:15). This baptism led Jesus along the way of the Suffering Servant, made manifest in his sufferings, death and resurrection (Mark 10:38-40, 45). By baptism, Christians are immersed in the liberating death of Christ where their sins are buried, where the "old Adam" is cru-

cified with Christ, and where the power of sin is broken.
Thus those baptized are no longer slaves to sin, but free.
Fully indentified with the death of Christ, they are buried
with him and are raised here and now to a new life in the
power of the resurrection of Jesus Christ, confident that they
will also ultimately be one with him in a resurrection like
his (Rom. 6:3-11; Col. 2:13. 3:1; Eph. 2:5-6).

B. Conversion, Pardoning and Cleansing

4. The baptism which makes Christians partakers of the mystery of Christ's death and resurrection implies confession of
sin and conversion of heart. The baptism administered by
John was itself a baptism of repentance for the forgiveness
of sins (Mark 1:4). The New Testament underlines the ethical
implications of baptism by representing it as an ablution
which washes the body with pure water, a cleansing of the
heart of all sin, and an act of justification (Heb. 10:22; I Peter
3:21; Acts 22:16; I Cor. 6:11). Thus those baptized are par-
doned, cleansed and sanctified by Christ, and are given as
part of their baptismal experience a new ethical orientation
under the guidance of the Holy Spirit.

C. The Gift of the Spirit

5. The Holy Spirit is at work in the lives of people before,
in and after their baptism. It is the same Spirit who revealed
Jesus as the Son (Mark 1:10-11) and who empowered and
united the disciples at Pentecost (Acts 2). God bestows upon
all baptized persons the anointing and the promise of the
Holy Spirit, marks them with a seal and implants in their
hearts the first instalment of their inheritance as sons and
daughters of God. The Holy Spirit nurtures the life of faith
in their hearts until the final deliverance when they will
enter into its full possession, to the praise of the glory of God
(II Cor. 1:21-22; Eph. 1:13-14).

D. Incorporation into the Body of Christ

6. Administered in obedience to our Lord, baptism is a sign
and seal of our common discipleship. Through baptism,
Christians are brought into union with Christ, with each
other and with the Church of every time and place. Our
common baptism, which unites us to Christ in faith, is thus
a basic bond of unity. We are one people and are called to
confess and serve one Lord in each place and in all the
world. The union with Christ which we share through baptism has important implications for Christian unity. "There
is ... one baptism, one God and Father of us all ..."

(Eph. 4:4-6). When baptismal unity is realized in one holy, catholic, apostolic Church, a genuine Christian witness can be made to the healing and reconciling love of God. Therefore, our one baptism into Christ constitutes a call to the churches to overcome their divisions and visibly manifest their fellowship.

COMMENTARY (6)

The inability of the churches mutually to recognize the various practices of baptism as sharing in the one baptism, and their actual dividedness in spite of mutual baptismal recognition, have given dramatic visibility to the broken witness of the Church. The readiness of the churches in some places and times to allow differences of sex, race, or social status to divide the body of Christ has further called into question genuine baptismal unity of the Christian community (Gal. 3:27-28) and has seriously compromised its witness. The need to recover baptismal unity is at the heart of the ecumenical task as it is central for the realization of genuine partnership within the Christian communities.

E. The Sign of the Kingdom

7. Baptism initiates the reality of the new life given in the midst of the present world. It gives participation in the community of the Holy Spirit. It is a sign of the Kingdom of God and of the life of the world to come. Through the gifts of faith, hope and love, baptism has a dynamic which embraces the whole of life, extends to all nations, and anticipates the day when every tongue will confess that Jesus is Lord to the glory of God the Father.

III. BAPTISM AND FAITH

8. Baptism is both God's gift and our human response to that gift. It looks towards a growth into the measure of the stature of the fullness of Christ (Eph. 4:13). The necessity of faith for the reception of the salvation embodied and set forth in baptism is acknowledged by all churches. Personal commitment is necessary for responsible membership in the body of Christ.

9. Baptism is related not only to momentary experience, but to life-long growth into Christ. Those baptized are called upon to reflect the glory of the Lord as they are transformed by the power of the Holy Spirit, into his likeness, with ever increasing splendour (II Cor. 3:18). The life of the Christian is necessarily one of continuing struggle yet also of contin-

uing experience of grace. In this new relationship, the baptized live for the sake of Christ, of his Church and of the
world which he loves, while they wait in hope for the manifestation of God's new creation and for the time when God
will be all in all (Rom. 8:18-24; I Cor. 15:22-28, 49-57).

10. As they grow in the Christian life of faith, baptized believers demonstrate that humanity can be regenerated and
liberated. They have a common responsibility, here and now,
to bear witness together to the Gospel of Christ, the Liber-
ator of all human beings. The context of this common witness
is the Church and the world. Within a fellowship of witness
and service, Christians discover the full significance of the
one baptism as the gift of God to all God's people. Likewise,
they acknowledge that baptism, as a baptism into Christ's
death, has ethical implications which not only call for personal sanctification, but also motivate Christians to strive for
the realization of the will of God in all realms of life
(Rom. 6:9ff; Gal. 3:27-28; I Peter 2:21–4:6).

IV. BAPTISMAL PRACTICE

A. Baptism of Believers and Infants

11. While the possibility that infant baptism was also practised in the apostolic age cannot be excluded, baptism upon
personal profession of faith is the most clearly attested pattern in the New Testament documents.

In the course of history, the practice of baptism has developed in a variety of forms. Some churches baptize infants
brought by parents or guardians who are ready, in and with
the Church, to bring up the children in the Christian faith.
Other churches practise exclusively the baptism of believers
who are able to make a personal confession of faith. Some
of these churches encourage infants or children to be presented and blessed in a service which usually involves
thanksgiving for the gift of the child and also the commitment of the mother and father to Christian parenthood.

All churches baptize believers coming from other religions
or from unbelief who accept the Christian faith and participate in catechetical instruction.

12. Both the baptism of believers and the baptism of infants
take place in the Church as the community of faith. When
one who can answer for himself or herself is baptized, a
personal confession of faith will be an integral part of the
baptismal service. When an infant is baptized, the personal
response will be offered at a later moment in life. In both

cases, the baptized person will have to grow in the understanding of faith. For those baptized upon their own confession of faith, there is always the constant requirement of a
continuing growth of personal response in faith. In the case
of infants, personal confession is expected later, and Christian nurture is directed to the eliciting of this confession. All
baptism is rooted in and declares Christ's faithfulness unto
death. It has its setting within the life and faith of the Church
and, through the witness of the whole Church, points to the
faithfulness of God, the ground of all life in faith. At every
baptism the whole congregation reaffirms its faith in God
and pledges itself to provide an environment of witness and
service. Baptism should, therefore, always be celebrated and
developed in the setting of the Christian community.

COMMENTARY (12)

*When the expressions "infant baptism" and "believers'
baptism" are used, it is necessary to keep in mind that
the real distinction is between those who baptize people at any age and those who baptize only those able
to make a confession of faith for themselves. The differences between infant and believers' baptism become
less sharp when it is recognized that both forms of
baptism embody God's own initiative in Christ and
express a response of faith made within the believing
community.*

*The practice of infant baptism emphasizes the corpo-
rate faith and the faith which the child shares with its
parents. The infant is born into a broken world and
shares in its brokenness. Through baptism, the promise
and claim of the Gospel are laid upon the child. The
personal faith of the recipient of baptism and faithful
participation in the life of the Church are essential for
the full fruit of baptism.*

*The practice of believers' baptism emphasizes the ex-
plicit confession of the person who responds to the
grace of God in and through the community of faith
and who seeks baptism.*

*Both forms of baptism require a similar and respon-
sible attitude towards Christian nurture. A rediscovery
of the continuing character of Christian nurture may
facilitate the mutual acceptance of different initiation
practices.*

In some churches which unite both infant-baptist and

believer-baptist traditions, it has been possible to regard as equivalent alternatives for entry into the Church both a pattern whereby baptism in infancy is followed by later profession of faith and a pattern whereby believers' baptism follows upon a presentation and blessing in infancy. This example invites other churches to decide whether they, too, could not recognize equivalent alternatives in their reciprocal relationships and in church union negotiations.

13. Baptism is an unrepeatable act. Any practice which might be interpreted as "re-baptism" must be avoided.

COMMENTARY (13)

Churches which have insisted on a particular form of baptism or which have had serious questions about the authenticity of other churches' sacraments and ministries have at times required persons coming from other church traditions to be baptized before being received into full communicant membership. As the churches come to fuller mutual understanding and acceptance of one another and enter into closer relationships in witness and service, they will want to refrain from any practice which might call into question the sacramental integrity of other churches or which might diminish the unrepeatability of the sacrament of baptism.

B. Baptism — Chrismation — Confirmation

14. In God's work of salvation, the paschal mystery of Christ's death and resurrection is inseparably linked with the pentecostal gift of the Holy Spirit. Similarly, participation in Christ's death and resurrection is inseparably linked with the receiving of the Spirit. Baptism in its full meaning signifies and effects both.

Christians differ in their understanding as to where the sign of the gift of the Spirit is to be found. Different actions have become associated with the giving of the Spirit. For some it is the water rite itself. For others, it is the anointing with chrism and/or the imposition of hands, which many churches call confirmation. For still others it is all three, as they see the Spirit operative throughout the rite. All agree that Christian baptism is in water and the Holy Spirit.

COMMENTARY (14)

(a) Within some traditions it is explained that as bap-

tism conforms us to Christ crucified, buried and risen, so through chrismation Christians receive the gift of the pentecostal Spirit from the anointed Son.

(b) If baptism, as incorporation into the body of Christ, points by its very nature to the eucharistic sharing of Christ's body and blood, the question arises as to how a further and separate rite can be interposed between baptism and admission to communion. Those churches which baptize children but refuse them a share in the eucharist before such a rite may wish to ponder whether they have fully appreciated and accepted the consequences of baptism.

(c) Baptism needs to be constantly reaffirmed. The most obvious form of such reaffirmation is the celebration of the eucharist. The renewal of baptismal vows may also take place during such occasions as the annual celebration of the paschal mystery or during the baptism of others.

C. Towards Mutual Recognition of Baptism

15. Churches are increasingly recognizing one another's baptism as the one baptism into Christ when Jesus Christ has been confessed as Lord by the candidate or, in the case of infant baptism, when confession has been made by the church (parents, guardians, god-parents and congregation) and affirmed later by personal faith and commitment. Mutual recognition of baptism is acknowledged as an important sign and means of expressing the baptismal unity given in Christ. Wherever possible, mutual recognition should be expressed explicitly by the churches.

16. In order to overcome their differences, believer baptists and those who practise infant baptism should reconsider certain aspects of their practices. The first may seek to express more visibly the fact that children are placed under the protection of God's grace. The latter must guard themselves against the practice of apparently indiscriminate baptism and take more seriously their responsibility for the nurture of baptized children to mature commitment to Christ.

V. THE CELEBRATION OF BAPTISM

17. Baptism is administered with water in the name of the Father, the Son and the Holy Spirit.

18. In the celebration of baptism the symbolic dimension of water should be taken seriously and not minimalized. The

act of immersion can vividly express the reality that in baptism the Christian participates in the death, burial and resurrection of Christ.

COMMENTARY (18)

As seen in some theological traditions, the use of water, with all its positive associations with life and blessing, signifies the continuity between the old and the new creation, thus revealing the significance of baptism not only for human beings but also for the whole cosmos. At the same time, the use of water represents a purification of creation, a dying to that which is negative and destructive in the world: those who are baptized into the body of Christ are made partakers of a renewed existence.

19. As was the case in the early centuries, the gift of the Spirit in baptism may be signified in additional ways; for example, by the sign of the laying on of hands, and by anointing or chrismation. The very sign of the cross recalls the promised gift of the Holy Spirit who is the instalment and pledge of what is yet to come when God has fully redeemed those whom he has made his own (Eph. 1:13-14). The recovery of such vivid signs may be expected to enrich the liturgy.

20. Within any comprehensive order of baptism at least the following elements should find a place: the proclamation of the scriptures referring to baptism; an invocation of the Holy Spirit; a renunciation of evil; a profession of faith in Christ and the Holy Trinity; the use of water; a declaration that the persons baptized have acquired a new identity as sons and daughters of God, and as members of the Church, called to be witnesses of the Gospel. Some churches consider that Christian initiation is not complete without the sealing of the baptized with the gift of the Holy Spirit and participation in holy communion.

21. It is appropriate to explain in the context of the baptismal service the meaning of baptism as it appears from scriptures (i.e. the participation in Christ's death and resurrection, conversion, pardoning and cleansing, gift of the Spirit, incorporation into the body of Christ and sign of the Kingdom).

COMMENTARY (21)

Recent discussion indicates that more attention should be given to misunderstandings encouraged by the socio-cultural context in which baptism takes place.

(a) In some parts of the world, the giving of a name in the baptismal liturgy has led to confusion between baptism and customs surrounding name-giving. This confusion is especially harmful if, in cultures predominantly not Christian, the baptized are required to assume Christian names not rooted in their cultural tradition. In making regulations for baptism, churches should be careful to keep the emphasis on the true Christian significance of baptism and to avoid unnecessarily alienating the baptized from their local culture through the imposition of foreign names. A name which is inherited from one's original culture roots the baptized in that culture, and at the same time manifests the universality of baptism, incorporation into the one Church, holy, catholic and apostolic, which stretches over all the nations of the earth.

(b) In many large European and North American majority churches infant baptism is often practised in an apparently indiscriminate way. This contributes to the reluctance of churches which practise believers' baptism to acknowledge the validity of infant baptism; this fact should lead to more critical reflection on the meaning of baptism within those majority churches themselves.

(c) Some African churches practise baptism of the Holy Spirit without water, through the laying on of hands, while recognizing other churches' baptism. A study is required concerning this practice and its relation to baptism with water.

22. Baptism is normally administered by an ordained minister, though in certain circumstances others are allowed to baptize.

23. Since baptism is intimately connected with the corporate life and worship of the Church, it should normally be administered during public worship, so that the members of the congregation may be reminded of their own baptism and may welcome into their fellowship those who are baptized and whom they are committed to nurture in the Christian faith. The sacrament is appropriate to great festival occasions such as Easter, Pentecost and Epiphany, as was the practice in the early Church.

IV
EUCHARIST,
RECONCILIATION,
AND RENEWAL

Reconciliation and renewal were themes of the last Roman Holy Year. Reconciliation is a "space" word. Renewal is a "time" word. Reconciliation has to do with bringing together, coming together; it is the reunion of the separated. Renewal has to do with a fresh start, the passage of the old and the beginning of the new; it is remaking, rebirth, resurrection. The purpose of God's redemptive work for humanity in Jesus Christ may be characterized as reconciliation of human beings and the world to God himself (Rom. 5:10f.; 2 Cor. 5:18-20; Eph. 2:16; Col. 1:20), as the renewal of human beings according to God's own image (Rom. 12:2; 2 Cor. 4:16; 5:17; Eph. 4:23f.; Col. 3:10; Tit. 3:5). Our redemption, because it is *God's* redemption of us, transcends space and time; but our redemption, because it is God's redemption of *us*, is operative in space and time. As a sacrament of our redemption, the eucharist is a sacrament of reconciliation and renewal. Let us look at the sacrament in its spatial and temporal structures. In the spatial circumstances of its celebration and in the use of space in its own ritual and verbal symbolism, the eucharist expresses the reconciliation between God and humanity and the reconciliation among human beings which is its corollary. In the temporal circumstances of its celebration and in the incidence of time in its own linguistic usage and imagery, the eucharist shows the part it plays in the renewal of man by his Maker.

I. THE EUCHARIST AS A SACRAMENT OF RECONCILIATION

It is the vertical reconciliation of humanity to God which is theologically primary; this reconciliation carries, however, as its horizontal corollary the reconciliation of human beings among themselves. It is *together* that people have been reconciled by Christ to God; Christ is "our peace," therefore, not only as between humanity and God but also as among human beings. My language has already started to echo the second half of Ephesians 2, and the repercussions will continue as we consider the eucharist, first, as a sacrament of reconciliation between humanity and God and, second, as a sacrament of reconciliation among human beings.[1] I shall go on to deal, third, with the universal scope of reconciliation; and, fourth, with its local beginnings.

1. Reconciliation between humanity and God

In the words of Ephesians 2:18: "Through Christ we both [= Jew and Gentile] have access in one Spirit to the Father." Here we have in a nutshell the scriptural basis of Origen's principle that the prayer of the Church is normally addressed *to* the Father, *through* Jesus Christ, *in* the Holy Spirit.[2] This is the "type" or pattern of the classical eucharistic anaphora, which managed to establish and maintain itself even at a period when the development toward full Trinitarianism in doctrine—and the need to meet resistance to this—reinforced the tendency which saw the Son and indeed the Holy Spirit as due recipients of worship along with the Father.[3] The eucharist is the place where Christians "together, with one voice, glorify God" (Rom. 15:6): with angels and archangels and all the company of heaven we cry "Holy, holy, holy," and we render him praise and thanks above all for his redemptive work, accomplished in Christ Jesus, of reconciling the world to himself. It is in the eucharist also that "with confidence we draw near to the throne of grace, that we may receive mercy and find grace to help in time of need" (Heb. 4:16): the eucharist has always contained, usually within the canon but also in the prayers of the faithful and at other points, an element of supplication made through Jesus Christ our great high priest. Because it is both a thankful commemoration of the reconciling work of Christ whose focus was the Cross and a prayer of supplication through our great high priest who has passed through the heavens, it is natural that sacrificial language should be used at the eucharist. Protestants traditionally insist that the "full, perfect and sufficient sacrifice" of Christ on the Cross (the phrase is from the Anglican Book of Common Prayer) can only be *thanked for* and *pleaded* at the eucharist: it is not, they would say, offered again, and there are difficulties even if the qualifications "bloodlessly" or "in a sacramental mode" are introduced. Modern work in biblical theology has restored a more "real" and "dynamic" sense to the notion of *memorial*, and this has enabled Protestant and Catholic theologians of the eucharist to come much closer together in their understanding of the sacramental *anamnesis*. Yet Protestants are still taken aback by the words of the new Eucharistic Prayer IV of the Roman rite: "Offerimus tibi eius corpus et sanguinem." Here is an area of theology where ecumenical work still needs to be done.[4]

But to return to our uncontroversial theme. In the eucharist we experience the reconciliation accomplished in Christ, and we express that experience in the language of space: we "have access" to the Father, we "draw near" the throne of grace. This restoration of humanity to God's fellowship is also expressed in terms of ascent and descent.

The principal expression of ascent is the dialogue which introduces and governs the great prayer of thanksgiving: the eucharistic president summons us "Lift up your hearts," and our reply is "We lift them up to the Lord"; as St. Cyril of Jerusalem explains, we are bidden to "have our hearts in heaven with the God who loves mankind";[5] in directly biblical terms, we are setting our mind on things that are above, where our life is hid with Christ in God (Col. 3:1-4). Within the great prayer of thanksgiving, some liturgies, doubtless borrowing from the story of the feeding of the 5,000,[6] insert in the institution narrative a reference to Christ's "looking up to heaven," and a rubric in the Roman canon says that the eucharistic president correspondingly *"elevat oculos ad caelum."*[7] Using sacrificial phraseology, several liturgies pray, at various points, that the oblations of the earthly Church may be accepted by God upon his heavenly altar, and the Roman canon, in the *Supplices*, asks that they may be carried there by angelic hands.[8] In the area of ritual action, the elevations of the eucharistic elements which may take place at various points bear multiple significance, but they may, at least under one aspect, be an expression, in symbolic up-

ward movement, of the reconciliation between humanity and
God once wrought through Jesus Christ and still operative
in him. Even the rising cloud of incense may, in smoke and
smell, signify humanity's access to God.[9]

There is also the language of descent. The upward *Sursum corda* finds its principal counterpart in the downward
epiclesis of the Holy Spirit. God is called on to send the
Holy Spirit down upon the people and the bread and wine:
*katápempson tó Pneúma son tó Hágion eph hēmás kaí epí
tá prokeímena dóra taúta* (Byzantine Liturgy of St. Chrysostom). The pneumatological epiclesis is characteristic of
all the classical anaphoras of the East; and in the course
of the recent widespread revision of eucharistic liturgies it is now, in various forms, finding its way back into
the West.[10] It is a further expression of the meeting between
God and humanity in the eucharistic celebration.

Still in terms of spatial imagery and of movement "from"
God, Christ may be invoked to "come" into the assembly of
those gathered in his name (Matt. 18:20). Thus it is now
widely agreed that the primitive *Maranatha* carries a eucharistic as well as a parousiac reference (1 Cor. 16:22;
Rev. 22:20: Did. 10:6).[11] Then there is the characteristic
Mozarabic invocation addressed to Christ: "*Adesto....*"[12]
This has been taken up again by the liturgy of the Church
of South India: "Be present, be present, O Jesus, thou good
High Priest, as thou wast in the midst of thy disciples, and
make thyself known to us in the breaking of the bread." In
the Byzantine tradition, the bringing of the bread and wine
from the table of preparation to the altar is decked out as the
processional entry of the divine king.

All these are expressions, in the verbal and ritual imagery
of space, of the meeting between God and humanity which
may now take place through the reconciling work of Christ.
But the reconciling work of Christ has, as we saw, the horizontal corollary of reconciliation among human beings, and
to that we now turn.

2. Reconciliation among human beings

From the first, the eucharist is an occasion of gathering, of
spatial assembly. From near and far they come. Justin Martyr
records that there was a eucharistic "coming together in one

place (*epí tó autó synéleusis*)" of all Christians who dwelt
in either the towns or the country (*Apology* 1, 67). In early
use, the phrase "come together in one place" appears to be
almost a technical term for liturgical assembling (see also
1 Cor. 11:20; 14:23; Ignatius, *Ad Eph.* 13:1). The Didache
(14:1) employs the verb *synágein* for the eucharistic gathering, and the noun *synaxis* was long used for the eucharistic
service.[13] The significant relation between gathering and
horizontal reconciliation is indicated by Didache 14:2: "No
one who has a dispute with his fellow should come together
with you until he has made it up (*diallagōsin*), in order that
your sacrifice be not polluted." This appears to depend directly on the Lord's word in Matthew 5:23f.: "If you are offering your gift at the altar, and there remember that your
brother has something against you, leave your gift there before the altar and go; first be reconciled (*diallágēthi*) to your
brother, and then come and offer your gift." Within the eucharistic symbolism, the special sign of good fraternal relations is the kiss of peace, which dates from New Testament
times (Rom. 16:16; 1 Cor. 16:20; 2 Cor. 13:12; 1 Thess. 5:26;
1 Pet. 5:14). In the Eastern liturgies, the peace is usually
exchanged before the eucharistic anaphora, wherein those
who live in harmony with one another will be praising God
with one heart and one voice (*homothymadón en hení stómati*, Rom. 15:6); and it is at the beginning of the properly
eucharistic part of the liturgy that most modern Protestant
revisions have reintroduced the Peace into the service.[14] The
new missal of Paul VI retains the *pax* in its traditional Roman
position before communion: fraternal harmony is thereby
expressed just before all partake of the one bread at the one
Table of the Lord.

Let us dwell for a moment on the symbolism of one bread.
This is based in Scripture, and several modern liturgies in
fact quote the words of Paul, at the Fraction, as the one bread
is being broken for distribution to the many: "The bread
which we break, is it not a participation in the body of Christ?
Because there is one bread, we who are many are one body,
for we all partake of the same loaf" (1 Cor. 10:16f.).[15] The
one bread is first a sign of existing unity. Thus Augustine
sees the eucharistic bread, which is made from many grains,
and the eucharistic wine, which is made from many grapes,

as the *mysterium* of the "one body" which the communicants have already been made by their baptism: unless they
behave peaceably toward one another, they are giving the
lie to the "Amen" which they say in response to the words
corpus Christi as they receive communion.[16] But those whose
unity is expressed and maintained through participation in
the one bread, which is spiritually the same wherever the
eucharist is celebrated, find themselves in daily life physically dispersed throughout the world: the anaphora of Ser
apion uses the theme of the one bread in a prayer for the
gathering of the geographically scattered Church in catholic
unity: "As this bread was once scattered on the mountains
and then, gathered together, became one, so also gather thy
holy Church out of every nation and every land and every city
and village and house and make one living Catholic Church."
In the Didache (9:4), where the eschatological perspective
is even clearer, the one bread serves as a prayer-sign for that
future and final gathering, when many shall come from east
and west, from north and south, and sit at table in the kingdom of God (Matt. 8:11; Luke 13:29): "As this bread which
we have broken was once scattered on the mountains and
then, gathered together, became one, so may thy Church be
gathered together from the ends of the earth into thy
kingdom."[17]

3. The universal scope of reconciliation

On God's side, the work of reconciliation is in principle complete. But he intends the reconciliation to be universal in
effect: Christ's blood was shed "for the many."[18] And not all
have yet, for their part, accepted reconciliation with God.
The broad sweep of the reconciling work of Christ is symbolized for the Byzantines by the arrangement of the pieces
of bread at the *proskomidé*, or preparation of the elements:
around "the Lamb" are placed pieces commemorating the
Virgin Mary, John the Baptist, the prophets, apostles, saints,
the faithful departed, and the Church on earth. In a Syrian
tradition of color symbolism, the red, the green, and the
white of the altar-cloths on which the eucharistic vessels are
placed represent respectively the fiery universe, the verdant
earth, and the holy Church: the Qurbana, as the sacrament
of Christ's reconciling work, is at the very center of God's

total economy of creation and redemption. The periphery
and the fullness will be reached when God's effective reign
becomes universal and all enjoy that perfect submission to
God the Father which the Son has enjoyed from all eternity,
so that God will be "all in all" (1 Cor. 15:24-28).

In the achievement of God's reign, the mission of the
Church has a part to play. Not only do the members of the
Church gather to celebrate a eucharist that expresses achieved
reconciliation: the communicants are also sent out (*Ite. . .*),
in order to serve as agents of reconciliation in a world which
still needs to hear the message "Be reconciled to God." The
role of the eucharist as a sacramental focus of the reconciliation for which thanks have already to be given but which
still needs extension throughout human society was perhaps
expressed in the practice of the ancient Church whereby the
Sunday communicants took bread home with them for communion during the week:[19] the sacramental sign of reconciliation was thus set up in the heart of daily life. Whatever
the merits and demerits of that particular practice, the daily
life of Christians, who themselves enjoy reconciliation sacramentally in the eucharist, ought to be a living summons
and aid to the spread of vertical and horizontal reconciliation
among those who have not yet found in Christ their peace
with God and with their fellow human beings.

The eucharist is a sign of that justice, peace, and joy in
the Holy Spirit which characterize the kingdom of God (Rom.
14:17): a rightly ordered eucharist exemplifies justice, because believers are all equally welcomed there by the merciful God into his table-fellowship and all together share in
the fruits of redemption and in the foretaste of the new heavens and the new earth in which right will prevail (see 2 Pet.
3:13); it exemplifies peace, because those who are reconciled
are there at peace with God and with one another; it exemplifies joy in the Holy Ghost, because the cup of blessing
conveys to all who partake of it a taste of that "sober intoxication" which the Spirit gives (see Eph. 5:18). Having
learned and experienced this in the paradigm of the eucharistic meal, the Church is committed to an everyday witness
in word and deed which will give the opportunity for all the
material resources of creation and all occasions of human
contact to become the media of that communion with God

and among fellow human beings which is marked by justice, peace, and joy in the Holy Ghost, and in which the kingdom of God consists. In a rhythmic movement of *systolé* and *diastolé*, the eucharistic and missionary Church celebrates and proclaims *reconciliation*.

4. The local beginnings of ecumenical reconciliation

My remarks in the previous paragraph could be endorsed by Christians of all denominations; and each would be thinking of "the Church" as his own ecclesial community, and of "the eucharist" as celebrated by his own ecclesial community. But much of the value of my remarks is in fact lost as soon as one recalls the existence of separated ecclesial communities, each of which celebrates its own eucharist from which the others are more or less excluded. Each community may know reconciliation *with God,* but as long as the communities are not reconciled *with one another*, they can hardly bear convincing witness before the world to Christ's reconciling work; for if the horizontal corollary is not in evidence, even the vertical achievement may be called into question. Is it possible that the eucharist, as a sacrament of reconciliation, may have a constructive part to play in the attainment of reconciliation among Christian communities whose separation stands in contradiction to their own message? For this to happen, the stronger stress will have to fall on the eucharist's value as *promoting* unity rather than on its value as *expressive of existing unity* (to borrow the distinction made by the well-known tag: *eucharistia significat et efficit unitatem ecclesiasticam*).

Consider for a moment the admirable description of dynamic unity proposed by the Third Assembly of the WCC at New Delhi in 1961:

> We believe that the unity which is both God's will and his gift to his Church is being made visible as all in each place who are baptized into Jesus Christ and confess him as Lord and Saviour are brought by the Holy Spirit into one fully committed fellowship, holding the one apostolic faith, preaching the one Gospel, breaking the one bread, joining in common prayer, and having a corporate life reaching out in witness and service to all and who at the same time are united with the whole

Christian fellowship in all places and all ages in such wise that ministry and members are accepted by all, and that all can act and speak together as occasion requires for the tasks to which God calls his people. It is for such unity that we believe we must pray and work.

In the long run, the "place" of the Church's unity must, if the universal scope of God's reconciling work be borne in mind, have no smaller limits than the whole world. But, as an interim measure, we may begin by understanding "place" in a more restricted sense. A "place" may be understood as the area from which Christians come together, at some convenient point within it, for the regular celebration of the eucharist. This is "the local church" gathering recurrently in eucharistic assembly and repeatedly returning to its sphere of everyday witness. The Orthodox theologian N. Afanassieff has insisted strongly on the eucharistic celebration as the "sacrament of assembly" in which the whole Church of God is present in the local church.[20] Vatican II spoke of the liturgical assembly as *praecipua manifestatio Ecclesiae* (Constitution on the Sacred Liturgy 41). This kind of ecclesiology makes it possible to say that the level of the local church— the local eucharistic assembly and the local area of the worshippers' everyday witness—is a proper level at which reconciliation among separated Christians may start. Just as denominational rivalry among Christians in everyday witness must cease, so also must rival eucharistic assemblies stop. A drastic solution would be that *all* eucharists should cease until the various groups had been reconciled among themselves: are we sure that God does not "despise our solemn assemblies" as long as we live in such disunity that we are unable to "glorify him with one heart and one voice"? To the penitent, however, God is gracious; and the common gathering of separated but peace-seeking brothers and sisters around a single table of the Lord does, I am persuaded, promote horizontal reconciliation. Our increased sharing together in the one eucharist will allow the Lord to bring peace among us; for such a eucharist will be the occasion for him to cast out from us whatever is amiss in us, to unite us more closely to himself and therefore to one another, and to join us together in common enjoyment of his presence and gifts.

I am well aware of the view that "the one bread" may not be shared together at all until there is agreement in "the one apostolic faith" and until "ministry and members" are already mutually acceptable among hitherto separated communities. Far be it from me to belittle problems of faith and order. But I would argue, as I have done in detail elsewhere,[21] that, where truth and love are in apparent conflict, love should prevail over truth as it is imperfectly apprehended; and that, in view of the urgent task of proclaiming the gospel, missionary witness to the reconciling work of Christ should take priority over questions of the internal ordering of the Church. Let the eucharist, as the *effective* sacrament of reconciliation, bring closer together those who are still in some degree held together by their common Lord and who already display a will to reconciliation with their temporary adversaries!

II. THE EUCHARIST AS A SACRAMENT OF RENEWAL

We now move from reconciliation to renewal, from spatial imagery and structures to temporal imagery and structures. In this second half, our thinking will again fall under four heads, roughly corresponding to the four heads of the first half. Where we talked first of the reconciliation between humanity and *God*, we shall now talk of the *divine agents* of renewal. Where we talked before of reconciliation among *human beings*, we shall this time talk of renewed *humanity*. To the section on the *universal* scope of reconciliation will correspond a section on the *permanent and ultimate* quality of the renewal. The paragraph on the *local* beginnings of ecumenical reconciliation will find its counterpart in a paragraph on the *present* call for ecumenical renewal.

1. The divine agents of renewal

We have already referred to the ways in which the entry of Christ into the midst of the eucharistic assembly is expected and enacted. Now the Bible presents Christ as the creative Word (John 1:3; Heb. 1:2; see also 1 Cor. 8:6; Col. 1:16f.): "Your Word through whom you made the universe" is the phrase used by *The Apostolic Tradition* and by the new Eucharistic Prayer II of the Roman rite. He is appropriately the agent also of re-creation, remaking, renewal. Regarding Christ as the agent of creation and re-creation, of making and remaking, the eucharistic liturgies have associated this aspect of his work particularly with a change wrought in the eucharistic elements of bread and wine. One thinks of the Roman Catholic doctrine, ritually demonstrated by genuflections and elevations, of the consecratory power and effect of Christ's words in the institution narrative as it is rehearsed by the priest acting *in persona Christi*. In the Armenian liturgy, the institution narrative begins thus: "Then taking the bread in his holy, divine, immortal, immaculate and *creative* hands, he blessed . . ."; and in an ancient Persian anaphora, thus: "He took bread and wine which *his own will had made*, and he sanctified it. . . ."[22] We may also think of the so-called Logos-epiclesis in Serapion's anaphora; and the Word is invoked as consecratory agent in some Gallican and Mozarabic prayers. Many Protestants would resist this pattern of understanding insofar as any change in the eucharistic elements beyond that of an enhancement of meaning and purpose (transignification and transfinalization) may fall into "objectivism" (transubstantiation); they also fight shy of "biological" imagery which suggests a special physical effect on the communicant through the physical reception of the elements. But they would be happy with the kind of "personalist" view which stretches from Theodore of Mopsuestia to Michael Schmaus, and which sees the eucharistic communion as an encounter with the risen and glorious Lord who already begins his work of renewing persons in anticipation of the Parousia: by drawing them into closer communion with himself, Christ is gradually transforming the faithful communicants into his personal likeness and giving them an earnest of the life of the final kingdom.[23] "Blessed is he who came and who is to come in the name of the Lord" is the form of the acclamation of Christ in the Syrian and Armenian anaphoras; the Byzantine and Western anaphoras use a form which focuses on his present coming: "Blessed is he that comes in the name of the Lord." In any case, the eucharist is an occasion and means of encounter with Jesus

Christ who is the same yesterday, today, and forever. As creator and re-creator, he is performing his work of renewal in all who receive him in faith, hope, and love.

We have mentioned also the prayer for the descent of the Holy Spirit upon the elements and the people engaged in the eucharistic action. The Byzantine anaphoras of *St. Chrysostom* and *St. Basil* both include "the communion of the Holy Spirit" among the benefits entreated in the epiclesis for those who participate in the sacrament. Now the Bible presents the Holy Spirit also as a divine agent of renewal: when Yahweh sends forth his Spirit, he creates and renews (Ps. 104:30; Ezek. 37); the Spirit operates in human rebirth (John 3:5-7; Tit. 3:5); he makes alive (John 6:63; 7:38f.; 2 Cor. 3:6), and through him we shall be raised in our spiritual bodies (Rom. 8:11; 1 Cor. 15:44). There is of course no competition between the work of Christ and the work of the Holy Spirit: we may say that the Holy Spirit "applies" Christ to the Christian and to the Church, or that it is "in the Holy Spirit" that Christ comes to the Christian and to the Church.

The renewing activity of the Holy Spirit in the eucharist is expressed in the words of a *post-secreta* in the *Missale Gothicum*: ". . . beseeching that thou wouldest deign to pour thy Holy Spirit into us who eat and drink the things that will confer eternal life and the everlasting kingdom."[24] The East Syrian liturgy of *Addai and Mari* prays thus: "And may there come, O my Lord, thine Holy Spirit upon this offering of thy servants and bless it and hallow it that it be to us, O my Lord, for the pardon of offences and the remission of sins and for the great hope of resurrection from the dead and for new life in the kingdom of heaven with all those who have been well-pleasing in thy sight."[25] Some Protestants would consider that these prayers attached too great an instrumental value to the eucharistic elements. But none would doubt the operation of the Spirit in the eucharistic celebration as a whole. Calvin, in particular, laid stress on the Holy Spirit as the "link" between Christ and the Church in the eucharistic action. And the Holy Spirit himself is for the Christian the firstfruits (*aparché*, Rom. 8:23) and earnest (*arrabón*, 2 Cor. 1:22; 5:5; Eph. 1:13f.) of eternal life.

2. Renewed humanity

In talking of the eucharistic encounter with the risen and glorious Lord which takes place in the Holy Spirit, we have so far stressed the divine agency in the work of renewal. Let us now look at the process from the viewpoint of the beneficiaries of that work of renewal: the people who are being renewed. We may do so in terms of "glory," which provides a way of talking about the progressive realization of God's purpose for human beings and their attainment of the destiny God intends for them.

As they behold or reflect his glory, Christians are being progressively changed into the likeness of the Lord, from glory to glory (2 Cor. 3:18). Now some patristic writers gave a eucharistic interpretation to the saying of the Johannine Jesus at the Last Supper: "The glory which thou hast given me I have given to them" (John 17:22).[26] And a few liturgies pursue the theme of glory on similar lines. Thus the eucharistic prayer of the Dêr Balyzeh papyrus takes up the phrase "full of thy glory" from the Sanctus and continues in this way: "Fill us also with the glory that is from thee. . . ." The final blessing in the liturgy of *Addai and Mari* includes these words: "May the Lord make our people glorious, which have come and had delight in the power of his glorious and holy and life-giving and divine mysteries." The hymn of dismissal in the Greek liturgy of *St. James* begins: "From glory to glory advancing, we hymn thee. . . ." The divine gift of glory to humanity is in fact returned by humanity to God in praise, in "doxology." The second epiclesis in the Alexandrian liturgy of *St. Mark* makes the closest relation between "renewal of body, soul and spirit," "participation in the bliss of eternal life," and our "glorifying of the all-holy name" of God. In the epiclesis of the anaphora in *The Apostolic Tradition,* the final purpose of the Spirit's descent is "that we may praise and glorify thee through thy Son Jesus Christ." In almost all eucharistic prayers, the Sanctus and the concluding doxology highlight the fact that the eucharist is the liturgical expression of humanity's rendering to God the glory he himself bestows.

To some, particularly Protestants perhaps, this talk of glory will seem altogether too "substantialist" and "cultic." But it may be possible to translate into more "existential" and "ethical" terms the truth of which the eucharist is the sacramental expression. Taking our clues from Romans 5–8 and 12:1-2, we may say that humanity's "glory" is its God-given "liberty," the proper exercise of which consists in the "filial service" of God such as that displayed by Jesus—and God himself is thereby "glorified."

Prominent examples of the renewal of humanity are to be found in the saints who have adorned the Church down the centuries of its history. At the eucharist, the saints are commemorated especially in the canon, but also in the litanies and (prominently in the West) in the propers of their feast days. The Greek liturgy of *St. James* makes it explicit that the heavenly assembly in whose worship of God the earthly Church joins at the Sanctus includes "the spirits of just persons and prophets, the souls of martyrs and apostles." According to the Mozarabic Easter mass it is "all the angels and *saints*" who do not cease from shouting "Holy."

3. The permanent and final quality of the renewal

According to Paul's account of the institution of the eucharist, Jesus said, "This cup is the *new* covenant in my blood" (1 Cor. 11:25). At Mark 14:24 also, manuscripts A f1 f13 700 and the Latin and Syriac traditions read "This is my blood of the *new* covenant." The newness of the New Covenant inaugurated by Christ's blood-shedding is a newness that will never grow old; like the eagle's (Ps. 103:5; see also Isa. 40:31), its youth is constantly renewed. The Roman liturgical tradition is not substantially wrong in the addition it makes to the words of institution: "Hic est enim calix sanguinis mei, novi *et aeterni* testamenti." The New Covenant, inaugurated through Christ, is permanent and definitive. There is therefore a sense in which the eucharist, as the covenant meal, already realizes the promise which Jesus made to his disciples, that they would drink wine "new" together in the kingdom (Mark 14:25; Matt. 26:29; Luke 22:18, 29f.). Yet it is equally clear that the fullness of the kingdom tarries: sin is not yet fully extirpated, not even from Christ's followers, let alone from the whole human race; the Parousia has not yet taken place. The eucharist bears the marks of this incompleteness: we do not yet see Christ face to face, but only the "sacramental veil"; our celebration is periodic, not yet perpetual; the service we offer is imperfect, not yet total; it is not yet the whole of "the many" for whom Christ's blood was shed, but only a part, which gathers at the Messiah's table.

The permanent and definitive quality of the New Covenant inaugurated through Jesus Christ is reflected in the fact that the same New Testament continues to be read as Scripture at the eucharist. In present thanksgiving, the Church then rehearses the redemptive events of the past to which those Scriptures bear witness. In present expectation, the Church looks forward to the full realization of the promises which the past events contain and to which the Scriptures also bear verbal testimony (*praestolantes alterum eius adventum / exspectantes ipsius adventum in gloria . . .*[27]). In the eucharist the Church prays that the effects of the redemptive events of the past may be made present and understands its participation in the meal as an anticipation of the full realization of the promises that still belongs to the future.

The relation between the present and the future, the "already" and the "not yet" of our renewal, has in fact been expressed in the liturgies and the eucharistic theologians by a variety of figures. The eucharist is a "pledge," an "earnest," a "sign," an "image," a "prefiguration," a "promise." All these terms express both a link and a distinction between present and future. But best of all (because we are talking of a *meal*), the eucharist is a "taste" of the age to come. To taste is to try the relish; and to say that the eucharist provides a taste of the kingdom therefore allows us to express both the provisional and yet the genuine quality of the kingdom as it flavors the present. As a Methodist, I may perhaps be allowed to quote from the *Hymns on the Lord's Supper* of John and Charles Wesley (hymn no. 108):

> For all that joy which now we *taste*,
> Our happy hallow'd souls prepare;
> O let us hold the *earnest* fast,
> This *pledge* that we Thy heaven shall share,
> Shall drink it new with Thee above,
> The wine of Thy eternal love.

The Methodist brothers were singing in the eighteenth century what Peter Chrysologus had said in the fifth, in his exposition of the fourth petition of the Lord's Prayer: Christ gave us the eucharist "in order that we may by it attain unto endless day and the very table of Christ, and there receive in fulness and unto all satiety that of which we have here been given the taste."[28] A link between taste and renewal is made in a prayer from the Gregorian Sacramentary: "Having been filled by the gift of thy salvation, O Lord, we humbly beg that the thing whose taste gladdens us may by its effect renew us."[29]

4. The present call for ecumenical renewal

In terms of the symbolism of time, Sunday is the eucharistic day *par excellence.* It is the day on which the Lord Jesus rose from the dead, "the head of another race which he himself regenerated" (as Justin Martyr calls him[30]). As "the Lord's day," Sunday prefigures *the* "Day of the Lord." The Fathers called Sunday "the eighth day," seeing it as the beginning of the age to come. The eucharist is the meal belonging to the interval between the first, and specially privileged, meals which the disciples shared with the risen Lord[31] and the final messianic feasting[32] which will take place when the form of this world will have passed away and all things will have been made new.[33]

In this time of tension between the Church's original institution and her attainment of her final destiny, what is the role of the eucharist? We have already referred to the permanent and definitive quality of the renewal begun by Christ. But it is a beginning, and not yet an end. Enough of the old world remains for the Church's holiness to be disfigured by the sin of her members, and for her catholicity to be diminished through the absence from her of the still unconverted. This shortfall in holiness and catholicity prevents the Church from yet being considered to embody a universal unity of love. Sin, which may also be called lack of love, has resulted in schism; mission has not yet reached all "the many." As a sacrament of renewal, the eucharist has a part to play in the healing of old divisions and in the carrying of the Christian witness into fresh fields. The gathering, when it is allowed to happen, of the separated but penitent brothers and sisters around the one table of the one Lord exemplifies before the world the holiness which consists in the overcoming of sin and in the growth of love; from the one table, which is itself a sign to the nations of the feast which the Lord is preparing for the whole of humanity (Isa. 25:6-9), the brothers and sisters are dispatched on a common mission throughout the world—a "catholic" mission—to invite everyone to share with them in the new life of love offered in Christ.

III. CONCLUSION

In all that I have said so far about reconciliation and renewal, I have concentrated almost exclusively on the way in which they affect *humanity*, neglecting what may be called their "cosmic" dimension. This is because the redemption of creation must somehow pass through the redemption of *humanity* (Rom. 8:19-23); the question of humanity is therefore prior. In conclusion, however, I wish simply to hint at the way in which cosmic reconciliation and renewal are signified in the eucharist. In its temporal unfolding, the properly eucharistic celebration passes through three main "moments": the *taking* of bread and wine, the *giving of thanks* over them, the *eating and drinking* of them. By this process, the material creation is being renewed—in the sense that it is now being put (the *taking*) to its proper use as the occasion (the *thanksgiving*) and medium (the *eating and drinking*) of humanity's fellowship with God. In their spatial frame of reference, the bread and wine of the eucharist are representative parts of creation which are already exhibiting in an exemplary way that total reconciliation which will finally be achieved when the whole of creation will find its peace in fulfilling the divine purpose and "God will be all in all."[34]

As a final word, let me quote two eucharistic hymns from my own Methodist tradition, both from the Wesleys' *Hymns on the Lord's Supper*. The first (no. 116) sees the eucharist as a sacrament of reconciliation: the restoration of humanity to fellowship with God. The second (no. 40) sees the eucha-

rist as a sacrament of renewal: the progress of humanity in
the transforming fellowship to which it has been restored.

1 Victim divine, Thy grace we claim
  While thus Thy precious death we show;
  Once offered up, a spotless Lamb,
  In Thy great temple here below,
  Thou didst for all mankind atone,
  And standest now before the throne.

2 Thou standest in the holiest place,
  As now for guilty sinners slain;
  Thy blood of sprinkling speaks, and prays,
  All-prevalent for helpless man;
  Thy blood is still our ransom found,
  And spreads salvation all around.

3 The smoke of Thy atonement here
  Darkened the sun and rent the veil,
  Made the new way to heaven appear,
  And showed the great Invisible;
  Well pleased in Thee our God looked down,
  And called His rebels to a crown.

4 He still respects thy sacrifice,
  Its savour sweet doth always please;
  The offering smokes through earth and skies,
  Diffusing life, and joy, and peace;
  To these Thy lower courts it comes,
  And fills them with divine perfumes.

5 We need not now go up to heaven,
  To bring the long-sought Saviour down;
  Thou art to all already given,
  Thou dost even now Thy banquet crown;
  To every faithful soul appear,
  And show thy real presence here!

---

1 Author of life divine,
  Who hast a table spread,
  Furnished with mystic wine
  And everlasting bread,
  Preserve the life Thyself hast given,
  And feed and train us up for heaven.

2 Our needy souls sustain
   With fresh supplies of love,
   Till all Thy life we gain,
   And all Thy fulness prove,
   And, strengthened by Thy perfect grace,
   Behold without a veil Thy face.

V
EUCHARIST AND CONCILIARITY

This essay is divided into four parts. The first part recalls certain moments in the linkage between eucharist and conciliarity as these two themes have been brought together in the recent evolution of ecumenical thought. In the second part, an attempt is made to state, both descriptively and programmatically, what conciliarity might mean in the life of the Churches and of the Church. The third part goes back to the early Church in search of a concrete model of conciliarity, paying particular attention to the eucharistic incidences in the ancient expression of ecclesial conciliarity. In the fourth and final part, I consider systematically what is the proper place and function of the eucharist in our own efforts toward a better conciliar practice.

I. EUCHARIST AND CONCILIARITY IN RECENT ECUMENICAL THOUGHT

The word "conciliarity" came into recent ecumenical prominence through the Uppsala Assembly of the World Council of Churches in 1968. But in summoning the member Churches to "work for the time when a *genuinely universal council* may once more speak for all Christians," the Uppsala Assembly was doing no more than to draw out—and dramatically sharpen through talk of *a council*—the *universal* implications of the processive description of Church unity already proposed by the New Delhi Assembly of the WCC in 1961. The New Delhi description sees the process of unity as follows: "We believe that the unity which is both God's will and his gift to his Church is being made visible as all in each place who are baptized into Jesus Christ and confess

him as Lord and Saviour are brought by the Holy Spirit into
one fully committed fellowship, holding the one apostolic
faith, preaching the one Gospel, breaking the one bread,
joining in common prayer, and having a corporate life reaching out in witness and service to all and who at the same
time are united with the whole Christian fellowship in all
places and all ages in such wise that ministry and members
are accepted by all, and that all can act and speak together
as occasion requires for the tasks to which God calls his
people."[1]

In the years immediately following New Delhi, it was the
local accent of the first part of the description which received
most attention: "all in each place." Yet the latter part of the
New Delhi description clearly opened up the *universal* dimension (". . . united with the whole Christian fellowship in
all places and all ages in such wise that ministry and members are accepted by all")—and even hinted at the possibility of a universal *council:* ". . . and that all can act and speak
together as occasion requires for the tasks to which God calls
his people." For our purposes it is important to note that
"breaking the one bread" is a component in the unity which
New Delhi declared to be both "God's gift" and "our task."

Uppsala's dramatic talk of a future universal council gave
rise to a more active exploration of the whole notion of conciliarity, though a certain stimulus may also have been provided by the recent event of the Second Vatican Council in
the Roman Catholic Church. The Uppsala Assembly itself
was aware that a "genuinely universal council" would not
arrive as a bolt from the blue: it was something which the
Churches needed to "work for."[2] The special event of a universal council would in fact be intelligible and practicable
only within the context of a continuing process of conciliar
life in and among the Churches. The Faith and Order consultation at Salamanca in 1973 on "concepts of unity and
models of union" was able to re-express New Delhi's processive description in the form of a "vision" which stands
before us as a "goal" to be "achieved"—and it did so in the
language of conciliarity: "Jesus Christ founded one Church.
Today we live in diverse churches divided from one another.
Yet our vision of the future is that we shall once again live

as brothers and sisters in one undivided Church. How can this goal be described? We offer the following description to the churches for their consideration: The one Church is to be envisioned as a conciliar fellowship of local churches which are themselves truly united. In this conciliar fellowship each local church possesses, in communion with the others, the fulness of catholicity, witnesses to the same apostolic faith and therefore recognizes the others as belonging to the same Church of Christ and guided by the same Spirit. As the New Delhi Assembly pointed out, they are bound together because they have received the same baptism and share in the same Eucharist; they recognize each other's members and ministries. They are one in their common commitment to confess the Gospel of Christ by proclamation and service to the world. To this end each church aims at maintaining sustained and sustaining relationships with her sister churches, expressed in conciliar gatherings, whenever required for the fulfilment of their common calling."[3]

Three points need to be added immediately. First, conciliarity was not intended by the Salamanca document as a substitute for organic union; rather, conciliar fellowship is full and visible communion among "local churches which are themselves truly"—explained as organically—"united."[4] Second, the Salamanca document develops the link between conciliarity and eucharist in this way: "Conciliar fellowship cannot but be eucharistic fellowship. United by one baptism, members of all local churches should be able to share everywhere in the celebration of the Eucharist. No council *(concilium)* can be held without celebrating the Eucharist." Third, the Salamanca "vision of a united Church as a conciliar fellowship" was positively integrated into the thinking of the Nairobi Assembly of the WCC in 1975.[5]

The next impulse to be picked up from recent ecumenical history comes direct from the Nairobi Assembly. Since that Assembly, the Constitution of the WCC now expressly states that the purpose of the WCC is to help the churches to advance to "visible unity in one faith and in one eucharistic fellowship."[6] In its early days the WCC felt obliged to minimize its own ecclesiological significance; it did so in the face of some Protestant fears of a "super-Church" and in the

face of Orthodox reticence concerning the ecclesial status of
non-Orthodox members.[7] The WCC was a "conseil," not a
"concile." But the years of common experience in shared
membership have produced in all parts of the confessional
spectrum a growing sense that the WCC does in fact carry
some ecclesiological consistency.[8] The Salamanca document
used the term "pre-conciliar" of "the councils of divided
churches (e.g. the World Council of Churches, National
Councils, etc.) which have come into existence in the ecumenical movement as instruments to promote the search for
unity and common witness." The prefix "pre" in "pre-conciliar" is of course restrictive, but on the other hand it is also
forward-looking in a positive sense. It is an indication of the
fact that we may already have been granted, even while in
some respects divided, a partial anticipation of the conciliar
life in which all Christians should be united. The gift also
imposes a task: we have to work, in the strength of the gift,
for the fuller realization of the common life. The goal itself,
in the manner of a "final cause," draws us on.

In connection with the eucharistic theme, it is important
to note that it is within the context of such "pre-conciliarity"
that the so-called "inter-communion" debate has taken place
from the beginning of the modern ecumenical movement.
On the one hand, there have been those who reject the implications of the prefix "inter" on the ground that eucharistic
communion among the Churches must await the achievement of complete unity in all matters of faith and life. On
the other hand, there have been those who reject the implications of the prefix "inter" on the ground that the table is
the Lord's, and that he already invites all Christians to gather
around it together, irrespective of their divisions. Between
the proponents of these extreme positions the conversation
has often been a dialogue of the deaf. The more hopeful
discussion has taken place on a middle ground where the
conversationalists have tried to gauge the point at which the
divided communities (will) have reached a sufficient measure of unity for eucharistic communion *both* to express a
certain substantial reality of existing fellowship *and* to foster
the increase of that measure of unity toward full achievement. If we wished to justify the prefix "inter" in "intercommunion," we could allege its suitably ambivalent char-

acter as pointing to a persisting division that is on the way to being overcome, a unity that is at least on the road to achievement.[9]

The final matter to which attention must be drawn in current ecumenical history is the movement toward agreement on baptism, eucharist, and ministry. The statement on which the Accra meeting of the Faith and Order Commission in 1974 agreed, *One Baptism, One Eucharist, and A Mutually Recognized Ministry,* was sent upon authority of the Nairobi Assembly to the member Churches of the WCC for consideration and response. A first round of responses was evaluated in a report presented to the Central Committee of the WCC in August 1977 under the title "Towards an ecumenical consensus on baptism, eucharist and the ministry." It was there recognized that the transition from Statements agreed by theologians to a consensus among the Churches would take yet more time. But two points must immediately be made in connection with our joint theme of conciliarity and eucharist. First, the characteristically conciliar processes of consultation and even (in a provisional way) ecclesial "reception" are felt to be "on the way" in matters of doctrinal importance and practical consequence. Diversities and even differences persist, yet the Churches should now become increasingly aware of how much they can affirm and practice in common. My own hope is that most of the differences may eventually be seen as tolerable, and even welcome, elements of diversity.[10] The second point to notice is the view expressed in the Accra Statement that the mutual recognition of "the one baptism," where it seriously takes place, constitutes a dynamic toward "eucharistic sharing," "common witness," and all the components of "full visible union."

After these brief indications of recent developments in the ecumenical movement from the viewpoint of our dual theme, we must now look a little more analytically at the meaning of conciliarity.

II. A DESCRIPTIVE AND PROGRAMMATIC ANALYSIS OF CONCILIARITY

To state the meaning of conciliarity it is necessary both to include the positive elements in known ecclesial practice

and, since our own enjoyment of conciliarity is imperfect, to
project a picture of a more complete conciliarity which we
might succeed in practicing in the future. Our definition of
conciliarity will therefore be in part descriptive, in part pro-
grammatic. This combination of experience and hope is found
in both sections of our analysis as we seek to analyze conciliarity first in spatial and then in temporal terms; but the
element of given experience will predominate in the spatial
analysis, and the element of active hope will predominate
in the temporal analysis.

In a spatial morphology of conciliarity, we may distinguish both various levels and various areas of extension.
First, the "levels" of conciliarity. There is, first of all, the
level of the deep structures. Here conciliarity is a condition
or a state (in the sense which that word bears, for instance,
in the expression "state of grace"). At this basic level, conciliarity is the state of *relatedness* (to borrow a term from the
Salamanca document). The Churches are bound together by
their common grounding in the love of God, the saving work
of Christ, and the gift of the Holy Spirit. To be without this
grounding is to be without any ecclesial character at all. Any-
one who draws the boundaries of the Church narrowly ex-
poses himself to all the problems of Cyprianic exclusivism.
On the other hand, supposedly Christian communities which
live in division from one another are contradicting the deepest nature of the Church.

The next level of conciliarity is that on which the Churches
give expression to their deep unity through the practice of
everyday living. I think this is more or less what the Salamanca document means by "sustained and sustaining *relationships.*" It is the level of day-to-day circulation,
communication, exchange, mutual help, common enterprise.
It is a level of mobility, of an active network of relationships.
In our examination of the ancient Church we shall note the
direct and indirect eucharistic incidences which operate at
this level of conciliarity.

The third level of conciliarity (or is it a special point on
the second?) is that of the council itself. Here the mobile
conciliarity of everyday relationships comes to a "gathering-
point," a point of concentration at which the communities

meet through the person of their representatives in order to draw deeply on the divine well which is their common source. For a moment the mobile relationships settle into a fixed *relation,* in which the deep relatedness is brought to the surface in a particularly evident way. In the early history of the Church, councils tended to be called only in the emergency of a dispute. It is a more modern practice, facilitated perhaps by greater ease of travel, for conciliar gatherings of various kinds to take place for purposes of consultation and coordination in the more ordinary affairs of the Churches. We shall note again the eucharistic incidences of conciliar gathering, whether in emergency or more ordinary circumstances.

The various "areas of extension" in the matter of conciliarity can be dealt with simply. The day-to-day and the gathered expressions of conciliarity all operate, according to circumstances, over geographical areas of varying extension, whether it be a city, county, department, state, province, region, country, continent, or the whole inhabited earth. The size of the area touched by a particular expression of conciliarity varies with opportunity and need. That all expressions of ecclesial conciliarity are *potentially* universal follows from their grounding in the one God.

Let us move now from an analysis in spatial terms to an analysis in temporal terms. To analyze conciliarity in temporal terms allows us to speak of the varying *quality* of the expression of conciliarity in the life of the Churches and of the Church. How well are the Churches expressing in their mutual relationships the *newness* of Christianity? How successfully are the values of the *future* kingdom being lived and displayed in the present relationships among the Churches? Because the final kingdom has not yet come, there is always still a flavor of the optative and the conative in the verbs we use in talking of unity and of conciliarity as its form. New Delhi ended its processive description of the Church's unity by saying "it is for such unity that we believe we must *pray* and *work.*" Unity is a *gift* to be *sought.* That resides in the nature of the case, and it will remain so until the consummation: the Church in history can do no more than approximate its eschatological calling until God grants it the perfection of the End. This would be the case even at those times, if there have been such times, when there was no institutional division among Christians: the love which integral conciliar institutions and practices express and facilitate would even then be called to continued growth.[11] When conciliar institutions and practices have wholly or partly broken down through sinful division among the communities, the summons to restore relationships is of urgent gravity as a prelude to common growth toward perfect love. Progress in conciliar expression thus becomes a concrete form of growth in mutual love.

In the search for a concrete model of conciliarity, we may now turn for inspiration to the early Church since the early Church is generally regarded by our Churches as possessing in some sense a normative function.

III. CONCILIARITY IN THE EARLY CHURCH AND ITS EUCHARISTIC INCIDENCES

In discussing the early centuries it is impossible to speak of "the undivided Church" in any simple historical sense. St. Paul reveals the existence of splits (schísmata) among the Corinthian Christians, and there is much in the New Testament about false teachers and false shepherds. From the doctrinal viewpoint, W. Bauer's work did enough to show the imprecision and fluidity of the boundaries between *Orthodoxy and Heresy in Earliest Christianity*. From the institutional viewpoint, S. L. Greenslade found much material for his study *Schism in the Early Church*. Such books provide a necessary corrective in a historiographical tradition which has been dominated by a view of "the great Church" as a doctrinally and institutionally united body *from* which heretics and schismatics were simply excluded. Nevertheless, *de mortuis nihil nisi bonum*. We may still turn to the early centuries for a practical example of how the Church *approximated* an *ideal*, perhaps better a *calling*, of unity.

In looking at the practice of the early Church in the matter of conciliarity, I shall be sensitive to its eucharistic incidences. It will not be necessary to limit ourselves to explicit mentions of sacramental practice. We shall notice more widely certain features of the Christian life which find a cultic focus in the eucharist while occurring more diffusely outside the liturgy. Eight features of conciliar life will be detected, each bearing a direct or indirect reference to the eucharist.

1. The apostolic bond

The first element of conciliar life to be noticed belongs in a strict sense to the apostolic period alone. It consists in the fact that the Christian communities were linked by the apostolic ministry exercised toward them. We know best the case of the apostle Paul. His itinerant and epistolary ministry provided a personal bond among the churches. When he was present at their assemblies, he appears to have both preached and presided at the eucharist (Acts 20:7-11). In his absence, his letters were read in the assembly[12]—and were on occasion passed on from one church to another (Col. 4:16). It was Paul's quality as a *minister of the gospel* which gave specifically Christian content to the personal bond which he constituted among the churches—and one of the chief "horizontal" uses of *koinōnía* and *koinōnoun* in his writings is to speak of fellowship in the service of the gospel (2 Cor. 8:23; Gal. 6:6; Phil. 1:5, 7; 4:14f.; see also Philem. 6, 17).[13] The apostles died. But wherever apostolic writings continue to be read in the liturgical assembly, the communities which read and hear them are still to that extent joined together in a conciliar fellowship by the apostles. The use of Scriptures from the apostolic Church makes for a participation in a single gospel and in a common faith. Insofar also as the communities receive their present ministers as "successors to the apostles," the apostolic link among the communities lives on in that form too.

2. The fellowship of prayer

The fellowship of prayer is everywhere presupposed in Paul's letters. He often mentions his prayers for the recipients and asks for theirs on his own behalf. 2 Corinthians 9:14 and Ephesians 6:18 are good examples of one community praying for Christians in other places. As traditional liturgical practice developed, prayer was made at the eucharist for other churches in the person of their bishop. The mention of episcopal names in the "diptychs," or the removal of such names from the lists, signified the maintenance or rupture of ecclesial communion among the communities. This background reveals the importance of the modern ecumenical practice of the divided Churches in praying for one another, a practice sharply focused in the Week of Prayer for Christian Unity when the Churches often meet together for this purpose. Faith and Order's ecumenical calendar of mutual intercession, *For All God's People*, is also significant in this regard.

3. Interchurch aid

A third element of conciliar life dates from the apostolic period also, and once more it is St. Paul who provides our best evidence. This third feature is the "interchurch aid" exemplified by St. Paul's famous "collection" among his Gentile churches to help the "saints of Jerusalem."[14] Another main use of *koinōnía* and *koinōnoun* in Paul's writings occurs in this connection (Rom. 12:13; 15:26; 2 Cor. 8:4; 9:13).[15] When the apostle instructs the Corinthians to "put something aside on the first day of the week" (1 Cor. 16:1-4), there is a strong possibility that their individual contributions were collected at the weekly liturgical assembly. In the second century, Justin Martyr reveals that the *local* diaconal service of the church issued from the liturgical assembly: "And the wealthy who so desire give what they wish, as each chooses; and what is collected is deposited with the president. He helps orphans and widows, and those who through sickness or any other cause are in need, and those in prison, and strangers sojourning among us; in a word, he takes care of all those who are in need" (*First Apology* 67, 6-7). This was entirely appropriate since the eucharistic meal is, on the "horizontal" plane, a sacrament of fellowship among Christians, and Christian fellowship implies practical service to needy brothers and sisters. (There is a kind of negative proof of this point in Ignatius' *Letter to the Smyrnaeans:* in chapters 6 and 7 he refers to people who abstain from the eucharist, apparently for "docetic" reasons, and who [correspondingly!] fail in practical care for the widow, the orphan, the distressed, the afflicted, the prisoner, the hungry, and the thirsty.)

Wherever material service is given and received between Christian communities, a bond of fellowship is forged between them; and it appears appropriate, and indeed required, that this bond should on some convenient occasions come to sacramental expression through some form of eucharistic communion between the communities.

4. Hospitality

A fourth feature of conciliar life is the practice of hospitality which the New Testament writers enjoined upon the Christian communities (Rom. 12:13; 1 Tim. 3:2; Tit. 1:8; Heb. 13:2; 1 Pet. 4:9). This is no doubt intended in the general sense of a welcome to hearth and home. But visiting Christians would naturally be invited to share also in the liturgical assembly and eucharistic communion of their hosts. It is significant that even such a normally "closed" communion as that celebrated by the Roman Catholic Church should in recent times have been courteously opened to non-Roman Catholics who through geographical or other circumstances are temporarily deprived of their own eucharistic communion.[16] Other Churches have long practiced such hospitality. In the other direction, it should be remembered that there is also a proper "courtesy of the guest": when one is hospitably invited to share in a family meal, one does not make one's acceptance conditional upon the *cordon bleu* qualities of the cook. Similarly a visiting Christian should not be too concerned with the credentials of the eucharistic president of the host community.

5. Eucharistic presidency by a visiting bishop

The fifth expression of conciliarity to be mentioned from the early Church is specifically eucharistic. We know that a visiting bishop could be invited actually to preside at the eucharist of the church he was visiting. From Irenaeus by way of Eusebius we learn that when Polycarp visited Rome, "in the church Anicetus [the Roman bishop] yielded the (saying of the) Eucharist to Polycarp, plainly out of respect" (*Historia Ecclesiastica* 5, 24, 17). This courteous surrender of the eucharistic presidency occurred even while the two "agreed to differ" on the proper date for the paschal celebration. By the time of the Council of Arles (314), the mood had changed: canon 17 was needed in order to forbid bishops to trespass in the affairs of another bishop; and, if the interpretation of Hefele and Leclercq is correct, canon 19 was needed in order to ensure that a visiting bishop was nevertheless allowed the courtesy of "a place to say mass" (that is, his *own* mass).[17]

6. The *fermentum*

The sixth expression of conciliarity from the early Church is the eucharistic *fermentum*.[18] Our first evidence for this practice of sending out a portion of the eucharistic bread to other congregations comes from Rome. At the time of the "quartodeciman controversy" over the date of the Pascha, Ireneaus recalls to Bishop Victor of Rome the earlier practice of tolerance in the days of Anicetus and Polycarp: "None were ever cast out on account of this particular custom [of the Asiatic date], but the elders before you, though they did not themselves observe it, sent the eucharist to members of those communities *(paroikíon)* who did" (Eusebius, *Historia Ecclesiastica* 5, 24, 15). The reference is probably not to the sending of a portion of the sacrament from Rome to churches in Asia but much rather to a *local* practice by which the Roman bishop sent a consecrated particle to the Asiatic, and possibly other, congregations in Rome as a sign of the unity of the total Christian community in the city.[19]

The *Liber Pontificalis* associates both Miltiades (311-14) and Siricius (384-99) with the practice of sending the *fermentum* to other churches in the city where the eucharist was being celebrated by presbyters.[20] In these reports, which have a juridical sound, the *fermentum* appears to be a kind of episcopal "authorization" necessary to the other celebrations. Such an episcopal action would concretize the sentiments of Ignatius of Antioch who already, with a view to safeguarding local unity, had written: "Let no one do any of the things belonging to the Church without the bishop. Let that be held a valid eucharist which is under the bishop or one to whom he has committed it" (*Smyrnaeans* 8; see also *Philadelphians* 4). The Eastern practice by which episcopally consecrated *mýron* is used by presbyters for baptismal chrismation would be another concretion of this principle.

Innocent I (401-17) answered in this way the query of Decentius concerning "the *fermentum* which we send to all city churches (*per titulos*) on (Easter) Sunday": "The presbyters of the churches situated inside the city, who are unable to gather with us on that day because of the people committed to their care, receive at the hand of acolytes a *fermentum* which has been confected by us, so that they may not reckon themselves cut off from communion with us on that day of all days. But I do not think this ought to be done for outlying parishes (*per parochias*), as the sacrament ought not to be carried too far; nor therefore do we send it to presbyters who are situated in the more scattered cemeteries, and the presbyters there have the right and permission of confecting the sacrament themselves."[21] The episcopal *fermentum* was added to the presbyteral chalice; and traces of the practice persist at Rome till the end of the eighth century.[22]

In the East, the practice of sending the *fermentum* appears to be reflected—though only on the occasion of its prohibition—in the canons of the mid-fourth-century Council of Laodicea.[23] The fourteenth canon decrees that "the holy things (*tá hágia*) are not to be sent as *eulogíai* to other *paroikíai* at the Easter festival." The meaning is probably not that the practice remained allowable at other times than Easter; rather, a characteristically paschal practice was now being forbidden altogether. The *paroikíai* are probably not "dioceses" (which would mean that only interdiocesan traffic was being stopped) but rather "parishes" within a single diocese (Innocent's letter uses *parochiae* for "parts of a diocese outside the main city"; see Basil, *Epistle* 240 [*PG* 32, 897]); so once again the meaning is a total prohibition. (Wiles suggests that the idea of an interdiocesan *fermentum* rests on a misreading of Irenaeus' letter to Victor, as though it referred to sending of the Roman particle to Asia itself.) I take it that *tá hágia* and *eulogíai* in the fourteenth canon of Laodicea mean the *consecrated* bread of the eucharist: the prohibition would no doubt be due to problems of transport in connection with an increasingly "realistic" understanding of the eucharistic presence in the elements. But even if the reference were merely to "blessed bread" (i.e. the *antidṓra*), we should have Eastern evidence of the one-time existence of at least a quasi-sacramental expression of conciliarity among the parishes of a diocese (or between dioceses, if that interpretation of *paroikíai* be preferred). In North Africa, Paulinus and Augustine appear to have sent each other gifts of bread as a sign of unity (Augustine, *Epistles* 25 [*PL* 33, 103], and 31 [*PL* 33, 125]; see also 24 [*PL* 33, 100]).

The practice of a sacramental, or (if the sense of *eulogíai* be minimized) quasi-sacramental, exchange among churches may also be reflected in the thirty-second canon of Laodicea, which forbids the acceptance of *eulogíai* from heretical groups on the ground that they are *alogíai* (nonsenses) rather than *eulogíai* (blessings). Or the canon might refer to the reception of communion by individuals at heretical hands. In any case, this canon would seem on the face of it to exclude "intercommunion." In similar vein, the thirty-third canon orders that "no one shall join in prayers with heretics or schismatics." But three remarks must immediately be made: first, the presupposed ecclesiology of the canons is that of Cyprianic exclusivism, with all its problems; second, there is today a wider awareness that issues of schism and heresy are not so clear-cut as they once appeared to be; third, the modern ecumenical movement sets a context of nonhostility, in which Christian unity is actively being sought by partners committed to a common search for a common goal.

7. The eucharistic assembly

In speaking of the liturgical assembly, St. Paul and the patristic writers use the language of "coming together" *(synérchesthai, synágein, synéleusis, sýnaxis)*, often with the addition of "in(to) one place" *(epí tó autó)* (1 Cor. 11:18, 20, 33, 34; 14:23; Ignatius, *Ephesians* 13; Didache 14; Justin, *First Apology* 67). The local eucharistic assembly therefore appears itself as a "syn-odical" event. Insofar as it is "the one eucharist" which is celebrated everywhere, the celebration of the eucharist is also a bond *between* the local churches. The eucharist is a sacramental expression of the profound relatedness which we saw as constituting the deepest level of conciliarity: the common grounding of Christians—viewed both locally and universally—in the love of God, the saving work of Christ, and the gift of the Holy Spirit. The conciliar character of every eucharistic assembly is a reminder, first, that all conciliar life should, like the eucharist, be characterized by a doxological intention; and, second, that all conciliar life is, again like the eucharist, dependent upon the divine grace.

8. Councils

Finally there are the councils themselves. Although regional synods took place earlier, it was not until the "peace of the Church" under Constantine that wider councils were held—first the Western council of Arles in 314 and then in 325 the "ecumenical council" of Nicea (*sýnodos oikoumenîkē* is the expression of Eusebius; *Life of Constantine* 3, 7). Earlier synods had a sense of dealing with matters of concern to the universal Church; thus the synodical letter from Antioch in 268 was addressed to "... the whole catholic Church throughout the world under heaven" (Eusebius, *Historia Ecclesiastica* 7, 30, 2); and in the early stages of the Arian controversy, Bishop Alexander of Alexandria wrote in these terms to communicate the decisions of the Alexandrian synod to his "fellow-ministers of the catholic Church everywhere": "Since the catholic Church is one body, and the Scriptures command us to maintain the bond of unanimity and peace, we have the practice of writing to acquaint one another with what happens among us, in order that if one member suffers or rejoices, we may sympathize or rejoice together" (Socrates, *Historia Ecclesiastica* 1, 6). To Nicea, however, the emperor now convoked bishops "from everywhere" (Eusebius, *Life of Constantine* 3, 6); and later, in connection with the Council of Chalcedon, Pope Leo talks of bishops gathering *ex toto orbe* for a *concilium universale* (*Epistles* 43 and 89 [PL 54, 823 and 930]); in fact, however, the Western representation was in each case very small in number, though the Bishop of Rome sent his delegates. Unfortunately we have very little information concerning the liturgical practice in and around the early councils. We know that the Nicene bishops met in a "house of prayer" which, "as though divinely enlarged," sufficed to contain them (Eusebius, *Life of Constantine* 3, 7); and there are mentions of prayers being said. Yet although the councils were largely occupied with questions of maintaining, breaking, or restoring "communion," I have found no reference to what might be called a "conciliar eucharist" in the accounts of the early councils, though Eusebius sees fit to mention the splendid banquet to which the Nicene bishops were invited by Constantine to celebrate the twenty years of his reign. On the basis of later and still current practice in their churches, Orthodox scholars argue that the anathemata pronounced by the early councils imply that those councils celebrated the eucharist: the anathemata are pronounced during the eucharistic assembly.

IV. THE EUCHARIST'S ROLE IN THE IMPROVEMENT OF OUR CONCILIAR PRACTICE

The first three parts of this chapter have already contained hints as to the place and function which I think the eucharist should occupy in our own efforts toward a better conciliar practice. In the fourth and final part, my aim is to state more systematically the perspectives in which I consider the eucharist should be understood and celebrated if we are seeking to improve our conciliar practice as the form of our movement toward the overcoming of remaining disunity and the growth into ever more perfect unity. The treatment here is necessarily brief, and for a fuller theological background and argumentation I must refer to my book *Eucharist and Eschatology* (1971; expanded ed. 1981).

The first perspective relates history and eschatology. The second relates the expressive and the productive functions of the eucharist. The third relates the particular to the universal character of the Church. In the fourth, our eyes are kept open to choices among anomalies.

1. History and eschatology

According to its divine calling, the Church *is* one: it *could* not be otherwise when there is only one God and Father, one Lord, one Spirit, one divine kingdom as the final object of hope. Nor *should* it be otherwise in matters where the human response to the call comes in: one body, one faith,

one baptism (to complete the allusion to Ephesians 4:1-6).
Yet the evidence of history is that, in matters of human response, the Church is *not* one: baptisms are not mutually
recognized among all (supposedly) Christian communities;
or, where baptisms are mutually recognized among some
communities, there is then a contradiction if those communities stay separated in other matters; nor do the separated
communities usually consider themselves to be properly
united in a single faith, for there are more or less weighty
doctrinal points at issue among them; as to a single body,
the historical picture is more obviously one of dismemberment. An ecclesiology which denies the existence of disunity
is exclusivist: "we alone constitute the true Church: other
people have split from us and fallen into an ecclesiological
void." An ecclesiology which denies the gravity of disunity
is docetist: "institutional unity is not important because true
Christians are known to the Lord and are inwardly one in
him." A more satisfactory ecclesiology recognizes the tension
between history and eschatology, recognizes the imperfec-
tion of present human response to the divine vocation. It
sees "working toward" and "praying for" the End as essential characteristics of the human response to God's call in the
period before God himself decides to bring his kingdom in.
It sees it as a mysterious part of God's providence—somehow connected with his respect for human freedom—that
there should be a "not yet" as well as an "already" about
human salvation and the divine kingdom at present. It does
not idealistically pretend that there is no difference between
the historical and the eschatological Church. Nor does it
deny that there is a connection between the two. Rather: the
Church *is becoming* what it *will be*. In this perspective, we
can both admit that some disunity *still exists* among Christians and see the need to *overcome* such disunity; we can
rejoice in the measure of unity which we *already have* and
at the same time commit ourselves to striving for its *increase*.
We do not shut our eyes against the existence and gravity of
schism: we work openly to heal it.

    At this point we may consider the role of the eucharist in
the healing process.

2. The expressive and productive functions of the eucharist

The eucharist *significat et efficit unitatem ecclesiasticam:* this adage of Pope Innocent III[24] sums up a view of the eucharist which has been held since much earlier times. The biblical and patristic teaching is that the eucharist both *expresses* an existing unity of the Church and *produces* such unity.[25] Let us see how the expressive and the productive functions of the eucharist are properly related.

To celebrate the eucharist together clearly requires some measure of existing unity. Complete disunity makes a common celebration improper if not unthinkable. The Lord's words in Matthew 5:23f. are recalled in many liturgies. When Augustine taught that fractious church-members give the lie to the "amen" which they say in response to the words *corpus Christi* as they receive communion,[26] he was re-expressing the warning which St. Paul gave to the Corinthians (1 Cor. 11:17-34; see also 1:10-17; 10:16f.). On the other hand, we may conclude from our previous paragraph on history and eschatology that it would be quite unrealistic to expect Christians to be already in perfect harmony with one another. Their love for one another needs to increase. That is where the productive function of the eucharist comes into play. The eucharist not only seals an existing unity brought from the past; it also "leads forward" the communicants into a future where the unity will be greater. The eucharist *effects*. It is a means of *grace*. As a creative anticipation of the future (a present "taste" which whets the appetite for the messianic banquet in the completed kingdom), the eucharist is fulfilling an eschatological function in history. Granted the final superiority of eschatology over history, the eucharist is more important for *what it makes of us* than for what it expresses as being already true of us. It is the future which takes precedence.

I suggest that all this is relevant not only *within* communities but also *among* them. We should be ready to allow common participation in the eucharist to promote reconciliation among partially disunited communities which are seeking to overcome existing differences and so come to a closer companionship in the progress toward the kingdom.

As a "projection" of the Lord's final Parousia,[27] the eucharist is an occasion when the Lord may exercise his eschatological functions of casting out from us in judgment what is amiss in us, of uniting us closer to himself in divine fellowship, and of joining us together in common enjoyment of his presence and gifts. It is when it is celebrated ecumenically that the eucharist can most truly fulfill its character as an effective sacrament of reconciliation and renewal.[28]

Let me now state briefly some of the circumstances in which eucharistic sharing seems to be appropriate.

First the case of mixed marriages. In connection with Catholics and Donatists, Augustine could rightly point to the absurdity of a situation in which "husbands and wives find unity in their marriage bed and disunity at the altar of Christ" (*Epistle* 33, 5 [*PL* 33, 131]). But in our day the right remedy is not immediate individual "conversion" (by which partner? in which direction?). Rather, interchurch marriages should be seen as promises of the future, as "domestic churches" with a creative part to play in stimulating the wider ecclesial communities toward unity; for the deepening of their married love and for the sake of the witness which their unity can make to the Churches, the couple should be allowed to communicate together in each of their Churches.[29] The "(pre)conciliar decisions," taken in Strasbourg and in Switzerland by the Roman Catholic and Protestant churches acting together, to give this permission to mixed Catholic and Protestant couples is entirely welcome. The couples themselves will thereby in turn make their contribution to uniting their communities.

Second, hospitality. Eucharistic hospitality should be offered and accepted in the normal circumstances of visiting. Without waiting for the emergency of the prison-camp or the jungle, it should be an open practice that individual Christians share in eucharistic fellowship wherever their travels take them.[30] When visits of whole congregations are arranged, over longer or shorter distances, the two Churches should communicate sacramentally together.

Third, on (pre)conciliar occasions. When divided Churches are serious enough in their commitment to the goal of Christian unity to meet officially together through their representatives, the circumstances are sufficient for holding a common eucharist for the sake of promoting the cause.

Fourth, Churches entering into covenant relationships. In such cases, the covenant is envisaged as a step on the way to fuller visible unity. Entry upon the covenant will mean that Churches welcome to communion all communicant members in good standing of the other covenanting Churches, and, in the future, initiation in the membership of the covenanting Churches will be by mutually acceptable rites; by the covenant, each Church will recognize the ordained ministries of the other Churches as true ministries of word and sacraments, with all future ordinations being performed in an agreed way. The Churches will also commit themselves to developing methods of decision-making in common: a part of the conciliar process.

3. The Church as particular and universal

With due allowances for the "eschatological reserve" which must qualify all statements about the historical Church (as in para. one of this section), it may be said that, by virtue of a "qualitative catholicity," the whole Church is present in every particular local church.[31] An excellent statement on this theme has been made in the recent *Report of Theological Conversations sponsored by the World Alliance of Reformed Churches and the Baptist World Alliance 1973-77.* It is there said that "the one holy universal Christian Church becomes concrete in the local congregation. The local congregation is not a sub-department of the one Church of Christ, but manifests and represents it." The Report then quotes Vatican II in support: "The Church of Christ is truly present in all local gatherings of believers" (*Lumen Gentium* 26). A further text from Vatican II is particularly relevant to our own theme. Chapter 41 of the Constitution on the Sacred Liturgy declares that "the principal manifestation of the Church (*praecipua manifestatio Ecclesiae)* consists in the full, active participation of all God's holy people in the same liturgical celebrations, especially in the same Eucharist, in one prayer, at one altar, at which the bishop presides, surrounded by his college of priests and by his ministers." It should follow from these principles that every member of the Church of Christ is in principle welcome to share in the communion of any local eucharistic assembly. Participation by members from other local Churches is in fact a valuable reminder that qualitative catholicity cannot properly be separated from quantitative catholicity. As the Reformed/Baptist Report puts it: "At the same time the local congregation is necessarily related to other local congregations. In itself, it is not the universal Church of Christ. The local congregation which isolates itself from its sister congregations impairs the character of the true Church, and becomes sectarian." This is entirely in harmony with our theme of conciliarity.

The eucharist is, in N. Afanassieff's phrase, "le sacrement de l'assemblée."[32] It is also a dispersion-point. As J.-J. von Allmen explains,[33] it is part of the vital rhythm of *systolé* and *diastolé* that the Church also moves out from its eucharistic gathering to its more dispersed tasks of witness and service. For our part, we may say that the Church must display before the world, and for the sake of the world's salvation, the values of the kingdom which she has discovered in the eucharist. Again, the local church has its local field of witness and service; but once more the wider vision is also needed. The Reformed/Baptist Report points out that the isolation of the local church "would cloud its vision with regard to the world as the one great field of mission. This call for mission unites the local churches and makes them interdependent." Conciliarity is thus shown—again with eucharistic reference— to imply not only the "gathering" of the Churches but also their "dispersal," in which they remain united by their common task of witness and service.

4. A choice among anomalies

In our final paragraph, we must admit the existence of anomalies in the present situation of the Churches. It is, of course, an anomaly that divided communities—each believing itself to be in some sense "Church" or "of the Church"— should do anything at all together as long as they remain divided on any matters of substance. Clarity and firmness are necessary when truth is at stake. So much we should learn from the Cyprianic view. The gospel which the Churches proclaim, and the faith which they confess, need to be recognizably the same, however great may be the variety of the formulations for reasons of tradition, culture, and context. Yet common prayer and action among divided communites is only a minor anomaly in relation to the major anomaly. The major anomaly is that Christians should be divided *at all*. Division contradicts the calling and true nature of the Church. We should be aggravating the major anomaly if we simply refrained from common prayer and action until total unanimity was somehow granted to us "out of the blue." Accepting gratefully what unites us already, we should choose the minor anomaly of praying and working together while still partly disunited: this is the only way of *striving* toward overcoming the major anomaly of our division. In my judgment, our human striving needs the grace of God which has the possibility of coming to us through eucharistic sharing. God's common gift of himself to us all in love will help us all together to see and speak the truth more adequately. It is appropriate to close by recalling the summons to recite the creed in the Orthodox liturgy: "Let us have love to one another, that so with one mind we may confess the Father, the Son and the Holy Spirit. . . ."

VI
ORDAINED MINISTRY

INTRODUCTION: THE ESSENTIAL MINISTRY

One of the chief gifts of the modern liturgical movement to the Western churches has been the return of Hippolytus' *Apostolic Tradition*. The influence of his eucharistic anaphora extends far and wide in recent official compositions. More narrowly, his prayer at the ordination of a bishop has been taken, with even less adaptation, into the *Pontificale Romanum* of 1968 and the 1979 *Book of Common Prayer* of the Episcopal Church in the United States. The episcopal ordination prayer of Hippolytus will supply the themes and, in coarse outline, the sequence of the theological reflections which follow. I give the text according to H. B. Porter's translation, although some of the expressions will require elucidation later:[1]

> God and Father of our Lord Jesus Christ, Father of mercies and God of all comforts, who dwellest in the heights and hast respect to the lowly, who knowest all things before they come to be, thou who hast set bounds within the Church through the word of thy grace, preordaining from the beginning the race of the just people of Abraham, establishing princes and priests and not leaving thy sanctuary without a ministry, thou since the beginning of the world hast had pleasure among those whom thou hast chosen to be given (*or* glorified).
>
> Pour forth now that power which is from thee, the princely Spirit, which thou gavest to thy beloved Son, Jesus Christ, which he gave to the holy apostles, who established in every place the Church, thy hallowing, to the glory and unceasing praise of thy name.
>
> Father who knowest the heart, grant to this thy servant, whom thou hast chosen for a bishopric, to feed thy flock; and to exercise high priesthood for thee with-

95

out rebuke, serving night and day, to propitiate thy
countenance unceasingly and to offer the holy gifts of
thy Church; by the Spirit of high priesthood to have the
power to remit sins according to thy commandment; to
give lots according to thy direction; to loose also every
bond according to the power which thou gavest to the
apostles; to please thee, too, by gentleness and a pure
heart, offering to thee an odour of sweet savour, through
thy Child (*or* Servant) Jesus Christ, through whom be
glory and power and honour to thee, to Father and Son
with the Holy Spirit, both now and world without end.
Amen.

On the basis of that prayer I will unfold my thoughts in a
development which is as familiar to Christians as the creeds:
I. theology, in the strict sense; II. christology; III. pneumatology; IV. ecclesiology; V. eschatology. A conclusion will face
a little more directly the fundamental question of the authority of the ordained ministry. But before starting on the
five central sections of this chapter I want in this introduction to make already some remarks on the essential place of
an ordained or special ministry within the Church.

According to the celebrated anglo-catholic symposium of
1946, edited by K. E. Kirk under the title *The Apostolic Ministry*, the "essential ministry" was the episcopate, understood in the sense of a lineal succession of local bishops
instituted by the apostles and spread wherever the Church
had since been implanted.[2] While the essentiality of the
episcopate has never been seriously questioned in the "catholic" churches of either East or West, at least since its clear
emergence as a universal feature by the late second century,
there is nevertheless a certain variety and controversy concerning its relationships with other parts of "the threefold
ministry." Thus the medieval and tridentine West predominantly saw special *priesthood* as the distinctive essence of
"orders," the *potestas ordinis* consisting above all in the
power to change the bread and wine into the body and blood
of Christ in the eucharistic sacrifice. But that left only a distinction of *jurisdiction* between the episcopate and the presbyterate. Even within the episcopate, there were questions
to do with the relationship of the other bishops to the bishop

of Rome: in what sense, if any, was it a relationship of dependence? Was the dependence essential or jurisdictional? These questions are still left unresolved by the *una cum* of Vatican II.[3]

And what more precisely of the relationships between episcopate and presbyterate? When at least from the third century, priestly language started to be used of the special ministry, it was the bishop who preeminently became *hiereus* or *sacerdos* (sometimes *archiereus* or *summus sacerdos*);[4] and when the bishop ordained presbyters, he called them "assistants to our weakness," "cooperators with our order," who obtained "the office of second dignity" (so the Roman ordination prayers).[5] But did these "priests of the second rank" (the phrase came from 2 Kings 23:4) not retain a corporate memory that the "monarchical" episcopate had developed from the elected presidency of the presbyteral council? That, in any case, was how the influential Jerome viewed the matter in his (re)assertion of presbyteral rights;[6] and continuing support might be found in the Alexandrian practice, whereby the new bishop was chosen by the presbyters from among their own number (although he also received tactile succession from the hand of his embalmed predecessor).[7] Or was more weight to be given to another probable factor in the historical origins of the episcopate, namely the more direct appointment of continuing local "supervisors," *epískopoi*, by the itinerating apostles and "other illustrious men" of whom 1 Clement 44:3 speaks?[8] Then indeed the models of participation or ("downward") delegation would become more appropriate for the part played by presbyters in an *essentially episcopal* ministry. This second view has long held sway in the Byzantine East ("monepiscopacy" already appears normal in the letters of Ignatius of Antioch), and it seems now to occupy the field in the documents of Vatican II.[9]

And what of the deacons? The diaconate (not to mention, for many centuries in the West, the subdiaconate) is regarded as a "major order." Occasionally it is reckoned as a third rank in the priestly order.[10] More usually, however, it is kept distinct from the priesthood, as already in the explanation given by Hippolytus of why only the bishop, and not the presby-

ters, lays on hands at the ordination of a deacon: "he is not
ordained for the priesthood but for the service of the bishop,
non in sacerdotio ordinatur sed in ministerio episcopi." The
matter is complicated by the sheer historical fact that, in the
West at least, the diaconate has for many centuries been a
mere stepping-stone to the presbyterate—or even, in the
dark ages, directly to the papacy.[11] As I shall be stressing
again soon, the real historical practice of the ministry is an
indispensable datum for theological reflection; this is made
abundantly clear in Bernard Cooke's monumental study,
Ministry to Word and Sacrament: History and Theology
(1976). Cooke himself, in a witticism at the expense of the
presbyterate, gives one amusing formulation to the problem
of the "threefold ministry": "Presbyters became deacons with
fuller powers, though they often preferred to think of themselves as bishops with lesser powers" (p. 200).

So far I have had in mind the "catholic" churches, especially in the West. But the Protestant Reformation did not
abandon the notion and practice of a special or ordained
ministry. Calvin sought to be more scriptural by adopting a
fourfold pattern of pastor, teacher (doctor), elder, and deacon.
Here again, however, there have proved to be problems. The
teacher has disappeared, except in the academy and as a
more informal function in the local church. The elder is
"ordained" yet considered "lay," especially in comparison
with the pastor, on whom the whole "ministry of word and
sacrament" has tended to be concentrated. From Luther
himself onward, Lutheranism has been satisfied with what
is fundamentally a single pastoral ministry, with bishop,
superintendent, and so on, being regarded as administrative
functions and titles.

A single pastoral ministry is also characteristic of the (British) Methodism to which I belong. Although Methodism and
liturgy (in the narrow sense of the word) are usually considered strange bedfellows, and although the ordained ministry
in my church will be judged "invalid" according to criteria
which are happily being rethought by all but the most die-
hard "catholics," I hope I may be allowed to advance a genuinely Methodist viewpoint on the special ministry which
helps to overcome the Catholic/Protestant debate on whether

ordination introduces a difference *in kind* from the general ministry of the Church. (These next remarks will at least serve to show where my prejudices lie, so that others may tacitly substitute their own in the rest of the chapter.) I will bypass the polemical or defensive statement from the 1932 Deed of Union (internal Methodist politics at the time of reunion in British Methodism are not our concern here), to the effect that there is "no priestly virtue inherent in the office" of the ordained ministry; though it might be interesting to develop positively the Deed's affirmation that the calling and setting apart of some Christians to the ordained ministry is "for the sake of Church order." Instead I will take up two themes from the *Statement on Ordination* passed by the British Methodist Conference of 1974: I mean the related notions of "focus" and "representation." The idea is that the special or ordained ministry brings the multi-faceted ministry of the whole Church to sharp or concentrated expression in such a way that all Christians may be stimulated and enabled to exercise the Church's ministry—and that the whole Church's ministry may also be clearly identified by those yet outside the Church to whom the gospel is being commended. The metaphor of focus indicates that the special ministry is not an *exclusive* ministry: from the beginning of Methodism, laypeople have officially preached (called "local preachers," in distinction from the itinerants whose evangelism kept them circulating), and laypeople have officially shared in the exercise of pastoral care (notably the "class-leaders"), while in some parts of the Methodist tradition, and now in the British Methodist Church as such, appointed laypersons have also presided at the Lord's Supper, especially in cases of sacramental need. Yet a focus is also *distinctive*, and this is confirmed by the notion of representation. The special character of the ordained ministry consists precisely in its being an efficacious sign in the furtherance of the divine purpose both in the Church and in the world to which the Church bears witness.[12]

There are two further remarks to be made concerning the essential ministry. The first underlines both the importance and the problematic nature of the relations between the apparently permanent official structures of the ordained min-

istry (whether these be threefold, fourfold, or simple) and
the mobile sociological styles and practical forms in which
that ministry is exercised in the varying historical circumstances of the Church. Because it used the word "patterns"
to cover both the official and the sociological/practical realities, the WCC Faith and Order statement *A Mutually Recognized Ministry* remained unclear.[13] It is obvious that,
sociologically and practically, *new* "patterns" of ministry are
being called for: the Church has always sought to adapt itself
to culture at this level. The question is how the Churches—
particularly perhaps the "catholic" Churches—will allow
these changes to affect the hitherto *fixed* "patterns" at the
level of the sacramental structure of the ordained ministry.
Must the "non-episcopal" Churches acquire bishops, presbyters, and (possibly) deacons? Or may the ecumenical future allow us to discover together a common but somehow
flexible sacramental embodiment of the abiding prophetic,
priestly, and royal ministry of the Church? The final WCC
text on *Ministry* recommends "development" of the "traditional threefold pattern" (= structure), while holding that
"a uniform answer" to the question of distribution of functions "is not required for the mutual recognition of the ordained ministry" (§§ 25, 28).

The second remark notes briefly the value of those enthu-
siastic Christian groups which, at certain times and places,
have called the institutional ministry radically into question.
They serve as a critical irritant in the history of Christianity.
For all the dangers involved, they can be seen *in optimam
partem* as instances of God's free operation in judgment and
(directly or indirectly) renewal, when institutional sclerosis
has affected the bigger communities. Like the martyrs, they
may be read as eschatological signs of that "levelling" process (up, not down) which the Christian vocation implies.
For are not all God's people called to be prophets, priests,
and kings?[14] But to that we shall return.

In the central sections of this chapter I shall now take for
granted a rough-and-ready agreement about the existence of
an "essential ministry" marked by ordination, although my
reflections will be variously appreciated according to the an-
swers already variously given to the questions raised in this

introduction—and others yet to arise. It is, then, to the "theological," christological, pneumatological, ecclesiological, and eschatological incidences of the ordained ministry that we shall in turn look. A further assumption is that the act of ordination—essentially an imposition of hands specified by verbal prayer—is the ritual sign of the continuing ministry which it sacramentally inaugurates. But again, more of that later.

I. THE "THEOLOGICAL" DIMENSION OF ORDINATION

The prayer of Hippolytus for the ordination of a bishop is addressed to the "God and Father of our Lord Jesus Christ." That is the God of salvation history. Himself transcendent *(qui in excelsis habitas),* he is related to all things as the universal Creator *(qui cognoscis omnia antequam nascantur).* From the start, he has a purpose for humanity *(ex initio saeculi).*[15] His purpose is one of love *(pater misericordiarum et Deus totius consolationis).* He himself sets the values *(qui humilia respicis).* The human attainment of God's purpose and values is itself the worship of God *(in gloriam et laudem nomini tuo).*[16] To facilitate the ultimate achievement of his purpose, God is ready to "elect": first, he "predestined from the beginning the race of the just people of Abraham"; among that people he "established princes and priests"; finally, "thou gavest the princely Spirit to thy beloved Son, Jesus Christ." In turn, Christ gave the Spirit "to the holy apostles, who established in every place the Church, thy hallowing, to the glory and unceasing praise of thy name." Christ is the focal representative and effective sign of God's saving design for humanity. One effect of the Old Testament typology common in patristic and medieval ordination texts is to set the Christian ministry in the line of the salvation history which is now being continued and expanded in and through the Church.[17]

One expression in the exordium of Hippolytus' prayer demands particular comment: *tu qui dedisti terminos in ecclesia per verbum gratiae tuae.* Parallels in later ordination prayers suggest that the "bounds" here have something to do with *order* or *orders.*[18] In the sacramentaries, the Roman

prayers at the ordination of bishops, presbyters, and deacons
begin respectively thus:

> God of all the honours, God of all thy worthy ranks,
> which serve to thy glory in hallowed orders. . . .
>
> O Lord, holy Father, almighty, everlasting God, be-
> stower of all the honours and of all the worthy ranks
> which do thee service, thou through whom all things
> make increase, through whom everything is made firm,
> by the ever-extended increase to the benefit of rational
> nature by a succession arranged in due order. . . .
>
> Assist us, we beseech thee, almighty God, giver of
> honours, distributor of orders, and bestower of offices;
> who abiding in thyself, dost make all things new, and
> disposest everything through thy Word, Power, and
> Wisdom, Jesus Christ thy Son our Lord; by thine
> everlasting providence thou dost prepare, and apportion
> to each particular time, what things are needful. . . .[19]

We may wish to take this in a sober and demythologized
way as placing the ecclesiastical ministry in relation to the
orderliness of creation and humanity with which the physical and social sciences are concerned: orderliness is part of
the nature and culture which grace presupposes, renews,
and perfects. More metaphysically, Augustine and pseudo-
Denys make Church order part of "the great order of being"—
and that, platonically, in a *hierarchical* way.[20] It is here that
another source of "order" language in connection with ecclesiastical ministry comes into play. In secular Rome, the
distinction was drawn between the *ordo* (the senate) or *or-
dines* (when the *equites* were added) and the *plebs* or *po-
pulus romanus* (outside the capital, the decurions constituted
the *ordo*).[21] Undoubtedly the secular distinction in dignity
was transferred into the Church when the language of *ordo*
came to be applied analogously to the "ordained" ministry
(and with the imperial establishment of Christianity, the use
became rather more than analogical in the case of a clergy
now with civil status). But the question must at least be
asked whether *hierarchical* ordering is not contrary to the
overall picture of the Church in the New Testament. The
whole *laos* is holy and called to holiness. All are elevated to
the dignity of *ordo*. An attempt is made to recognize this in

occasional talk of the "order of laity," but this appears still
to assume a gradation among the orders (plural).[22] True, the
Matthaean and Lucan Jesus promises *the twelve* that they
will sit on thrones and rule the twelve tribes of Israel (Matt.
19:28; Luke 22:30). But Luke, particularly by placing the
bequest of the kingdom in the context of the eucharistic institution and by linking it with Jesus' reversal of the pagan
idea of rule into one of Christ-like service (Luke 22:24-27),
appears to intend the extension of regality to every Christian.
The Apocalypse describes all Christians as kings and priests
(Rev. 1:6; 5:10). In St. Paul's body-ecclesiology (Rom. 12;
1 Cor. 12), there is *diversity* of function *for the common
good*. This certainly implies *orderliness*, but not necessarily
rank. The tortuous passage about the more and less honorable parts of the body is in fact directed precisely against
those who claim higher value for this or that gift over against
others.[23] If St. Paul does make an ordered list, the sequence
clearly favors the primary ministry of spreading the gospel:
first apostles, second prophets, third teachers (1 Cor. 12:27f.;
see also Eph. 4:11f.). This is far removed from a *cursus honorum*, an ecclesiastical career structure modelled on the civil
service.[24]

II. THE CHRISTOLOGICAL DIMENSION
OF ORDINATION

Christians are kings and priests (Rev. 1:6; 5:10), a royal
priesthood (1 Pet. 2:9), a prophetic community (Acts 2:17f.,
38f.). They are these things because they are the people of
Jesus *Christ*, the Spirit-anointed prophet, priest, and king.[25]
Jesus is the eschatological prophet, and more: the Word of
God incarnate. Jesus is the high priest, who offered *himself*
and secured an eternal redemption for humanity. Being the
divine kingdom in person (Origen calls him *autobasileía*),
Jesus "reigned from a tree"[26] and God the Father has exalted
him and bestowed on him the supreme name of Lord. Baptism is the sacrament of entry into participation in the prophetic, priestly, and royal dignity of Christ. Using the term
in at least a semitechnical sense, we may say that baptism

is the effective sign by which Christ's prophetic, priestly, and royal "character" is stamped on the believer.

Character, in the technical language of medieval Western sacramental theology, is defined by Aquinas as conformation to Christ and, consequently, a deputation to function in the Church's worship.[27] Unfortunately, the baptized (and confirmed) functioned only rather passively in the liturgy of the Middle Ages. It needed the somehow closer conformation to Christ conferred in ordination for an active part to be played in the cult. With the modern reactivation of the *total* liturgical assembly, it becomes possible to see the ordained ministry, in its cultic aspect, as *enabling* or, if you dislike the sociological jargon, simply *leading* the worship of the whole people. Although at some points in the life of the Church preachers may need to speak out *against* the community in which they are set, the opposition is only provisional and aims at bringing the whole community back to its own prophetic role in the world. The deacon is summoning the entire priestly people to intercession: "Let us pray to the Lord." The eucharistic president is voicing the *sacrificium laudis* which the whole assembly is offering: "Let us give thanks to the Lord our God." Rule in the Christian assembly is the rule of the shepherd who "feeds God's holy flock" and who, like the Good Shepherd himself, is ready to give his own life for the sheep.[28]

Baptismal and ordained character has never been simply a somehow external conformation to Christ, and its exercise in worship has never meant a merely external obedience in the performance of rites once instituted by Christ. Rather Christ himself becomes formed in those who are conformed to him, and he makes himself present in the word and the sacraments which he gives to his Church. It was in an anti-Donatist context that St. Augustine elaborated his doctrine of Christ as the real minister of the sacraments: when Peter or Paul or any other minister, were it Judas, baptizes, *Christus est qui baptizat*.[29] But the idea is found also in Chrysostom: "It is not only the priest who touches the head, but also the right hand of Christ, and this is shown by the very words of the one baptizing. He does not say 'I baptize so-and-so,' but 'so-and-so is baptized,' showing that he is only the min-

ister of grace and merely offers his hand because he has
been ordained to this end by the Spirit."[30] The theme continues into the Middle Ages, in both East and West.[31] It is
picked up by Vatican II when the Constitution on the Sacred
Liturgy delineates the multiform presence of Christ in the
liturgical assembly:

> To accomplish so great a work (of salvation), Christ is
> always present in his Church, especially in its liturgical
> actions. He is present in the person of his minister, "the
> same now offering, through the ministry of priests, who
> formerly offered himself on the cross", but especially
> under the eucharistic species. By his power he is pres-
> ent in the sacraments, so that when a man baptizes it
> is really Christ himself who baptizes. He is present in
> his word, since it is he himself who speaks when the
> holy scriptures are read in church. He is present, lastly,
> when the Church prays and sings, for he promised:
> "Where two or three are gathered together in my name,
> there am I in the midst of them." Christ indeed always
> associates the Church with himself in this great work
> wherein God is perfectly glorified and men are
> sanctified.[32]

In sum, the liturgical assembly is the effective-symbolic-
focus of the Church's growing up into Christ, its Head (see
Eph. 4:14-16).

Mention may be made of a picturesque medieval statement of the way in which Christ is the source, exemplar, and
continuing empowerment of Christian ministry. I refer to
those texts recently studied by Roger Reynolds and called
by him "the ordinals of Christ."[33] The various orders, both
minor and major, are given origins in a saying of Christ or
an event in his ministry. The grave-digger, who later van-
ished from the minor orders, was early associated with the
raising of Lazarus. The doorkeeper is sanctioned by the "I
am the door" saying, by the harrowing of hell (sometimes
verbalized in the word to the penitent thief), or in later ver-
sions by the cleansing of the temple. The lector's office is
rooted in Christ's reading the scroll at the synagogue in
Luke 4 (often confused with the boy Jesus' debate with the
doctors in the temple). The favored exorcisms are those of

the deaf and dumb man and of Mary Magdalene. The acolyte, who comes into prominence in France and Italy, is sanctioned by "I am the light," by Christ's illumination of the
blind, and by his call to "follow me" (see especially John
8:12).[34] The subdeacon started off with the temple-cleansing
but later acquired the *pedilavium* instead. The foot-washing
was transferred from the deacon, to whom was allotted the
distribution of the eucharistic elements. That was because
the presbyter's ministry was now epitomized by the *consecration* of the bread and wine, though also by "the altar of
the cross." Presbyter and bishop sometimes coalesce.[35] When
the bishop figures distinctly, the originating event of the
episcopate is usually Christ's lifting of his hands in blessing
at the Ascension and his gift of the Spirit. These last twin
events implicitly make up a substantial cause of the continued efficacy of all the ministries "instituted" by the Christ
who is now the heavenly bestower of spiritual gifts.[36] Other
ways in which the ordinals of Christ appear to understand
the present effectiveness of ministries in the Church are the
notion of a *recapitulation* of Christ's earthly ministry (so in
the earlier "chronological" ordinals) and the relation of all
ministries to the *eucharist* in which Christ was now un-
questionably present and active (so in the later "hierarchical" ordinals).

A final paragraph in this christological section must em-
phasize the revolution brought by Jesus to the idea and exercise of *rule*. It was the incarnate *God* who reigned from
the tree. Jesus revealed the essence and character of God to
be self-gift for the life of others (that is the case both within
the Trinity and in relation to creation). The lord and master
washed his disciples' feet, and his unparalleled example left
them an obligation of mutual service, a "new commandment" (John 13). Standing among them "as one who serves,"
Jesus taught his followers the total contrast between pagan
dominance and service in the divine kingdom (Luke
22:24-30). Therefore ministry in the Church must never be
confused with worldly honor but must rather advance others
to salvation: *episcopus nomen est operis, non honoris* (Isidore of Seville).[37] The very term "ministry" is significant,
and the name "deacon" is not one which other "orders"

should refuse.[38] Yet service itself may be subtly perverted: Gregory the Great's claim to be *servus servorum Dei* was an embryonic claim to "universal immediate jurisdiction." But the prayers of ordination point the pastor to the Good Shepherd who laid down his life for the sheep.[39] And "judgment" in the Church is properly nothing other than the love which shows up its contrary for what it is. Pastoral discipline, and even excommunication, must envisage the offender's salvation, in however long a run (1 Cor. 5:1-5). According to Hippolytus, the bishop's ministry is to "remit sins" and "loose every bond"—in order, we may add, that the sinner may be set free for the service of him "whom to serve is to rule."[40]

III. THE PNEUMATOLOGICAL DIMENSION OF ORDINATION

Nunc effunde eam virtutem quae a te est, principalis spiritus, quem dedisti dilecto filio tuo Jesu Christo: such is the prayer of Hippolytus' text at the ordination of a bishop. In the case of the presbyter, the prayer is that God may "impart to him the Spirit of grace and counsel for presbyters." In the case of the deacon, God is asked to "give the Holy Spirit of grace and care and diligence to this thy servant." It will be noticed that on each occasion the epithets attached to the Holy Spirit help to specify the gifts which are sought for the ordinand in his particular ministry. In the Byzantine rites, the common invitatory for bishops, presbyters, and deacons runs as follows: "Divine grace which heals all that is infirm and supplies what is wanting chooses N. as bishop/presbyter/deacon. Let us pray for him, that the grace of the Most Holy Spirit may come upon him." In any case, as P. M. Gy insists in his study of the theology of the ancient rites, the ordination prayer is essentially an epiclesis.[41] The first and fundamental point to be made in this pneumatological section is very simple and can be stated very briefly: all Christian ministry is and remains dependent on the Spirit's empowerment.

But the texts so far quoted all pertain to official ministry. Do not the great Pauline letters and the contemporary charismatic renewal alike suggest a much more free and informal

picture of the distribution of spiritual gifts for ministry?[42]
Church history knows a recurrent tension between "institution" and "event." Certainly there is abundant evidence
that God works through continuing ecclesiastical institutions, but it is also clear that institutions develop, if Roman
Catholics will forgive the pun, a tendency to petrification. It
is also evident that the more spontaneous movements of the
Spirit must quickly take on a more structured form if they
are not to evaporate: John Wesley's organizational ability was
a necessary support for his evangelism. Ideally, *logos* and
pneuma, coherence and energy, go together. But in the interval before the Parousia, the Church appears to receive the
influx of the two in variable proportions.

According to St. Paul, the Holy Spirit is a principle of both
unity and diversity. The image of the body and the members
shows that there is properly no contradiction here, but only
complementarity. Special gifts of the Spirit are given to *each*
for the common good of *all;* for it is by the *one* Spirit that all
have been baptized into *one* body, and all have been made
to drink of the *one* Spirit (1 Cor. 12). Since there is only one
body and one Spirit, the various gifts have been given for
the building up of the whole in love (see Eph. 4). Developing the thought of the Jesuit Donald Gelpi in his *Charism
and Sacrament*,[43] we may locate ordination in the morphology of the Church somewhere between baptism and the
"service gifts." Sacramentally, the one baptism which is administered to all is the sign of the things which all Christians
have in common in the one body: the one God and Father,
the one Lord, the one Spirit, the one faith, the one hope
(Eph. 4:1-6). Baptism is the outward sign of the fundamental
unity which the Spirit gives. It is fitting that entry upon this
basic and, in intention, universal and permanent unity should
be marked by a single ritual sign: baptism. Within the body,
however, there are many and varied "service gifts" (Gelpi),
which may be temporary and local in their exercise. These
lend themselves less easily to signification by a permanent
and universal rite; though Gelpi, from the viewpoint of the
developed Roman Catholic sacramental system, allows to the
historically "extra" sacrament of confirmation the meaning
of a "public profession of personal readiness to respond to

whatever gift(s) of service the Spirit may choose to give in the course of one's development as a converted Christian." In Christian tradition, the *ordained* ministry is related, in the one direction, to the universal and permanent unity signified by baptism and, in the other direction, to the various gifts of temporary and local service which usually remain unritualized. In intention, ordination has given a person a permanent place and function within the structures of the universal Church as constituted by baptism (though problems arise in connection with both baptism and ordination, as we shall see, on account of the factual failure of Christians to live the unity which the sacraments signify). Now if, as I shall later allow, an essential function of the ordained ministry is "oversight" or "supervision" (for which the aid of the Spirit is also needed), one of the most important expressions of *episkopé* is the coordination of the individual service gifts for the edification of the total community. It is the business of the supervisory ministry both to discern the gifts and to distribute the charges in which they are to be employed.[44] None of this is too far removed from the prayer of Hippolytus that the bishop may "give lots according to thy direction, *dare sortes secundum praeceptum tuum.*"[45] In traceable Christian history, it is always "the bishop" (by whatever name and in whatever form) who has presided at ordinations, and it has been the constant duty of the ordained ministry to recognize, foster, and harmoniously exploit the gifts of all the members.

IV. THE ECCLESIOLOGICAL DIMENSION OF ORDINATION

In this section we shall relate the ordained ministry to the four notes of the Church. The sequence will be regrettably untidy: 1. apostolicity; 2. holiness; 3. unity; 4. catholicity.

1. Apostolicity

According to the prayer of Hippolytus, it was to the apostles that Christ first gave the Spirit, and their mission was to "establish in every place the Church." In their cap city as original witnesses to the gospel and founding fathers of the

Church, the apostles are historically and theologically unique. Yet the gospel must continue to be proclaimed in all its truth. Down the centuries, that responsibility has been focally and representatively borne by the ordained ministry, and notably by "the episcopate" (by whatever name and in whatever form). In the patristic and medieval periods, the bishop's duties were recognized to include evangelizing, preaching, and teaching.[46] It was the bishop who, in one way or another, presided at the initiation of new Christians. The "ministry of the word" stands at the heart of the eucharistic synaxis. In our ecumenical days, the Anglican Anthony Hanson has suggested that the proper criterion of ministerial authenticity is the spread of the gospel: his book is significantly entitled *The Pioneer Ministry*.[47]

But, it will be said, it must indeed be the *gospel* which is spread. "Catholics" have made a close link between the truth and episcopal succession. Ever since St. Irenaeus, "order" has carried a diachronic dimension: *ordo successionis;* and the language of *diadoché* figures right in the ordination prayer of Serapion.[48] Everyone now knows that it is not simply a question of *verbally repeating* the apostolic message (though all the churches significantly continue to read the New Testament Scriptures in worship): there is the question of *translating* the original message in differing historical and geographical circumstances; there is the question of doctrinal *development,* which is a brute reality for all the churches; there is the question of the *hermeneutics* of Scripture and of the developed and variegated tradition. Yet the "catholic" churches recognize in one form or another a permanent *magisterium* in the Church and uphold in one sense or another the fundamental infallibility of this "teaching office." Protestants view the relation between evangelical truth and the historical Church's preaching and teaching in a much more dialectical fashion; and there are those who would consider the "break" of ministerial succession at the Reformation not so much as a "loss" but as a necessary (albeit regrettable) "counter-sign" of a return to the gospel.

Three more points may be briefly made under this heading of apostolicity. First, the apostolic vocation and quality of the Church as a whole means that there can be no simple division between *ecclesia docens* and *ecclesia discens*, the teachers and the taught. Certainly the teaching office needs a personal (not necessarily individual) focus. But the magisterium must also learn from the whole people and, as the Anglican/Roman Catholic International Commission (ARCIC) statement on Authority declared in a rare fit of courage, somehow be "assessed" by it.[49] And the task of teaching the gospel to the world belongs to the Church in its entirety.

Second, there is the matter of apostolicity and locality. For St. Irenaeus the apostolic *sees* were important.[50] And the tendency now is to decry the "absolute" ordinations practiced in the Middle Ages: ordination must be to a local charge.[51] But the human sciences teach us that place is a complex notion.[52] And our planet is becoming, in M. McLuhan's phrase, "a global village."[53] Methodist ordinations are rather absolute, but then John Wesley's evangelistic vocation led him to "look on the whole world as my parish."

Third, there is the ministry of the theologian. At least since the twelfth century, theology has been a professional occupation in the undivided service of truth and the Church. It sits uneasily, however, across the distinction between ordained and lay. We have here an example of mismatch between sacramental structures and concrete practice.

2. Holiness

The prayer of Hippolytus designates the Church *"sanctificationem tuam."* The sanctification is both passive and active: God hallows the Church *(gregem sanctam tuam)*, and the Church hallows God's name *(in gloriam et laudem indeficientem nomini tuo)*. Within the priestly people, the bishop's ministry is a high priesthood *(primatus sacerdotii)*. This priesthood is cultic: ... *servientem noctu et die, incessanter repropitiari vultum tuum et offerre dona sancta* (or *sanctae) ecclesiae tuae*. It is also ethical: ... *placere autem tibi in mansuetudine et mundo corde, offerentem tibi odorem suavitatis.* Worship and conduct are theologically inseparable: the rites of a wicked people stink in God's nostrils; contrariwise, it is in the liturgy that a believing people perceives the values of God's kingdom and receives the grace

to enact them in daily living. It is important that the episcopal ordination prayer in Hippolytus is followed immediately by a sample eucharistic anaphora for the bishop's use,
and it is significant that ordinations traditionally take place
within the eucharistic liturgy. I have been equally impressed
by the way in which traditional ordination prayers seek moral
gifts for the ordinand. Against Donatism, it is vital that the
congregation's salvation not be thought to depend on the
worthiness of those who minister God's sacraments to it. Yet
the good example of a pastor has brought many people closer
to God and his kingdom. At least since the Pontifical of Dur-
andus in the thirteenth century, Roman priests have been
exhorted to "imitate what you handle, *imitamini quod trac-
tatis.*"[54] The same expectation is shared for themselves by
all who participate in the Easter sacraments: "Grant that the
sacraments we have received at Easter may continue to live
in our minds and hearts"; "Grant that we who have celebrated the Easter ceremonies may hold to them in life and
conduct"; "Grant that we may imitate and achieve what we
celebrate and profess."[55]

Holiness would perhaps be the proper rubric under which
to consider a number of questions which are controversial
today: the question of full-time and part-time service, which
is not quite the question either of "worker-priests" or of "non-
stipendiary ministry"; then also the question of "ordination
for life" or "temporary ordination" (I understand this is currently a matter of debate in the French Reformed Church);
and finally, particularly in the Roman Catholic Church, the
question of clerical celibacy. The battle lines cross in these
controversies, but I suspect that the underlying issue is always that of the *quality of commitment* which the ordained
ministry is meant to represent and stimulate in the whole
Christian body.

3. Unity

Hippolytus' bishop is a pastor. The image of the shepherd
has constantly been associated with the unity of the Church
(see John 10:16). Although it is rather in virtue of his analogous representation of God the Father (another traditional
theme), the bishop appears already in the letters of Ignatius
of Antioch as the guardian of unity in the local church: "Let

that be reckoned a valid eucharist which is under the bishop or a person appointed by him."[56] It is in the eucharistic assembly that unity comes to focal expression—or fails to. From Cyprian's *De unitate ecclesiae* onward, the *ordo episcoporum* is clearly seen to have a collegiate responsibility for safeguarding the unity of the universal Church.[57] It is chiefly with reference to the universal level that the ARCIC statement *Ministry and Ordination* can declare: "The communion of the churches in mission, faith, and holiness, through time and space, is thus symbolized *and maintained* in the bishop."[58] As one who for the last two hundred years has not belonged to an "episcopal" church in the "catholic" sense of the term, I am taken aback that two churches with *rival episcopates* should make that affirmation together. Ideally, the episcopate *would* maintain the universal unity of the Church. But the members of ARCIC have a notable difficulty in distinguishing between the ideal and the actual (as their statement on Authority demonstrates even more obviously). Yet the eschatological tension between the already and the not yet is a fundamental datum for theological reflection in ecclesiology. All movements toward Christian unity—which will probably remain asymptotic until the Parousia—had better take that polarity into account if there is to be further practical progress. Mercifully, there has already been progress beyond the position of Cyprian, who reduced "schismatic" baptisms and ordinations to charades, and of Augustine, who allowed their "validity" only in the sense that they were not to be repeated when return to the "catholic" church made them "fruitful"; but even where mutual "recognition" has been achieved, the churches have not always gone on to communion and unity. Despite my present nonepiscopal allegiance, I should myself welcome a unifying episcopate with many of the values indicated by (though not equated with) the notion of apostolic succession. It is not yet clear whether Faith and Order's description of "the episcopal succession as a sign, though not a guarantee, of the continuity and unity of the Church" will prove helpful to the churches in their search for "a mutually recognized ministry."[59] I like the suggestion of the Groupe des Dombes that "*vigilance*" and "*unité*" are the two notes that should chiefly characterize the ministry of the "*épiscope*" (*épiscope* is a neologism created to avoid both *évêque* and *surintendant* or even *inspecteur*).[60]

4. Catholicity

One aspect of catholicity has already been touched on under unity: the intentionally worldwide, universal character of the Church and its ministry. There is, however, another sense to catholicity. I cannot find any point of attachment in Hippolytus for a discussion of women's ordination. In a baptismal passage, St. Paul teaches that life in Christ transcends all divisions of race, culture, economic condition, and sex (Gal. 3:27f.). This does not imply undifferentiated uniformity. The sexually differentiated contributions which men and women make to the whole Christian community will vary according to psychological and social circumstances, which appear themselves to depend on a mixture of biological and cultural factors. In the modern West, the judgment is growing that it is wrong to schematize the properly diverse contributions of the sexes by restricting the eucharistic presidency and the more general oversight of the Church to male Christians. The exclusion of women from these focal offices and functions is now widely felt to be untrue to the Church's vocation to catholicity.[61]

V. THE ESCHATOLOGICAL DIMENSION OF ORDINATION

The prayers of Hippolytus are disappointing on eschatology. True, the doxological themes are strong, but that fact might almost serve to confirm M. Werner's thesis about the delay in the Parousia and the consequent and compensatory dissolution of eschatology into cult.[62] However, later ordination prayers in both East and West reintroduce the future prospect. The angle is that of responsibility and reward.

Oversight can be given an eschatological depth in terms of *vigilance*.[63] The episcopal "watchman"[64] has *ultimate* responsibility for the congregation. Thus the Byzantine ordinal prays that the bishop may "imitate thee, the true pastor . . . so that having formed in this life the souls entrusted to him, he may stand without shame before thy judgment-seat and receive the great reward which thou hast prepared for those who have done battle for the preaching of the gospel." For the presbyter the prayer is that "at the second advent of our great God and Saviour Jesus Christ thy only Son, he may receive by thy bounty the reward of good stewardship in the affairs of thy house."[65] The Roman prayer at the ordination of presbyters is *ut bonam rationem dispensationis sibi creditue reddituri, aeternae beatitudinis premia consequantur.* A strong sense of continued dependence on divine grace till the end shines through the Spanish *completuria:* "Accomplish, Lord, what we ask and finish what we seek; and be ever thus gracious that thou, having been called upon, may not in any respect fail us."[66]

CONCLUSION: THE SOURCE OF AUTHORITY

In considering the authority of the ordained ministry, let us first search the Scriptures. According to Mark 3:14f., Jesus "made" twelve: "I have chosen you to be with me. I will also send you out to preach, and you will have authority to drive out demons." They were thus set in the service of God's kingdom. According to John 20:22f., the risen Lord breathed on the disciples and said, "Receive the Holy Spirit. If you forgive people's sins, they are forgiven; if you do not forgive them, they are not forgiven" (see Matt. 16:18.; 18:18). At the conclusion of St. Matthew's gospel (28:18-20), the risen Jesus says to the remaining eleven: "I have been given all authority in heaven and on earth. Go, then, to peoples everywhere and make them my disciples: baptize them in the name of the Father, the Son, and the Holy Spirit, and teach them to obey everything I have commanded you. And I will be with you always, to the end of the age" (see Acts 1:8). We have already indicated ways in which the ministry of the apostles is both unique and yet must be continued. The New Testament starts to show us (a) how certain individuals were appointed to the continuing task, and (b) the place they then occupied in the Christian community as a whole.

As to the manner of appointment, Max Thurian looks to

four passages for an embryonic rite of ordination: Acts 6:3-8; 13:1-4; 1 Timothy 4:13; 2 Timothy 1:6f. From these texts we may see that the Holy Spirit is "both the master and the criterion" in the Church's choice of candidates for ordination; that ordination is performed on the responsibility of those who already carry authority in the Church; that the act of ordination consists in prayer and the laying on of hands;[67] and that the fruit of ordination is the charism of ministry.[68] As to the location of particular ministries in the overall structure of the Christian communities, modern New Testament scholarship concedes that the picture is rather obscure and probably includes local variations.[69] Such uncertainty and complexity in the New Testament evidence is of theological importance when a scriptural component is being sought for the authority of the ordained ministry or (more especially) certain particular forms of it. An interesting element has been introduced into recent discussion by the notion of "trajectory."[70] But even if it is possible to detect accurately the direction of incipient movements in the matter of ministry in the New Testament period, the questions remain: whether the course they factually took in the patristic period was the necessary one; and why, the notion of development once being admitted, the structures reached at a certain point in the development have traditionally been considered "fixed" (bishop, presbyter, deacon), whereas the concrete exercise of representative ministries of word, sacrament, and rule has varied considerably. The fundamental theological question is, of course, that of God's guidance of the Church in history. In the present and more limited context, I can do no more than suggest that clues to the churches' understanding of the authority of the ordained ministry are to be found in (a) their rites and ceremonies of ordination, where the ministries are sacramentally inaugurated,[71] and (b) the configuration of their regular liturgical assemblies, where the patterns of authority within the community come to symbolic expression.

First, the rites and ceremonies of ordination. Homilies, invitatories, and prayers—whether ancient, Catholic, or Protestant—show widespread agreement that the call, choice, and gifting of the ministers come from God.[72] But some differences emerge concerning the human role in translating

ꜱ

the divine choice into ecclesiastical reality. All are agreed in praying that the Holy Spirit may confirm those gifts of grace which have already to some extent been recognized in the candidates and which will fit them for a particular ministry in the public life of the Church. The problem is: *Who*, ecclesiastically, decides that *these* individuals are divinely called to positions in which the responsibility (and authority) which accompanies the divine gift will be exercised?

For several centuries in the early Church it appears that Christian communities shared in the election of their own bishop.[73] The part played by other local bishops in the imposition of hands and, by one of them, in voicing the ordination prayer, marked his aggregation to the episcopal college within the Church universal.[74] The next development transferred the making of the choice to metropolitans and patriarchs, and notably the pope. At Rome, the pope himself was elected by the local clergy, notably the cardinal deacons. In Byzantine and Gallican rites, popular consent to the new bishop found expression in the acclamation "He is worthy" at the ordination service. In time, the people's role in the election of bishops became limited to a failure to object when the question of impediments was asked. It is important, however, that the whole community's *prayer* remains a constituent part of the ordination, whether in silence, or in a litany, or in the *Veni creator,* or at least in the Amen when the presiding bishop speaks the ordination prayer. The recent tendency is toward restoring the people's say in the whole process of election. (There is no room here to treat the issues raised when civil authorities act in the appointment of a bishop.) In the Presbyterian and Independent traditions, a pastor may be "called" only by a local church; and it was a Congregationalist practice—where laypeople shared also in the imposition of hands—that the professional minister must be ordained anew if he moved to another congregation.

Among the secondary ceremonies in the ancient ordination rites, the placing of the gospel-book on the bishop's head and shoulders strikes me as the best epitome of ministerial authority. The accompanying Byzantine formula mentions the *yoke* of the gospel. It is the bishop's existential submission to the gospel which will win him personal au-

thority. He will thus share in the *power* of the gospel itself
(Dom Bernard Botte's interpretation of the ceremony)—the
gospel whose proclamation, in and through the Christian
community, the Christian community appoints him, with
prayer for God's grace, to lead.[75] In a nutshell: the minister
has authority insofar as, by life and word, he or she represents the gospel.

Second and last: the configuration of the worship assembly. Vatican II spoke of the worship assembly as *praecipua
manifestatio Ecclesiae:* there is no mistaking the theological
importance of its "human shape."[76] The modern liturgical
movement has emphasized the variety of functions in the
worship assembly.[77] Even Protestants are questioning the
dominance of the isolated preacher-theologian in "his" pul-
pit. On the Roman Catholic side, Vatican II's Constitution
on the Sacred Liturgy envisages "the full, active participation of all God's holy people in the same liturgical celebrations, especially in the same eucharist, in a single prayer at
one altar, at which there presides the bishop surrounded by
his college of priests and ministers" (para. 41).[78] The council
was cautious; but let no one doubt the significance of the
shift in the assembly's "human shape" in the question of
authority. Listen first to Archbishop Lefebvre:

> It is obvious that this new rite is, if I may put it this
> way, of an opposing polarity, that it supposes a different
> conception of the Catholic religion. It is no longer the
> priest who offers the Holy Sacrifice of the Mass, it is
> the assembly. Now this is a complete programme. From
> now on it is also the assembly which will replace au-
> thority in the Church. . . . It is the weight of numbers
> which will give the orders from now on in the holy
> Church. And all this is expressed in the Mass precisely
> because the assembly replaces the priest, to such an
> extent that now many priests no longer want to cele-
> brate the Holy Mass if there is not an assembly there.
> Very quietly, it is the Protestant idea of the Mass which
> is creeping into the holy Church. And this is in accor-
> dance with the mentality of modern man, with the men-
> tality of modernist man, completely in accordance, for
> it is the democratic ideal which is fundamentally the
> idea of modern man. That is to say that power is in the
> assembly, authority is vested in men, *en masse,* and not

in God. . . . This Mass is no longer a hierarchic Mass,
it is a democratic Mass.[79]

Yves Congar remarks on the oddity of making the exercise
by the faithful of their baptismal priesthood equivalent to a
denial that power comes from God; he also maintains that
the liturgical "presidency" in no way excludes the appointed
person from acting "in persona Christi" *toward* the
community.[80]

Drawing on Congar's own historical studies of changing
conceptions of ecclesiastical authority, the leading English
Catholic theologian Nicholas Lash has welcomed the recent
move away from the clerical authority structure of the pre-
ceding generations, the liturgical embodiment of which was
the mass celebrated by an individual agent supplied with
attendants and an audience.[81] The vision of the eucharistic
assembly promoted by the liturgical movement is characterized by the principle of "distribution of function" and is
reflected in article 28 of Vatican II's Constitution on the Liturgy: "In liturgical celebrations, whether as a minister or as
one of the faithful, each person should perform his role by
doing solely and totally what the nature of things and liturgical norms require of him." Lash comments: "Article 28, for
all its low-key abstractions, is important because it is one of
a number of conciliar texts that point to that recovery of a far
richer, more ancient and biblical vision of the church, which
was one of the major doctrinal achievements of the council.
. . . A profound shift in liturgical structures and self-understanding has both stimulated and expressed an underlying
shift in ecclesial consciousness, the nature of which may be
indicated by speaking of the recovery of a functional model
of ministry. . . . The shift in catholic liturgical practice in
recent decades has brought about, or is bringing about, a
corresponding shift in the manner in which, pre-reflexively
and informally, authority in the church is experienced and
understood." All this, says Lash, is in accordance with the
"principle of the public accountability of office-holders,"
which is important for the healthy exercise of authority in
any society: "they are answerable to the community for their
stewardship"; in terms of the Church and theology, it represents a recovery of "the ancient doctrine of the consent of
the church, the *consensus ecclesiae*."

VII
SACRAMENTAL TIME

I. ECCLESIAL TIME

The taste of a madeleine dunked in tea evoked in the proustian narrator's memory seven or eight volumes of "lost time" for re-exploration.[1] In the holy eucharist the believer is invited to "taste and see the goodness of the Lord"; Psalm 34:8 is a traditional communion-verse. It is the Christian conviction that the Lord Jesus Christ there makes himself present—the same yesterday, today, and forever. The sacramental *anamnesis* and *epiclesis*, remembrance and invocation, mediate an encounter with the man raised by God from the dead and appointed by him to judge the world one day. "Blessed is he who came and who is to come": thus the Syrian rites greet his advent in the liturgical celebration. In "the time of the Church," the Lord's meal is a proclamation of his death until his coming again. Let me start this first section by bringing out, in a gentle contrast with the novelist, three characteristics of an ecclesial experience of time as qualified by Christ.

First, the presence of Christ to his Church, epitomized in the eucharist, has more ontological substance than a psychological event in the mind of the individual. "Mere memorialism" has found no home except in the Zwinglian tradition, and even there the problem was caused by the astronomical location of the ascended Christ at God's right hand. Calvin, with a more "relational" conception of space,[2] exploited the *Sursum corda* to do better justice to the believer's communion with Christ at the supper. Taking a more consistently instrumental view of the bread and wine than Calvin, the Orthodox and Catholic traditions look on the eucharistic elements as the bearers of a "real presence." Whether the emphasis fall on the elements or be distributed throughout the

120

action of taking, thanking, eating, and drinking, Christ is experienced by the Church as present "in the order of signs," to use a scholastic phrase more recently taken up again by the Catholic poet and painter David Jones.[3] As both Calvin's talk of the Holy Spirit as "link" and the characteristic Eastern forms of epiclesis express it, Christ's presence is a pneumatological reality. In the words of a Wesleyan hymn on the Lord's Supper, it is the function of the Holy Ghost to "realize the sign."[4] The claimed experience of Christ's personal presence in the Spirit would be illusory if his resurrection did not set him in a realm beyond death. Put the other and more positive way: the Church's continued testimony to his eucharistic *parousía*, his advent and presence in the sacrament, is a witness to the event which the New Testament speaks of as his resurrection. "We know that Christ being raised from the dead will never die again; death no longer has dominion over him. The death he died he died to sin, once for all, but the life he lives he lives to God" (Rom. 6:9f.). In a seminal article[5] O. Cullmann showed the part played in the origin of the Church's eucharist by the post-resurrection meals: Christ's presence in the midst has continued to be sensed by the community gathered in his name (the phraseology of Matt. 18:20 is adopted in several Syrian anaphoras).

Second, the Church's eucharist not only recalls the past but also anticipates the future. In some Eastern anaphoras the technical anamnesis[6] stretches from the conception and birth of Christ through his death, resurrection, and ascension and on to his second and glorious advent in which he will judge the living and the dead. It is Western practice to restrict remembering to things past and to turn to a verb of expectation for things still to come: *et praestolantes alterum eius adventum* (Roman eucharistic prayer III). Combining the two emphases: the present is qualified by both the past and the future work of the one Christ as ground and goal respectively. It is on the basis of what he has already done for the inauguration of God's kingdom and human salvation that we may now pray for their final consummation. This understanding runs right through liturgical history and does not stand or fall with J. Jeremias's exegesis of 1 Corinthians 11:25f.: "that God may remember me" ... "with a view to [the Lord's] coming."[7] In classical eucharistic anaphoras, the past acts of God in Christ are rehearsed in thanksgiving, and supplication is made that we may stand in the final judgment and be given a share in the bliss of the definitive kingdom. How, more precisely, is present communion related to the past and future events?

Work in biblical theology around the *zkr* root has concentrated on the relation between present and past.[8] It is sometimes suggested that the effect of liturgical commemoration is to transport the present generation back to the decisive occasion in the past. In Christian terms: "Were you there when they crucified my Lord?" Others rather envisage liturgical *Vergegenwärtigung* as bringing the original event into the present by reenactment: the unbloody sacrifice of the mass or the "mystery-memorial" of O. Casel.[9] Similarly with respect to the future: if the final Parousia of Christ will take place (the detailed scenario is not my concern, only let it stand for the certainty of a consummation of judgment and salvation in Christ), the eucharist may be seen either as its pro-jection from the future (the future coming into the present) or as its anticipation (the present reaching out for the future):

> By faith and hope already there,
> Even now the marriage feast we share.[10]

For those who have difficulties, even in the order of signs, with the idea that a past event can be repeated or an expected event preempted, it may perhaps be sufficient to speak of the influence or effect of such events on the present. But I think that justice would be done to the vividness of the Church's sense of past and future in the eucharist only on condition that the personal presence be recognized of a Christ clothed with his past and future acts, or less metaphorically a Christ who once gave himself for humanity to the point of death and is our appointed judge and savior. The central Christian understanding was expressed by J.-J. von Allmen in an essay entitled "pour un prophétisme sacramentel":[11]

> Sacrament occurs wherever the age to come elects, touches, exorcises (or pardons), occupies and conse-

crates an element of this age and thus makes itself present there. A sacrament is an echo of the first coming of
Jesus Christ and a pledge of his second coming, Christ
himself being the sacrament *par excellence*. The sacrament is prophetic in the sense that it is for the present
age both a threat and a promise, signifying both its end
and its future, calling it to both repentance and hope.

Third, the eucharistic evocation of Christ is far from
accidental:

Jesus, we thus obey
Thy last and kindest word;
Here, in thine own appointed way,
We come to meet thee, Lord.[12]

Although our reading of the institution narratives might be
more critical than the Wesleys', even a cult-legend is a retro-
jection from what is experienced as a given and sought
presence.[13] The point is: Christ is believed to have committed himself to time. According to a structuralist decipher-
ment of the rite, L. Dussaut holds the eucharist to be a
symbolic commemoration of the whole of Christ's earthly
life between the poles of the Incarnation and the Passion;[14]
he thereby rejoins Thomas Aquinas: "The body of Christ
represents the mystery of the incarnation . . . while the blood
of Christ represents sacramentally the passion."[15] The Incarnation and finally the death of Christ are the profoundest
expression of a movement begun in creation. God's decision,
by an irreducible act of will, to create a temporally structured
universe means that he must, in B. Hebblethwaite's words,
"relate himself to it in a mode appropriate to its temporality.
This is part of God's self-limitation, his *kenosis*, in creation."[16] In submitting himself to time, the servant Lord becomes time's redeemer: his sovereignty is exercised for the
benefit of creatures whose drift is toward decay if they fail
to let themselves be included in his irreducible purpose of
love. More of the negativities shortly. Here I simply want to
bring eucharistic testimony to our dependence on the divine
availability and enablement if we are not to let the opportunities of creaturehood slip by. From our angle, the whole

eucharistic action is prayer, epiclesis. The evocation depends on invocation. The Wesleys take up a pneumatological image from the Clementine liturgy:

> Come, thou Witness of his dying,
> Come, Remembrancer divine,
> Let us feel thy power applying
> Christ to every soul and mine.[17]

The Holy Spirit is also firstfruits (*aparchḗ*), and earnest (*arrabṓn*), of the End.

What I have said so far may appear too *heilsgeschichtlich* for the taste of some. Let me try to sugar the pill by briefly talking more formally in terms of intention and purpose. Without some notion of a divine intention and purpose for creation, and particularly for humanity, it seems to me that we have no chance of making theological sense of time. Time is a condition for the realization of intention, for the achievement of purpose. In the words of the Orthodox theologian Olivier Clément: time is the God-given opportunity to learn to love.[18] F. W. Dillistone speaks of the self-giving career of Christ as an "arrow of history," indicating the direction of God's gracious design, which is to bring many sons to glory.[19] Transformation into the moral and spiritual likeness of God takes place wherever and whenever humans freely requite his love. To revert more obviously to the *Heilsgeschichte* in the narrower sense: the period between the Crucifixion and the Parousia is time-for, time for the Church to preach the gospel of God's self-giving love in Christ and so facilitate a sharper response to the divine offer. Where the love of God does not find an answer (which will show itself also as love of the neighbor), deliberate refusal is a self-inflicted judgment. Issues of ultimate destiny are being played out in time. (Sacramentally: failure to "discern the body" [1 Cor. 11:29; see also Heb. 10:29] is, according to the exegesis of C. F. D. Moule and G. Bornkamm, "a culpable failure to recognize, to discern, that the life which was surrendered [on the Cross] was that of the Lord himself," and in a eucharistic context that means failure to be "alert to the meaning with which the bread and wine are charged both in regard to the incarnate Christ given for us and in regard to the fellow members

of the Body which that surrender created." That is why the
unbrotherly and unsisterly Corinthians are said to be eating
and drinking judgment upon themselves.)[20]

After time as experienced by the Christian community I
want now to concentrate on time as experienced by the
Christian individual. From ecclesial time to existential time.

II. EXISTENTIAL TIME

We may begin with baptism. It is the sign which marks
Christian existence: *baptizatus sum* (Luther). It is an anticipation of individual death, which is "also a baptism." As the
sacrament of justification (1 Cor. 6:11), it is also an anticipation of final judgment. It is these because it signifies participation in the baptism of Christ on the Cross. "I have a
baptism to be baptized with, and how I am constrained until
it is accomplished" (Luke 12:50; see also Mark 10:38f.). Passage through death and judgment may open out into the
broad land of resurrection. It was the case with Christ. He
continues to issue the call to follow him. "If any one would
come after me, let him deny himself and take up his cross
and follow me. For whoever would save his life will lose it;
and whoever loses his life for my sake and the gospel's will
save it" (Mark 8:34f.). In E. Jüngel's words: love, and God,
is "a unity of death and life, to the advantage of life."[21] When
a heart hitherto turned in upon itself opens out and surren-
ders itself in love, it receives back its new identity from the
other or certainly from the Other. In Pauline terms: it becomes "dead to sin and alive to God in Christ Jesus" (Rom. 6).
What has all this to do with time?

Time may readily be experienced as decay: *nascenti mor-
imur*. A physically closed system is subject to increasing en-
tropy. Biologically, a closed system is moribund if not already
dead. *Homo in se incurvatus*, "man turned in upon himself"
(Luther), is on the road to ruin. But time may also be experienced as growth. Moral and spiritual growth takes place
through death to self. "Unless a grain of wheat die. . . ." Our
old self is crucified, so that we may walk "in newness of life"
(Rom. 6). In the Bible, the theologically significant uses of
"new" connote qualitative newness: the Johannine equiv-

alent to the Pauline "newness of life" is "eternal life." The old Roman canon aptly spoke of "the cup of the new and eternal covenant." To share in newness of life is to have your youth constantly renewed like the eagle's (Ps. 103:5; see also Isa. 40:31). In the words of the old Roman entrance psalm:

> I will go in to the altar of God:
> To the God who rejoices my youth.

Worship is well compared to the serious play of children (R. Guardini, *Vom Geist der Liturgie*).[22] This "spirit of the liturgy" should also characterize the ethical life of Christians, who are being daily renewed after the image of their creator (Rom. 12:2; 2 Cor. 4:16; 5:17; Eph. 4:23f.; Col. 3:10; Tit. 3:5). For they have already "passed from death to life" (John 5:24).

Why then do Christians still die? The problem already posed itself to the Pauline congregations (1 Thess. 4:13-5:11; see also 1 Cor. 15). It cannot be said that the apostle gave them a clear answer. Perhaps there is some help to be found in E. Jüngel's suggestion that a certain definitiveness is needed for the constitution of identity,[23] but we must be careful not to underestimate the need or possibilities of transformative grace even at the end of a Christian life well lived on earth. We must in fact face up to the reality of post-baptismal sin, before which St. Paul found himself at such a loss that he could only resort to rhetorical questions and *reductio ad absurdum* arguments (Rom. 6:1f.; 1 Cor. 1:10-13). The Church came to see the necessity of repeatable penance. An Anglican absolution (1928 English from Sarum) prays for "time for the amendment of life." It is Orthodox custom to receive the sacrament of the sick at least yearly, thereby acknowledging one's continuing need of the Physician. That is why Christian burial liturgies still commend the departed to the mercy of God. Only where eschatology is totally realized has death quite lost its sting. The martyr, whose death is entirely self-gift, has immediate access to heaven: the martyr has "learned to love."

The classical liturgies of the eucharist testify to the earthly Church's sense of being surrounded by a cloud of witnesses.

In the Sanctus of the Greek *St. James,* the Church on earth
joins a heavenly assembly which includes "the spirits of just
people and prophets, the souls of martyrs and apostles." Our
prayer is that we may have part with the saints in the kingdom. Although the saints are believed already to enjoy the
nearer presence of God, their condition still contains an element of waiting: "How long?" (Rev. 6:9-11). Nicholas Ca-
basilas was embarrassed at the thought that the Church on
earth might pray for the saints when we rather stood in need
of their prayers, but some Syrian and Armenian commentators take the *offerimus pro* in these cases to mean that the
saints themselves have not yet quite reached perfection.[24]
We may here have a clue concerning why the second advent
of Christ and the final resurrection are still awaited. Because
of the communal nature of humanity and salvation, none is
perfect until all are perfect. The kingdom will (have) come
only when each and all of its beneficiaries have been irre-
versibly transformed into the moral and spiritual likeness of
God.

Meanwhile the eucharistic liturgies provide language for
expressing the relation between Christian existence now and
the life of the kingdom then. As the epitome of Christian
existence, the eucharist is a "pledge," an "earnest," a "sign,"
an "image," a "prefiguration," a "promise," a "seed." All
these terms express both a link and a distinction between
present and future. But most characteristically (for the sacrament takes the form of a meal), the eucharist is a "taste"
of the age to come. To taste is to try the relish; and to say
that the eucharist provides a taste of the kingdom therefore
allows us to express both the provisional and yet the genuine
quality of the kingdom as it flavors the present. A Gregorian
post-communion prays "that what rejoices us by its taste may
by its effect renew us" *(ut cujus laetamur gustu, renovemur
effectu).* Or in the words of the Wesleys:

> For all that joy which now we taste,
> Our happy hallow'd souls prepare;
> O let us hold the earnest fast,
> This pledge that we thy heaven shall share,
> Shall drink it new with thee above,
> The wine of thy eternal love.[25]

The prefiguration is creative: God's bread feeds, strengthens, and transforms. "We trust that we have been strengthened by the reception of this sacrament, so that what we here possess meanwhile by hope we may enjoy in its true fruits when we dwell in heaven" (Stowe missal). Hope mobilizes (J. Moltmann).

Having in a movement of concentration reduced ecclesial time to existential time, let me in a third part spread into the public area of creation and society. On now to what may be called cosmic time.

III. COSMIC TIME

At the end of the Flood story the Lord promises: "While earth remains, seedtime and harvest, cold and heat, summer and winter, day and night, shall not cease" (Gen. 8:22). Insofar as humanity falls or falls short, the order of creation becomes an order of (mere) preservation by which God maintains fallen humanity in existence with a view to their redemption. Without redemption there is a limit to preservation, whether for the individual or for the race: "as long as the earth remains" is also a threat. Insofar as redeemed humanity responds to the divine vocation, the orders of creation and preservation pass into an order of salvation. The love which moves the sun and the other stars is the love which bled on Calvary; on an early medieval tomb-sculpture in Salamanca cathedral the outstretched hands of the Crucified are upholding the moon and the sun. The temporal substructure in which God's purpose for personal beings is played out can at least be experienced as redeemed and may even itself thereby be brought into the realm of salvation.

There are daily, yearly, and weekly rhythms. When accepted with thanksgiving, they are sanctified (see 1 Tim. 4:4f.). Day and night are consecrated by the morning and the evening sacrifice, by the "cathedral offices" of lauds and vespers:[26] everyday existence is thereby acknowledged to be received from the hands of God. In biblical Israel, the annual rhythm was given a special linkage with redemption through the association of the feasts with the events of exodus, Sinai, and settlement. The Christian Church was to claim by direct takeover the natural pagan feast of the winter solstice as the birthday of Christ, the sun of righteousness. Earlier, the Church had seen the deliverance celebrated in the Jewish passover as having been re-new-ed and universalized by the exodus which Christ accomplished at Jerusalem. While Christmas had begun life as an anniversary, and even Easter ran that risk with the historicism which accompanied Constantinianism,[27] the primary feast of Sunday—attested already by Acts 20:7, 1 Corinthians 16:2, and Revelation 1:10— kept clearer the eschatological significance of Christ which his resurrection had confirmed and displayed. It may have been the relative insignificance of the weekly rhythm from the natural point of view (I know about the moon but also about weeks of other duration than seven days in some cultures) which fitted the weekly Sunday for the eschatological-symbolic role in Christianity which the weekly sabbath had apparently come to occupy in Judaism (see the Letter to the Hebrews). In Christian understanding, the resurrection of Christ marked the beginning of the End: Christ was the first-born of many brethren (Rom. 8:29; see also Col. 1:18), the "head of another race which he himself regenerated,"[28] and his resurrection was the start of creation's renewal.[29] As the day of Christ's resurrection, Sunday was the "eighth day," the sign of the future age.[30] It was the most appropriate day for the gathering of Christians to receive "the medicine of immortality, the antidote against death and for life in Jesus Christ for ever."[31] From Theodore of Mopsuestia to M. Schmaus and E. Schillebeeckx, Christian commentators have interpreted eucharistic communion as a transforming encounter with the risen and glorious Christ. That encounter is so close that it has seemed appropriate to speak of "participating" in Christ.[32]

The moral and spiritual transformation is to be tested, exercised, and prolonged in everyday life. E. Käsemann rightly sees that liturgical language is employed in an ethical sense in Romans 12:1f. and elsewhere in the New Testament: "the service of God in the everyday world."[33] But, rather like the Quakers with the sacraments, he cannot abide a special holiness of times and places, what he pejoratively calls the cult; the whole of life is lived "before God," *coram deo*. But this is a secular version of the attempt to force the Parousia, just as a round-the-clock monastic office would be a sacred version of overrealized eschatology. In an *inaugurated* eschatology the focal moments of rite are rather experienced as (already) given and (still) needed to clarify the vision, nerve the will, sustain the action. This applies not only in the field of personal ethics. In the public arena, individual Christians and the Church have the prophetic responsibility of reading the signs of the times in relation to the kingdom of God. By symbolic gestures, both sacramental and paraliturgical, they must seek to keep before the eyes of the world the values of the divine kingdom which may and should find at least provisional embodiment in society and politics. To follow this analogical line discerned by K. Barth in *Christengemeinde und Bürgergemeinde*,[34] and developed by W. Pannenberg in *Die Bestimmung des Menschen*,[35] is to exclude the false alternatives of either the apolitical Christianity advocated by E. R. Norman in *Christianity and the World Order* or the "politicization" of Christianity which the 1978 Reith lecturer was attacking.[36]

To talk of provisionality is to admit a "not yet" and to point forward to a "one day." The last section of this chapter is largely concerned with that prospect.

IV. WHEN SACRAMENTS CEASE

I have spoken—intelligibly, I hope—of the character and opportunites of time without seeking a lexical base in *chrónos* and *kairós*.[37] But some may consider that I should at least address myself to another part of the legacy from the Biblical Theology movement of a generation ago: the notions of linear and cyclical time. Cyclical time comes closest to what I have called cosmic time: salvation might then be experienced as absorption into the circle. But that would scarcely match the sense of direction which so strongly characterizes biblical experience that O. Cullmann could see salvation-history stretched along rectilinear time.[38] That comes closest to what I have called ecclesial time. In fact, however, my cosmic and ecclesial times are not simply cyclical and linear respectively. There is much interference between the two; there is a mutual qualification. The unifying concept is purpose. A unifying figure might be spiral. Would the spiral open upward? or narrow downward? Might existential time allow us to see? Pastorally, I have known cases where physical decay unto death has been accompanied and contradicted by the finest flowering of spiritual life, perhaps possible only because the seeds had been planted earlier and had been growing modestly if not secretly. On the other hand, physical death may sometimes appear as the outward and visible sign of an inward and spiritual gracelessness. Or if no one is left ungraced, might false freedom not finally decline into nothingness? Are some human beings on an upward spiral, others on a downward (whether reversible or not)? What figure would be appropriate for the human race as perhaps a solidary and cumulative whole? I am dizzy. Let us leave geometry and speak rather in value language.

"Temps perdu" is ambiguous: *wasted* time is irretrievably *lost*. But time in which the divine presence has been savored acquires an eternal quality. It becomes part of a personal relationship which God intends to be permanent: "Man's chief end is to glorify God and to enjoy him for ever." The Westminster Shorter Catechism thus captures the vision of a thousand communion prayers. Eucharistic rites recognize that there is an "already," a "not yet," and a "one day" about our fellowship with God. They lend themselves admirably— if indeed they do not give rise—to an interpretative principle which has wider applications: in the eschatological prospect one is confirming and enhancing whatever is positive in the present, while removing those limitations which are due to sin but not those which are due to creaturehood.

> We now are at his table fed,
> But wait to see our heavenly king;
> To see the great Invisible
> Without a sacramental veil,
> With all his robes of glory on,
> In rapturous joy and love and praise
> Him to behold with open face,
> High on his everlasting throne.[39]

It will be easiest for me to repeat some of the systematic conclusions drawn from study of the liturgical evidence in my *Eucharist and Eschatology*: "At the eucharist Christ is present to the eyes of faith: at his table in the final kingdom we shall see him face to face. The eucharist is a periodic celebration: in the final kingdom the worship and rejoicing will be perpetual. In the eucharist a part of mankind and a part of the world serve the glory of God: in the final kingdom God will be all in all. The people who celebrate the eucharist are imperfect in their obedience: in the final kingdom their submission to the rule of God will be total. Eucharistic joy is marred by our persistence in sin: the joy of the final kingdom will be full. No schema of general eschatology is acceptable which fails to take into account the constitutive relation between the 'now' and the 'then', the 'here' and the 'there', and within that relation the polarities of hiddenness and visibility (contestability and incontestability), interruption and permanence, limited extension and universal scope, incomplete obedience and complete service, spoilt joy and perfect bliss."[40]

The eucharistic symbolism is meal symbolism, and the Bible's favorite picture for the final kingdom is that of feasting. This twin fact must influence any identifiably traditional position on two questions which are at present somewhat controversial in philosophical theology. First: objective storage in the memory of God is an inadequate conception of eternal life. Subjective experience of salvation is implied in the feasting and so also in talk of seeing, knowing, praising God. Christian worship is a free, active, reciprocal relationship between God and human beings. The divine kingdom and human salvation must be conceived on that model. Secondly, eucharistic and other liturgical symbolism includes the element of duration. For creatures at least, whatever it means for God in himself, the final kingdom is expected to *go on*. The eschatological images of bodily resurrection and new heavens and a new earth suggest the same thing. Could it be otherwise, if creatures are to explore the inexhaustibility of God?

A final remark on method. I hope that what I have written will not be mistaken for liturgical fundamentalism. I have done no more than allude to some tensions within the worship tradition of the Church which can serve as stimuli for internal criticism. Nor have I been able to do more than hint at some philosophical questions which it may be proper to address to the liturgical experience of the Church from without. My chief contention is that the liturgical experience of the Church, with its own more or less naive self-interpretation, supplies primary data for any more reflective theology of time and eternity which would be identifiably Christian. For a more detailed justification and exemplification of this approach I must refer to my systematic theology written from the perspective of worship under the title *Doxology*.[41] Meanwhile, with St. Patrick

> I bind this day to me for ever,
> By power of faith, Christ's incarnation;
> His baptism in the Jordan river;
> His death on Cross for my salvation;
> His bursting from the spicèd tomb;
> His riding up the heavenly way;
> His coming at the day of doom:
> I bind unto myself today.

VIII
BETWEEN GOD AND WORLD

Christian liturgy, and the eucharist in particular, epitomizes not only the relations between the Church and God but also the relations between the Church and the world. It would be a mistake simply to designate these two sets of relations the vertical and the horizontal respectively. That would risk obscuring any direct contact between God and the world. Nevertheless the Church does occupy a mediating place and function between God and the world, between the world and God. The Church has the missionary task of proclaiming God's gospel to the world. In the other direction, the Church's responsibility is to represent the world before God in worship. The Church's mission in the world is not only evangelistic but also liturgical. The Church's worship of God finds not only liturgical but also evangelistic expression. Nor may liturgy and evangelism be separated from ethics: everyday behavior takes place before God, and the conduct of Christians is part of their witness to the world; the liturgy brings the ethical and evangelistic offering to a symbolic focus, from which point the love of God may irradiate the world the more brightly for having once again expressed itself in its own appointed way. In words from John and Charles Wesley's *Hymns on the Lord's Supper:*

> Jesu, we thus obey
> Thy last and kindest word,
> Here in thine own appointed way
> We come to meet Thee, Lord.

My intention in this chapter is to indicate some of the perennial questions involved in the Church's existence at the hinge between God and world.[1] In some cases, I will sharpen the issues to their acute contemporary form. The headings of the discussion are five prominent New Testament themes, which will be typified by some Pauline or near-Pauline texts. The titles are: I. Reconciliation; II. Evangelism; III. Ethics; IV. Intercession; V. Kingdom.

I. RECONCILIATION

1. Through Christ we both have access in one Spirit to the Father. (Eph. 2:18)

In the second half of chapter 2, the writer of the Letter to the Ephesians grounds the newly created peace between Jew and Gentile in the reconciliation which the cross of Jesus Christ has effected for Jew and Gentile alike with God (v. 16). When Christ himself is said to be "our peace" (v. 14), a "peace-offering" may perhaps be understood, as the reference to Christ's blood in verse 13 suggests. The scope of the reconciliation is truly universal: making peace by the blood of Christ's cross, God was pleased to reconcile to himself all things, whether on earth or in heaven (Col. 1:20). The blood by which we are justified, the death by which we are reconciled to God, are those of God's Son; the initiative and work of reconciliation are therefore God's: "God shows his love for us in that while we were yet sinners Christ died for us" (Rom. 5:6-11). That is why the liturgy which derives from the completed work of Christ is first and foremost the "presence and act of the trinitarian God."[2] As the Greek Orthodox theologian Nikos Nissiotis continues: "Worship is not primarily man's initiative but God's redeeming act in Christ through his Spirit. The eucharistic sacrifice as the centre of Christian worship implies the absolute priority of God and his act before man's 'answer' and 'acknowledgment', as we usually describe Christian worship."

But then Christian worship *is* our response, for through Christ we do have access in the Spirit to the Father (Eph. 2:18). Christ offered himself, through the eternal Spirit, without blemish to God (Heb. 9:14); and because we thus have a great high priest who has passed through the heavens, we may now with confidence draw near to the throne of grace (4:14-16) and are thereby enabled to serve the living God

(9:14 again; see also 10:19-25). *Prosérchesthai,* to draw near, and *latreúein,* to serve, are cultic terms. In his treatise *On Prayer,* Origen argued—in his own way—that prayer is properly addressed to God through Christ in the Spirit. As Basil the Great was to show a century later against the Arians in his work *On the Holy Spirit,* this is the proper pattern for thanksgiving even according to developed trinitarian theology. It has remained the classical form of the mass, where we celebrate and enjoy our reconciliation to God.

2. So we are ambassadors for Christ, God making his appeal through us. We beseech you on behalf of Christ, be reconciled to God. (2 Cor. 5:20)

God was in Christ reconciling *the world* to himself (2 Cor. 5:19). Those who, with the apostle, have let themselves be reconciled to God through Christ have thereby themselves been given "a ministry of reconciliation" (v. 18). The embassy is addressed to all humanity: let yourselves be reconciled to God (v. 20). The ambassadorial style is that of plea and persuasion: "the request is the evangelical form of authority."[3] It is of the nature of reconciliation that it only takes place when the offer is received. The manner of the Church's message must respect the dignity of those from whom, through its medium, God is seeking a free response. Only so will the Church's preaching be *hypér Christoú,* the phrase used twice in 2 Corinthians 5:20. The preached "word of Christ" (Rom. 10:17) must correspond to the Word made flesh, who in christological self-surrender offered himself to humanity for acceptance or rejection. The best sacramental match to the news of the gospel is baptism upon profession of faith in the God who, by the Holy Spirit (1 Cor. 12:3), enables people to recognize the lordship of Jesus Christ who in cross and resurrection embodied the saving reconciliation of sinners to the Father, so that "they might live no longer for themselves but for him who for their sake died and was raised" (2 Cor. 5:15). As St. Paul puts it in a baptismally flavored passage: "If you confess with your lips that Jesus is Lord and believe in your heart that God raised him from the dead, you will be saved" (Rom. 10:9).

3. May God grant you to live in such harmony with one another, in accord with Christ Jesus, that together you may with one voice glorify the God and Father of our Lord Jesus Christ. (Rom. 15:5f.)

Since the reconciling God is "a God of peace" (1 Cor. 14:33), those who let themselves be reconciled to him are expected to live harmoniously together (Rom. 12:16). Only so will they be able to worship God fittingly, that is, glorify him with one heart and one voice, *homothymadón en hení stómati* (Rom. 15:6). This applies not only when the assembly takes a charismatic turn, as in the situation which Paul is trying to regulate in 1 Corinthians 14. Divisive behavior also nullifies the Lord's Supper as such, as Paul teaches in 1 Corinthians 11:17-34. That passage contains hints, especially in verses 21f. and 33f., that the factions may have had a social and economic base, as is explicitly the case in the reproved discrimination between rich and poor in James 2:1-7. In contemporary Latin American Christianity, such is the tension between political oppressors and politically oppressed that "participation in the Eucharist, as it is celebrated today, appears to many to be an action which, without an authentic Christian community underlying it, becomes an exercise in make-believe."[4]

Gustavo Gutiérrez recognizes also the potential of the eucharist for "the building up of a real human brotherhood." On the more private level, the modern liturgical movement's reintroduction of the exchange of peace among the congregation—already the Church of South India borrowed the practice from the Syrian communities—has proved to be a salutary encouragement to better personal relationships even in congregations composed of undemonstrative English people. The "success" of the gesture is a tribute of intended obedience to the dominical injunction recorded in Matthew 5:23f.: reconciliation within the Christian family was early expressed and preserved by the "holy kiss" mentioned several times in the New Testament epistles, though the *pax* before sharing together in the eucharist regrettably assumed a clericalized form in the classical Byzantine and Latin rites.

Denominationalism being theologically unjustifiable, indeed absurd (1 Cor. 1:10-17), the separated communities have the plain duty to press urgently on toward that "visible unity in one faith and in one eucharistic fellowship" which the member churches of the WCC set themselves to achieve. As an English Methodist, I make once more an evangelical appeal to the Church of England to join wholeheartedly in the reconciliation which other churches in the country are seeking. Attempts at reconciliation are undergirded by the Lord's own prayer "that they all may be one." From the beginning, the modern ecumenical movement has seen Christian unity to be part and parcel of the Church's witness to the world: "that the world may believe" (John 17:20-23). Disunity among Christians is active counter-testimony to the gospel of reconciliation.

4. If possible, so far as it depends on you, live peaceably with all. (Rom. 12:18)

That Christians should, as far as others allow, extend evangelical behavior beyond the limits of the Church is a clear implication of the dominical teaching represented by Matthew 5:43-48 and already reflected in Romans 12:14-21. In their worship assembly, Christians have learned and experienced peace, and all the other values of the divine kingdom, in an "interior" and "definitive" form; they should therefore, according to the analogical movement set forth by Karl Barth in his essay *Church Community and Civil Community* (1946), seek the furtherance of these same values, at least in an "exterior" and "provisional" way, in the broader social realm. The particular importance of prayer for peace will be mentioned later.

Reconciliation is a key New Testament category for the statement of the gospel. The theme of this opening section has therefore been fundamental to all that now follows.

II. EVANGELISM

1. I am already on the point of being sacrificed; the time of my departure has come. (2 Tim. 4:6)

The martyrdom which St. Paul expected was but the culmination of an apostolate marked by "afflictions, hardships, calamities, beatings, imprisonments, tumults, labours, watching, hunger" (2 Cor. 6:4f.). He bore on his body the marks of Jesus (Gal. 6:17). In the trials of apostleship Paul believed that he was "carrying in the body the death of Jesus": "While we live we are always being given up to death for Jesus' sake, so that the life of Jesus may be manifested in our mortal flesh. So death is at work in us, but life in you" (2 Cor. 4:7-12). The cultic roots of this sacrificial language become unmistakable when the apostle writes: "Even if I am to be poured out as a libation upon the sacrificial offering of your faith *(allá ei kaí spéndomai epí tế thusía kaí leitourgía tếs písteōs hymôn)*, I am glad and rejoice with you all" (Phil. 2:17). The self-spending of the gospel-preacher is part of the larger offering that includes the converts' faith. The modern spread of Christianity in black Africa was dependent, under God, on the willingness of missionaries from our churches to enter "the white man's grave": African Christians thankfully recognize that as a cause for rejoicing, whatever the ambiguities introduced by concomitant colonialism.

2. On some points I have written to you very boldly, by way of reminder, because of the grace given me by God to be a minister [leitourgón] *of Christ Jesus to the Gentiles in the priestly service* [hierourgoúnta] *of the gospel of God, so that the offering* [prosphorá] *of the Gentiles may be acceptable, sanctified by the Holy Spirit.* (Rom. 15:15f.)

The offering of the Gentiles—it matters little whether the genitive is objective or subjective—is their "obedience," which is "the obedience of faith" (Rom. 1:5). As we have just seen under 1, the evangelist's evangelizing activity is itself worship of God: St. Paul uses the verb *latreúein* in Romans 1:9, whose sense C. K. Barrett correctly captures with "God, to whom I render spiritual service in proclaiming the gospel of his Son."[5] When, in response to the preacher's message, conversions are made, the eucharistic chorus is thereby augmented: "Since we have the same spirit of faith as he had who wrote, 'I believed, and so I spoke,' we too believe, and so we speak, knowing that he who raised the Lord Jesus will raise us also with Jesus and bring us with you into his presence. For it is all for your sake, so that as grace extends to more and more people, it may increase thanksgiving, to the glory of God" (2 Cor. 4:13-15).

In this connection, two questions may arise. First: Is the liturgical assembly of the Christians itself directly evangelistic? Second: How is the worship of others apart from Christians to be evaluated? These questions we address in turn.

3. But if all prophesy, and an unbeliever or outsider enters, he is convicted by all, he is called to account by all, the secrets of his heart are disclosed; and so, falling on his face, he will worship God and declare that God is really among you. (1 Cor. 14:24f.)

The context in 1 Corinthians 14 makes clear that the prophetic message spoken in the Christian assembly is intended for believers. Believers need constantly to be confirmed in the gospel they have accepted. Yet when God's word is intelligibly spoken (the contrast is made with speaking in tongues), the apostle's expectation is that any entering unbelievers or outsiders will be persuaded to adoration (whereas from glossolalia they will infer madness). Insofar as a *disciplina arcani* was observed in the early Church, its justification will have lain in the threat and actuality of persecution to which Christians were exposed. The deliberate closure of any occasion on which the gospel is proclaimed appears theologically contrary to the latter's character as an "open secret."[6]

But how far may the unconverted actively participate in what they witness? In 1 Corinthians 14:16, St. Paul *may* be envisaging the possibility that an outsider will be led to say "Amen" to *the* eucharistic prayer. The Didache used the dominical injunction not to cast pearls before swine in order to exclude the unbaptized from sharing in the agape or eucharist. The Lord himself appears to have liberally fed all comers in the messianically significant desert-feedings. John Wesley considered the Lord's Supper a "converting ordinance" and encouraged "seekers" to communicate (admittedly he could presuppose an infant baptism, though the regeneration had been "sinned away" and conversion was needed). My own view is that no one should be refused communion who has been moved by the celebration of the gospel sign then in progress to seek saving fellowship with the Lord through eating the sacramental bread and drinking the sacramental wine. Then such a person should be brought to the sealing commitment of baptism as expeditiously as possible.[7]

4. For, "every one who calls upon the name of the Lord will be saved." (Rom. 10:13)

The question may appear differently when it is a matter of "dialogue with other religions" or of the "religious" marking of "civil" events in a religiously pluralist society. How far may non-Christians be invited to share in Christian worship? How far should Christians accept any invitations they may receive from adherents of other religions? Are "joint services" permissible? In the contexts envisaged, the intention to "convert" is generally reckoned to fall foul of the rules or spirit of the game. In some respects, the questions sound similar to those raised in the early days of the modern ecumenical movement among Christians; but a qualitative difference may be introduced by the issue of the uniquely saving name of the Lord Jesus Christ (see Acts 4:12).

The relations between Christ(ianity) and other religions will become an increasingly urgent question in the next generations, both in the "one world" and in what used to be "Christendom." It would probably be premature to attempt an answer already to what may be an old question but one which is now being posed in relatively new circumstances. John Hick desires a "copernican revolution" in religious and theological understanding, whereby God would replace Christ at the center, and Christianity join the other religions as the circling planets.[8] From a Christian viewpoint, it is hard to see how that could happen without such a forfeiture of devotional and doctrinal substance from our faith as to denature and devitalize it. It is more likely, and appropriate, that Christians will frame the debate in terms of an *exclusive* or a more *inclusive* understanding of the unique status and universal significance ascribed to Jesus Christ by the Christian confession of faith.

The inclusive alternative is as old as the view of Justin Martyr that the ancient Greeks who lived according to the Logos were Christians *avant la lettre*. It is expressed in a eucharistic prayer composed for the experimental *New Orders of the Mass for India* which have since been forbidden by Rome, apparently at the request of less "inclusivist" Indian Catholics. The preface made successive allusions to the animistic religions, to Hinduism (with its three paths to salvation: *karma, jnana, bhakti*), to Buddhism and Jainism together, and finally to Islam:

> God of the nations,
> You are the desire and hope
> of all who search for you with a sincere heart.
> You are the Power almighty
> adored as Presence hidden in nature.
> You reveal yourself
> to the seers in their quest for knowledge,
> to devout who seek you through sacrifice and
>   detachment,
> to every man approaching you by the path of love.
> You enlighten the hearts that long for release
> by conquest of desire and universal kindness.
> You show mercy to those who submit
> to you inscrutable decrees.

The optional reading from Indian Scriptures was justified in terms of their containing "seeds of the Word." On the other hand, the second- and third-century Fathers, including Justin, looked upon the pagan mysteries as diabolical counterfeits of the Christian baptism and eucharist. The exclusivist position, corresponding to "Christ against culture" in H. R. Niebuhr's typology of attitudes, will doubtless continue to be maintained also, making reciprocal participation and common worship appear impossible between Christians and others.[9]

III. ETHICS

1. I appeal to you therefore, brethren, by the mercies of God, to present your bodies as a living sacrifice (thysían), *holy and acceptable to God, which is your spiritual worship* (logikén latreían). *Do not be conformed to this world but be transformed by the renewal of your mind, that you may prove what is the will of God, what is good and acceptable and perfect.* (Rom. 12:1f.)

The ethical worship of God is made possible and necessary by the indwelling presence of the Holy Spirit. The cultic metaphor of the body as temple can be given an individual application: "The immoral man sins against his body. Do you not know that your body is a temple of the Holy Spirit within you, which you have from God? You are not your own; you were bought with a price. So glorify God in your body" (1 Cor. 6:18-20). Or a rather more communal one: "What agreement has the temple of God with idols? For we are the temple of the living God; as God said, 'I will live in them and move among them, and I will be their God, and they shall be my people. Therefore come out from them, says the Lord, and touch nothing unclean; then I will welcome you, and I will be a father to you, and you shall be my sons and daughters, says the Lord Almighty.' Since we have these promises, beloved, let us cleanse ourselves from every defilement of body and spirit, and make holiness perfect in the fear of God" (2 Cor. 6:16–7:1).

The association, indeed identification, between sin and idolatry is made also in Colossians 3:5: "Put to death therefore what is earthly in you: fornication, impurity, passion, evil desire, and covetousness, which is idolatry. On account of these the wrath of God is coming." And again in Ephesians 5:5: "Be sure of this, that no fornicator or impure man, or one who is covetous (that is, an idolater), has any inheritance in the kingdom of Christ and of God." It is significant that baptismal imagery pervades the context of these verses: dying and rising with Christ (Col. 3:1-4), putting off the old and putting on the new (Col. 3:5, 8, 10, 12, 14; Eph. 4:22, 24, 25, 31), being renewed (Col. 3:10; Eph. 4:23), enlightened (Eph. 5:7-14), sealed (Eph. 4:30). Since Christians have passed through "the washing of regeneration and renewal in the Holy Spirit" (Tit. 3:5-7), the apostle has an indicative basis for the imperatives of Romans 12:1f.: the renewed mind is to discern the will of God, and what is there found acceptable *(euáreston)* is the criterion for bodily conduct which can be described as a sacrifice acceptable to God *(tō theō euráreston)*. The transformation of the believer means an end to conformity with this world. Ethics thereby become part of the Christian witness.

> **2. Maintain good conduct among the Gentiles, so that in case they speak against you as wrongdoers, they may see your good deeds and glorify God on the day of visitation. (1 Pet. 2:12)**

The passages mentioned under 1 contrast the behavior expected of Christians with the behavior that characterized them before their conversion and still characterizes the pagan environment. The "new creation" is ethically distinguishable from the old. When the First Letter of Peter evokes the eschatological prospect of "the day of visitation," the thought may be partly of the *confusion* of nonbelievers as they are made to see the ultimate reversal of this-worldly values. But with 1 Corinthians 14:24f. in mind, it may be possible to "realize" the eschatology in such a way that nonbelievers are already conceived as being brought to repentance and faith and so to the positive glorification of God ... by the witness of a distinctively Christian life. The judgmental aspect of Christian "light" in respect of the world appears uppermost in Philippians 2:14-16: "Do all things without grumbling or questioning, that you may be blameless and innocent, children of God without blemish in the midst of a crooked and perverse generation, among whom you shine as lights in the world, holding fast the word of life, so that in the day of Christ I may be proud that I did not run in vain or labour in vain." The sentence used from Matthew 5:16 at the almsgiving in the communion office of the English *Book of Common Prayer* envisages positive doxology resulting: "Let your light so shine before men, that they may see your good works, and glorify your Father which is in heaven." By "good works" which the world can understand, the Church witnesses to the *gracious end* into which the transitory world, if it will let itself be converted, is passing.[10]

IV. INTERCESSION

1. Continue steadfastly in prayer, being watchful in it with thanksgiving; and pray for us also, that God may open to us a door for the word, to declare the mystery of Christ, on account of which I am in prison, that I may make it clear, as I ought to speak. (Col. 4:2-4)

St. Paul's letters abound in the apostle's assurances to the recipients that he gives thanks to God for their having come to believe, and that he prays for the strengthening of their faith in whatever way circumstances require[11] (see, e.g., Rom. 1:8f.; 1 Cor. 1:4-9; Eph. 1:15-23; 3:14-19; Phil. 1:3-11; Col. 1:3-14; 1:29–2:7; 1 Thess. 1:2f.; 2:13-16; 3:9f.; 2 Thess. 1:3-12; 2:13-17; 2 Tim. 1:3-14). As we saw under II 2 and III 2 in particular, the faith and works of the converts are themselves a continuation of the Christian message before the world. In return, St. Paul frequently asks the churches to pray for him in his apostolic labors (see, e.g., Rom. 15:30-32; 2 Cor. 1:8-11; Eph. 6:18-20; Phil. 1:12-26 [especially v. 19]; Col. 4:2-4; 1 Thess. 5:25; 2 Thess. 3:1-3).

Solidarity in mutual intercession is particularly valuable when engagement with a world which needs but resists the gospel brings Christians into distress. The famous Pauline "collection" for the saints at Jerusalem makes concrete such solidarity and is a forerunner of modern programs of interchurch aid.[12] An encouraging feature in the recent history of the WCC is the realization that material aid goes hand in hand with intercessory prayer: the Faith and Order Commission has produced an ecumenical prayer calendar which facilitates informed intercession for sister churches throughout the world.[13]

2. First of all, then, I urge that supplications, prayers, intercessions, and thanksgivings be made for all men, for kings and all who are in high positions, that we may lead a quiet and peaceable life, godly and respectable in every way. This is good, and it is acceptable in the sight of God our Saviour, who desires all men to be saved and to come to the

*knowledge of the truth. For there is one God, and
there is one mediator between God and men, the man
Christ Jesus, who gave himself as a ransom for all,
the testimony to which was borne at the proper time.
For this I was appointed a preacher and apostle . . . a
teacher of the Gentiles in faith and truth.* (1 Tim.
2:1-7)

In the case of the secular authorities, the thanksgiving urged
by the apostle will be on account of their God-given ministry
to "approve good conduct" and to "execute God's wrath on
the wrongdoer" (Rom. 13:1-7; see also 1 Pet. 2:13f.), to "truly
and indifferently minister justice, to the punishment of
wickedness and vice, and to the maintenance of thy true
religion, and virtue" *(Book of Common Prayer).* The thanksgiving for all people will be on account of God's universal
saving intention (1 Tim. 2:3f.); the "general thanksgiving" of
the *Book of Common Prayer* is a perfect example.

"Supplications, prayers, and intercessions" for rulers have
classically centered on their peacekeeping responsibilities:
besides being an analogous reflection of the *shalom* of the
divine kingdom, peaceful conditions facilitate the travels and
tasks of the evangelist. Prayers for "all sorts and conditions
of men" are most vitally prayers for the conversion of the
world; such prayers figure prominently in the "prayers of the
faithful" in the ancient liturgies.[14] It is a patristic thought that
Christian prayer contributes to the *preservation* of the world,
so that all people may have time and opportunity to arrive
at the faith before the final advent of Christ in judgment.[15]
In all these ways, the Christian liturgy—performed through
the one Mediator—appears truly as a *leitourgía,* a "public
service" to the world.

There is a groaning wherever Satan blocks the birth of the
new creation, whether through unbelief, idolatry, individual
sin, social injustice, physical suffering, or mental torment.
The same word "groan" is used at Romans 8:22 for the sigh-
ing of creation *(systenázei),* at 8:23 for the struggles of believers as they await full redemption *(stenázomen),* and at
8:26 for the Spirit-inspired prayers of Christians *(stenagmoís
alalḗtois).* Christians pray that the whole world may be set

free to share in the glorious liberty that is the hope of the
sons and daughters of God.[16]

V. KINGDOM

1. The kingdom of God is not food and drink but righteousness and peace and joy in the Holy Spirit. (Rom. 14:17)

The context of St. Paul's remark is disputes over meat-eating
and wine-drinking: the apostle rebukes those who, "for the
sake of food, destroy the work of God." According to St. Luke,
the Lord will at the judgment reject the claim of the "workers
of iniquity" to have eaten and drunk in his presence (Luke
13:25-27). Yet the kingdom of God is pictured as a feast: "And
people will come from east and west, and from north and
south, and sit at table in the kingdom of God" (Luke 13:29).
It would capture the gist of biblical teaching concerning the
messianic banquet if we were to paraphrase the apostle thus:
The kingdom of God is food and drink *only insofar as* eating
and drinking express justice, peace, and joy in the Holy Spirit.

When any creature of God is received with thanksgiving
(see 1 Tim. 4:3-5), its use becomes thereby an occasion and
medium of communion with God. In what it does with the
bread and wine over which it has given thanks, the eucharistic liturgy makes exemplary use of all food and drink as a
medium of communion with God which cannot make abstraction of communion with fellow humans (see 1 John
4:7-21). Moreover, the general way in which people use all
food and drink is itself a test of the way in which they are
living before God and among themselves. Since the eucharist is representative of all meals, and since all food and drink
is representative of the totality of human life, the sacrament
should be so ordered that it shows the kingdom of God to
be food and drink *only upon condition that* their use em-
bodies justice, peace, and joy in the Holy Ghost. A properly
ordered eucharist exemplifies justice because grateful people are all equally welcomed there by the merciful Lord into
his table-fellowship and all together share in the fruits of
redemption and in the foretaste of the new heavens and the

new earth in which right will prevail (see 2 Pet. 3:13); it exemplifies peace, because reconciled people are there at peace with God and with one another; it exemplifies joy in the Holy Ghost, because the cup of blessing conveys to all who partake of it a taste of that "sober intoxication" which the Spirit gives (see Eph. 5:18). Having learned and experienced this in the paradigm of the eucharistic meal, the Church is committed to an everyday witness in word and deed which will give the opportunity for all the material resources of creation and all occasions of human contact to become the medium of that communion with God and among human beings which is marked by justice, peace, and joy in the Holy Ghost, and in which the kingdom of God consists.

A eucharist understood and practiced in that way will not fall victim to the Marxist critique of unconcern with this-worldly happiness. By its refusal, however, to abandon the strictly eschatological prospect, it will offer to satisfy the hunger which the sensitive among its Marxist despisers feel for a transcendence and an ultimacy over which death will not triumph: the definitive and eternal kingdom of God.

CONCLUSION

By letting the liturgy appear as the ritual focus of the Church's evangelism and ethics, I hope to have pointed impatient evangelists and ethicists to some values of the liturgy.[17] Granted the insights of cultural anthropology concerning the place of symbols in human existence, one could even speak of the *necessity* of the liturgy in respect of evangelism and ethics. In the other direction, I hope to have encouraged liturgists in their belief that evangelism and ethics are their concern, too.

It will be fitting to conclude with the passage from the First Letter of St. Peter which integrates ethics and evangelism into a liturgical edifice clearly shaped by baptism and eucharist:

You have been born anew, not of perishable seed but of imperishable, through the living and abiding word of God. . . . That word is the good news which was preached to you. So put away all malice and all guile and insincerity and envy and all slander. Like newborn babes, long for the pure spiritual milk, that by it you may grow up to salvation; for you have tasted the kindness of the Lord. Come to him, to that living stone, rejected by men but in God's sight chosen and precious; and like living stones be yourselves built into a spiritual house, to be a holy priesthood, to offer spiritual sacrifices acceptable to God through Jesus Christ. . . . You are a chosen race, a royal priesthood, a holy nation, God's own people, that you may declare the wonderful deeds of him who called you out of darkness into his marvellous light.

IX
REVOLUTION AND QUIETISM

At first sight, revolution and quietism are political opposites. This appears to be true even when both terms are taken *in optimam partem*. Viewed in the most favorable light, revolution is the active overthrow—in the name of freedom and justice (by what means is a question which may initially be left open)—of an oppressive and unjust system. For its part, quietism, benevolently considered, is the temporary acquiescence in an oppressive and unjust state of affairs whose wrongs will, the quietist hopes, eventually disappear.

The purpose of the present theological critique is to examine how far a Christian may condone, support, or indeed initiate a politics of revolution which seeks to overturn an existing "establishment" which he or she adjudges oppressive and unjust; it is also an attempt to appreciate the reasons which have led many good Christians to adopt a quietist attitude in a situation of recognized oppression and injustice. The solution finally proposed is neither simply revolutionary nor simply quietist.[1]

One's experience and practical possibilities will of course vary according as one is or is not oneself a victim of oppression and injustice; but even allowing for the part which experience and practice properly play in reflection,[2] it should be feasible for Christians, whatever the form and degree of their existential involvement, at least to understand one another in discussion of the theological and ethical foundations of their political attitudes in the face of oppression and injustice.

The question of revolution and quietism raises a number of major issues in Christian theology. The first three sections of this essay will be devoted to three of them: the relations between the order of preservation and the order of salvation; the respective roles of God and humanity in the achievement of the divine kingdom which is also human salvation; the nature, status, and scope of Jesus' ethical teaching and example. The fourth and final section of the essay will propose a solution which looks like a double paradox but which is really an attempt to transcend a partially false opposition.

I. THE ORDER OF PRESERVATION AND THE ORDER OF SALVATION

Traditional Christian theology has distinguished between the order of preservation and the order of salvation. The classical relation between the two orders may briefly be expressed thus: God preserves the life of sinful humanity with a view to bringing it from sin to salvation. But this needs to be spelled out in a little more detail.

The order of *preservation* is that disposition of the world and human society by which God maintains fallen humanity in earthly existence (it is the fact of "the fall" which makes the difference between the order of preservation and the order of creation insofar as the latter may "still" be discernible). God preserves the earth as humanity's temporal habitat and the scene of its history: after the crisis of "the flood" (itself a divine judgment on sin), God promised—though well aware that "the imagination of man's heart is evil from his youth"—that "while earth remains, seedtime and harvest, cold and heat, summer and winter, day and night, shall not cease" (Gen. 8:21f.). God preserves the bodily life of even sinful humanity: for fallen Adam and Eve God "made garments of skin, and clothed them" (Gen. 3:21); childbirth and the cultivation of the soil remain possible, if only in pain and sweat (Gen. 3:16-20). Even in a human society given to fratricide, God preserves some kind of order which limits the destructive effects of humanity's crime: this seems to be the intention of the "mark of Cain" (Gen. 4:15).[3] Moving from universals expressed in mythical terms, we find, when we come to history, that in Old Testament Israel the king had a duty, in the order of preservation, to administer civil justice (e.g. Jer. 22:1-5). In the time of the New Testament,

the civil authorities as such (in this case, pagan Rome; it can
no longer be a question of any kind of Israelite theocracy)
are seen by some Christian writers as God's servants, instituted and appointed by him in order to punish the wrongdoer—for the good of those who do right (Rom. 13:1-7;
1 Pet. 2:13-17); prayer is to be made "for kings and all who
are in high positions, that we may lead a quiet and peaceable
life" (1 Tim. 2:2). It is with the political aspect of the order
of preservation that we shall be chiefly concerned in this
chapter.

But first we must delineate the order of *salvation*. The
order of salvation is introduced by God's intervening in human history with the redemptive purpose of "restoring" the
fallen human race to that fellowship with God for which
humanity was made, and which has as its corollary loving
relationships among human beings. Through the person and
work of Jesus of Nazareth, so Christians believe, divine salvation has in an unparalleled way broken into human history
from "beyond." Full salvation will be realized only in the
definitive kingdom of God, which may be pictured as "new
heavens and a new earth" (2 Pet. 3:13). Then all resistance
to God's saving purpose will have been overcome. But already the "age to come" is—since Jesus, and through the
continuing work of the Spirit whom he bestows—actively
present in the midst of the old world which is now passing
away: through Jesus Christ human beings are finding fellowship with the heavenly Father and are beginning to love
their brothers and sisters. In the final kingdom of God—
whether that come during their earthly lifetime or only after
their death and "resurrection" (however we are to interpret
that)—their communion with God will be complete and mutual love will prevail among fellow human beings.[4]

In traditional Western theology, the distinction between
the order of preservation and the order of salvation has been
a fairly sharp one, even more in Protestant than in Catholic
thinking.[5] One recalls the *zwei Reiche* of Luther.[6] But even
the Reformers saw the order of preservation as positively, if
rather indirectly, oriented toward the order of salvation: the
civil authorities (to concentrate on the political aspect of the
order of preservation) had at least the duty of preserving the

peace *in order that there might be "room" for the gospel of salvation to be preached without hindrance*.[7] Still within terms of a fairly classical distinction between the orders of preservation and salvation, it is possible also to hope for a kind of feedback effect of the gospel upon the civil order; thus Karl Barth, in *Christengemeinde und Bürgergemeinde* (1946), expounded a principle of analogy whereby the "interior" freedom, justice, peace, and humanity of the gospel (to which the "Christian community" exists to bear witness) should, in an appropriate (i.e. "exterior" and "provisional") way, be reflected in the life of the polis (this principle is not to be laughed out of court simply on account of one unfortunate example which Barth gave: he argued that the "openness" of the Christian revelation had as its analogue the end of secret diplomacy).

In much recent theology, however, there has been a tendency for the distinction between the orders of preservation and salvation to break down, or at least for the edges to become greatly blurred. In different ways and at different levels, a number of factors have contributed toward this. I may mention five.

First: the "Greek" distinction between the "material" and "spiritual" components of the person has, after a long period of influence on theology, at last given way to the view which predominates in the Bible: the person as a *total being* who is related *in his or her totality* to both God and other persons. This change of perspective would not necessarily lead to a loss of distinction between the orders of preservation and salvation; but insofar as preservation had (in an unbiblical way) become associated with the "body," and salvation with the "soul," the distinction between the orders has *to that extent* broken down.

Second: Christian thinkers have become more aware of the "problem" posed by the existence of people of other faiths and those of none. Inspired by the idea of God's "universal will of salvation" (see 1 Tim. 2:4), theologians have sought ways in which non-Christians might be given a saving place within their understanding of God's plan (consider, e.g., R. Panikkar's "unknown Christ of Hinduism" and K. Rahner's "anonymous Christianity"). In itself, this comprehensiveness would not necessarily lead to a loss of distinction between the orders of preservation and salvation; but insofar as salvation had become exclusively associated with the institutional Church, and non-Christians had been seen as simply "preserved" until the gospel could be preached to them by Christians, the distinction between the orders has *to that extent* broken down.

Third: Christian theologians have assimilated the basic Marxian insight of a correlation between politics and economics. Once the relation between economic power and the acquisition and maintenance of political power has been seen, it becomes more difficult (Luther could still inveigh against the Peasants' rising) to look on the "existing authorities" as "ministers of God" for the preservation of peace: justice calls for the rights of "the poor" to be affirmed, even if that means the overthrow of the "powers that be." In itself, this revolutionary attitude would not necessarily lead to a loss of distinction between the orders of preservation and salvation; but insofar as the existing civil authorities have, in their *injustice*, come to be seen as *contrary* to God, their overthrow—even though it might theoretically remain within the order of preservation—is practically experienced as "salvation." The influence of Marxist thought upon the theologians has become the greater as they have become increasingly sensitive to the Marxist accusation that Christianity has been an alienating ideology which diverts the attention of the poor from their miserable condition; and even the theologians have begun to think that they should go in less for "interpreting" the world and more for "changing" it.

Fourth (and this may be theologically the most fundamental point): the work of biblical scholars on the relation between the Exodus and Creation in the Old Testament has made it appear appropriate to talk of Creation itself as "the first *saving* act" of God: salvation is the "intention" written into creation; or (to put it another way), the whole of history is "salvation-history"; or again, both creation and history have the eschatological goal as their "inner ground." Moreover, the saving act of the Exodus has its *political* dimensions: liberation of the children of Israel from oppression in Egypt, conquest and settlement of the Promised Land. In giving a transcendent scope and definitive quality to salvation (the age to come; the resurrection of the body; eternal life...), the New Testament relativizes but does not abolish the reality of salvation in its present earthly expression: the freedom, justice, peace, and love made possible in Christ must—at least until the Parousia—find earthly form, and because salvation is the "intention" of all creation, they cannot satisfactorily be kept internalized, privatized, even ecclesiasticized; rather, their own dynamic will press them toward the fullest and widest visibility of expression, and that will include the political. On this understanding, there is little room for an order of preservation between the order of creation and the order of salvation.

Fifth (and this is linked to the last point made): there has been something of a shift in the theological understanding of sin, and this obviously affects the order of preservation since the order of preservation is traditionally "that disposition of the world and human society by which God maintains *fallen* humanity in earthly existence." J. Hick's *Evil and the God of Love* (1966) may be taken as typical of the view that makes sin part of God's (human) creation from the very start: the "fall" is already given with creation (as humanity emerges in the evolutionary process)—it is entailed in that "epistemic distance" between Creator and creature which will alone give the creature room to discover God by faith and grow into communion with him. If the creature is thus "created as a fallen being," even sin is in a sense saving. Although most theologians would not push their language so far, some such view is probably implied in the generally optimistic, evolutionary view of humanity often associated with the name of Teilhard de Chardin and which was represented in liberal Protestantism by the "secular" theologians of the 1960s (Harvey Cox, *et al.*). If the evil of sin is thus deradicalized, the boundary between the order of salvation and any order of preservation that may be left is inevitably softened.

How does all this relate to the precise question of revolution and quietism? It is probably fair to say that the sharper the distinction Christians draw between the order of preservation and the order of salvation, the more likely they are

to adopt a political attitude of quietism in the face of present
oppression and injustice; though they may, where the "re-
formist" kind of way is open to them, seek to remove material
hindrances to the preaching of the gospel of salvation (here
belongs that form of "developmentalism" which says that
the "poor" must be fed *before* the saving gospel is preached
to them). If, on the other hand, they should blur or even
abolish the distinction between the orders, they are more
likely to undertake impatient political intervention in order
to hasten the fulfillment of God's kingdom, or at least to
allow it to reach its most complete earthly expression; such
Christians will be optimistic about the possibility of defeating the sin whose political expression is unjust and oppressive structures.[8] Revolutionary Christians have heard the
"prophetic perfects" of the Magnificat and seek to aid their
implementation on a universal scale:

> My soul doth magnify the Lord. . . .
> He hath put down the mighty from their seat,
>   and hath exalted the humble and meek;
> He hath filled the hungry with good things,
>   and the rich he hath sent empty away.
>   (Luke 1:46, 52f.)

Adrian Hastings comments: "As God works through secondary causes, the implication here is no less than the divine
countenancing of social revolution" (*Mission and Ministry*,
p. 54). But here we already touch on the second issue in
Christian theology which the question of revolution and
quietism raises: that of the respective roles of God and humanity in the achievement of the divine kingdom which includes human salvation.

II. THE ROLE OF GOD AND THE
ROLE OF HUMANITY

Although all Christians agree that the initiative in salvation
is God's, there exists what may roughly be called a "Catho-
lic/Protestant" disagreement concerning the extent to which
human beings "cooperate" with God in the achievement of
their salvation, if indeed they may be said to make any active

contribution at all. Classical Protestantism (though not the more modern, liberal, particularly Anglo-Saxon kind, which could cheerfully talk of building God's kingdom on earth) laid such stress on the radical fallenness of humanity and on the "by grace alone" that, not surprisingly, little was expected of human beings in the way of an active contribution to their own salvation; and such political activity as they undertake is not (even in Barth) "salvific."[9] Catholic theology, on the other hand, has seen human beings as actively cooperating with divine grace in their own salvation—from Mary's consenting *fiat* (Luke 1:38) to a view of faith and works which has smacked to Protestants of works-righteousness (as though one *earned* one's salvation). Consequently, the "Constantinian" notion of a "Christian civilisation"[10] and nowadays the active engagement by Christians, as Christians, in the construction of humanity's *cité fraternelle* both find a ready home in the Catholic tradition.

The difference between the "Protestant" and the "Catholic" approaches may be illustrated by a comparison between the attitudes toward revolution on the part of Jacques Ellul and Gustavo Gutiérrez. Ellul is a French lay theologian, a lawyer by profession, who has stuck closer to the "Protestant" approach than most of his coreligionists who have written recently on our question: his most relevant study is entitled *Violence* (1970). Gutiérrez is a Roman Catholic priest from Peru, and his book is called *Teologia de la liberación* (1971; ET *A Theology of Liberation* [1973]). For Ellul, "the world" is and remains a wicked place. This has not been "changed" by either the Incarnation or the Lordship of Christ.[11] Indeed, technical progress has brought an increase in "pride" and "materialism." The wickedness of the world is typified by "the chain of violence," "the circle of fear and hate" that "necessarily" characterizes sinful human society. It is only the revelation brought by God's word which liberates the believing *individual* from the grip of the world; and although this may have in some sense "revolutionary" social consequences (the future but secretly present kingdom of God makes us dissatisfied with any existing state of society), yet there must be no talk of human *self*-redemption.[12] Gutiérrez, on the other hand, talks of humanity's "conquest" of freedom, of the "struggle for a just society" which is "in its own right very much part of salvation history," and even of humanity's "self-creation" through political liberation—and this in the most universal context of the whole of humanity: "Every human act which is oriented towards the construction of a more just society has value in terms of communion with God—in terms of salvation" (ET p. 238). It is significant that Ellul's book is a rejection of the use of violence as a Christian option in the cause of justice: although other factors are involved in the question of violence (we shall return to it later), it may be noted here that Ellul's repudiation of violent action is entirely consonant with a classical Protestant rejection of any step which—no matter how modest the talk of "cooperation"—may seem to threaten the all-sufficiency of grace or wrest the initiative from the hands of God. On the other hand, Gutiérrez, though he strongly advocates "social" and "cultural revolution," never really faces up to the question of Christian participation in revolutionary violence: he is doubtless keeping his options open in a Latin America where the question is unresolved among those Christians who are actively engaged in the liberation struggle; and against the nonviolence of Archbishop Helder Cámara there must be set the example of the martyr-figure Camilo Torres, the Catholic priest who, when he joined the Colombian guerrillas, took up arms and soon fell in battle.

Turning to the liberal Protestantism of the United States, we may find (though they would not all perhaps relish the comparison) contemporary theologians who correspond—at least in the matter of the respective roles of God and humanity in the work of salvation—to the advocates of that "social gospel" which in the 1920s found itself opposed in the early ecumenical movement by the continental European "theologians of the Word" who were reviving orthodox Protestantism.[13] In tracing "the biblical sources of secularisation," Harvey Cox, in *The Secular City* (1965), treats the Exodus as "the desacralisation of politics." Although Yahweh "speaks" through it, the deliverance from Egypt is largely interpreted as a human act: "It was an act of insurrection against a duly constituted monarch, a pharaoh whose relationship to the sun-god Re constituted his claim to political sovereignty. . . . It symbolised the deliverance of man out of a sacral-political order and into history and social change, out of religiously legitimated monarchs and into a world where political leadership would be based on power gained by the capacity to accomplish specific social objectives." Although Cox says secularization is "the work of God for man," God is so well "hidden" that the chief accent throughout the book falls on the action of human beings now "come of age" as they "take responsibility for directing the tumultuous tendencies of [their] time."[14] For Paul Lehmann, in his book *The Transfiguration of Politics* (1975), social revolutions of a politically left-wing kind are bearers of a divine righteousness. In opposition to "the existing authorities," the revolutionary is "nearer to the centre and direction of God's purposes for human life in and for the world." The stress falls distinctly on human activity, although in virtue of an "incarnational hermeneutics" revolutionary human activity may be seen as the outworking of the "pressure upon the shape of things to come of the sovereign, freeing and fulfilling purpose and power of God": "To read and understand the Bible politically and to understand and practice politics biblically is to discern in, with and under the concrete course of human events, the presence and power of God at work, giving human shape to human life."

In a similar way to some black U.S. writers, the Liberian churchman Burgess Carr, in his address as General Secretary to the All Africa Conference of Churches at Lusaka in 1974, spoke of the salvific effect, in certain circumstances, of violent human action: "Any outright rejection of violence is an untenable alternative for African Christians. If for no other reason, we must give our unequivocal support to the Liberation Movements, because they have helped the Church to rediscover a new and radical appreciation of the Cross. In accepting the violence of the Cross, God, in Jesus Christ, sanctified violence into a redemptive instrument for bringing into being a fuller human life." This is indeed a "revolutionary" understanding of the Cross; for it is generally thought that the Redeemer did not commit but rather *suffered* violence on Calvary (Acts 2:23). But having come again to the question of Christian participation in revolutionary violence, we must now in fact face the issue of the nature, status, and scope of Jesus' ethical teaching and example.

III. THE ETHICAL TEACHING AND EXAMPLE OF JESUS

Recent "political theology" has revived interest in the question of Jesus' relationship to the Zealots.[15] The Zealot movement, whose nationalism was not without a religious motivation, aimed to liberate Palestine from the Romans by force of arms. One of Jesus' disciples certainly was (or had been) a Zealot: Simon Zelotes (Luke 6:15; Acts 1:13; also called, in Mark 3:18 and Matt. 10:4, *ho Kananaíos*, which is derived from the Aramaic word for Zealot); and O. Cullmann has suggested links in the case of other disciples also: Judas Iscariot (his surname may be connected with *sicarius*, "cutthroat," the Latin name for the Jewish resistance; see Acts 21:38), James and John (their nickname "sons of thunder" is of a piece with their violent reaction in Luke 9:54; and their request, in Mark 10:37, to be given the seats next to Jesus when he is enthroned as king is characterized by Cullmann as "a typically Zealot request"), and Simon Peter (Cullmann sees Mark 8:31-33 as a political temptation; see John 18:10f.).[16] There seems to be no doubt that *from the Roman point of view* Jesus was executed as a political criminal, a messianic pretender, the "king of the Jews" (Mark 15:2; Luke 23:2f.; John 19:12-22). Some have seen in Jesus' "cleansing of the temple" the action of a Zealot.[17]

Does it then belong to an attempt on the part of later Christians to whitewash Jesus for the sake of their own acceptability in the eyes of the Romans, when the Fourth Gospel presents Jesus as denying that his kingdom is "of this world," else his servants would fight to save him (John 18:36)? S. G. F. Brandon, in *Jesus and the Zealots* (1967), dates the origin of "the concept of the pacific Christ" to St. Mark's Gospel, where responsibility for the execution of Jesus is transferred from Pilate to the Jewish leaders and where Jesus is depicted as endorsing the Jewish payment of tribute to

Rome (Mark 12:13-17); the pacific teaching of the Sermon on the Mount (Matt. 5–7) is regarded by Brandon as an early Christian development along the same line.

In the light of modern critical scholarship, there can be no question of a simplistic appeal to the Gospel texts as they stand, but a modest "quest for the historical Jesus" does appear to be demanded of us since an appeal to the teaching and example of Jesus is now made by revolutionaries as well as by quietists. One might start with the text which Brandon places at the head of his study: "Think not that I came to bring peace on the earth: I came not to bring peace, but a sword" (Matt. 10:34). There is nothing improbable in the Evangelists' *metaphorical* understanding of the sword as the divisiveness of the proclamation of Jesus as it calls human beings to decision in face of the coming of God's (not directly political) kingdom (Matt. 10:35-39; Luke 12:49-53; 14:26; Mark 3:31-35; 13:12f.). When a *real* sword is drawn by his friend in the Garden of Gethsemane, the word of Jesus has an authentic ring: "Put your sword back into its place; for all who take the sword will perish by the sword" (Matt. 26:51-53; see also Luke 22:49-51; John 18:10f.).[18] One of the best-attested features of Jesus' ministry (and Brandon fails to meet—or even to see—this point) is that he made friends with the *publicani*, the tax collectors who "collaborated" with the Roman authorities (e.g. Mark 2:15f. and parallels; Matt. 11:19=Luke 7:34); there is then nothing unlikely in the fact that Jesus should have taught that a man compelled to carry a Roman soldier's pack for a mile should voluntarily go with him for a second mile (Matt. 5:41), or that Jesus should have healed the centurion's boy (Matt. 8:5-13=Luke 7:1-10). It is all part of the teaching and example of Jesus concerning love for the enemy (Matt. 5:43-48), "nonresistance" to evil (Matt. 5:39)—or, as Paul rightly interprets it, the overcoming of evil with good (Rom. 12:14-21). It is the peacemakers whom Jesus pronounces blessed (Matt. 5:9), and those who suffer persecution for righteousness' sake (Matt. 5:10). He taught, and practiced, forgiveness and reconciliation (e.g. Matt. 5:23f.; 6:12, 14f.; 18:21-35; Mark 11:25; Luke 17:3f.; 23:34). Jesus saw his own vocation in terms of *suffering* and called on his followers to share in that destiny (e.g. Mark 8:31-38 and parallels; Mark 10:38f.; see also John 21:18f.; 2 Cor. 4:7-12; 1 Pet. 2:18-24). The "political temptation" doubtless stood close to Jesus, but he rejected it (Matt. 4:8-10 = Luke 4:5-8); and although the crowds may more than once have "tried to make him king" (John 6:15; Matt. 21:9), it was *humbly*, "mounted on an ass" (Matt. 21:1-7; contrast the quoted Zech. 9:9f. with Pss. Sol. 17:23-27[19]), that Jesus entered Jerusalem, a peaceful "king." To return to the Fourth Gospel: the source and quality of his kingship were not "of this world." The Spirit that his death released numbers "love, joy, peace, patience, kindness, goodness, faithfulness, gentleness, self-control" among its fruit (Gal. 5:22f.). The *nature* of Jesus' teaching and example is clear: it is unarmed love; but there are still questions as to its *status* and *scope*.

Some scholars have given to the teaching and example of Jesus the status of an *Interimsethik:* it is seen as guidance for conduct in the relatively short period that Jesus and the early Christians expected to intervene before "the End" (so, most recently, O. Cullmann). In the matter of violence, the Christian writers of the early centuries generally considered military service incompatible with membership in the Church. Thus Tertullian: "Is it right to occupy oneself with the sword, when the Lord proclaims that he who uses the sword shall perish by the sword? And shall the son of peace, for whom it is unfitting even to go to law, be engaged in a battle?"[20] However, a new situation arose when the expectation of an imminent Parousia finally declined (persecutions had no doubt helped to keep the hope alive), and when Christianity became first recognized (under Constantine) and then established as the imperial religion (under Theodosius); from then on, theologians started to justify the factual participation of Christians in military service (Ambrose and Augustine launched the concept of a "just war" which reached its classic definition in Thomas Aquinas[21]). Ellul calls this "compromise"; but it may be more sympathetically seen as an answer to the problem which arose when the implementation of the political side of the order of preservation in the face of external threat could no longer be left (as it could in New Testament times) to a "pagan" civil authority while Christians "kept their hands clean." And if, within a given society, a "prince" (even a "Christian" prince) should turn tyrant, there have been, at least since the sixteenth century, "Christian" theories of tyrannicide.[22] In some such way as this, the Christian would-be revolutionary of today may consider the possibility of embarking on a "just revolution," with violence regarded as a regrettable but necessary *ultima ratio*.[23] He or she might even claim the sixteenth-century precedents of Thomas Müntzer and John of Leyden, for whom revolution in favor of "the poor" certainly bore even salvific (millenarist) significance. It should not be forgotten, however, that a strand of witness to the "Sermon on the Mount" position has reemerged from time to time throughout the period of "established Christianity": from Francis of Assisi to modern "conscientious objectors" to military service and the nonviolent witness of Martin Luther King against internal injustice and oppression. For these the "last resort" in the face of injustice and oppression is *prayer*, "trust in God," and a willingness to lose their life in "this world" for the gospel's sake. For such people, the teaching and example of Jesus are clearly more than an *Interimsethik* which ceased to be applicable with the failure of a quick Parousia: the proximity of the kingdom is not a question of time but a question of values.

What, then, is the *scope* of the teaching and example of Jesus on the question of violence? One historic tendency in interpretation has been to distinguish between "evangelical precepts" and "counsels of perfection"—so that not even all Christians, but only (say) the monks or the clergy, are expected to accept the ethical teaching of Jesus in all its radical demand. But this is not satisfactory, for the demand is grounded in the very character of God: "Love your enemies and pray for your persecutors; only so can you be children of your heavenly Father, who makes his sun rise on good and bad alike, and sends rain on the just and the unjust" (Matt. 5:45f.). Such a divine basis ultimately means that the claims of Jesus' teaching are incumbent not merely on all Christians, but on *all people*—though the possibility of their being met will depend on the scope of divine grace and the degree of human willingness to accept both the demand and the gift. The scope of Jesus' ethical teaching is, then (at least potentially), *universal*.[24] There is, however, yet one more problem. While it is, in principle, easy to see how the teaching and example of Jesus concerning unarmed love apply to (all) individual persons,[25] the existence of social structures— where those willing and those unwilling to respond to Jesus are *ab initio* bound together in a transindividual totality— appears to raise such insuperable difficulties for the practice of the teaching and example of Jesus that we are (compared to the case of an individual person's life) in the presence of a qualitatively different situation. How are the "ethics of Jesus" to be carried out within the context of those economic, political, socio-psychological, and communicational structures of planetary life which some modern theologians have gone so far as to compare or even identify with the "principalities and powers" of the New Testament? It is not easy to see, even in principle, how this may be done. The universal scope of Christ's *victory* (e.g. Rom. 8:31-39; Col. 1:15-20; 2:15) gives to the Christian, however, *hope* that even this may turn out to be possible—though perhaps not short of the Parousia.

Even though human activity cannot bring in the definitive kingdom of God (the fact that we can only *await* Christ's "final Parousia" safeguards God's exclusive role in this respect), yet Christians—mobilized by the hope of the final kingdom—must push toward the universal and ultimate expression of the permanent values of the kingdom which have already been embodied in the teaching and example of Jesus: freedom, justice, and peace, all springing from self-giving love. Even the strictest Protestant ought to be able to agree to that, on the basis of his or her own "ethics of gratitude": having been "set free" by God, such a person expects to show his or her thankfulness by practicing the ethics of Jesus (without considering that this *earns* final salvation). In political terms, I suggest that this approach means allowing revolution and quietism to qualify each other—so that we may speak of a quiet revolution and a revolutionary quiet.

IV. QUIET REVOLUTION AND REVOLUTIONARY QUIET

Let me look at the matter largely from the viewpoint of a middle-class, white, Western Christian. Insofar as I am myself, as a citizen of a nation and of the world, party to political and social structures of oppression and injustice, I have no moral right to oppose revolutionary action undertaken by the victims of the system, even though their action may involve violence against me; I am rendered the more helpless by my membership in a Church which, as an institution, has been in fact associated with the offending civil powers. Yet as a Christian charged with preaching further the gospel of Jesus Christ, I must—even to the victims of oppression and injustice—call violence into question and proclaim rather the message of forgiveness and reconciliation grounded in love. How to bridge the "credibility gap"? A solution must be sought in the direction of repentance and solidarity.

1. Revolutionary quiet

My first attitude must be to place myself under *judgment*. As a member (at least by culpable acquiescence) of the oppressing "establishment," I must submit (this time in penitent acquiescence) to the judgment falling upon that establishment. According to the book of Jeremiah, social oppression and injustice within the nation were part of Israel's unfaithfulness to Yahweh (Jer. 2:34; 5:28; 7:5f.; 21:12; 22:3, 13-17); and for this the people were to submit, said the prophet, to the Babylonian invasion as to divine judgment (Jer. 21:1-10; 37–38). Within our present world community, revolutionary action on the part of the oppressed classes and peoples should be understood as divine judgment upon the oppressing classes and peoples. This I must allow to bring me to *repentance*—which is itself a *revolution* (in Hebrew *shub;* in Greek *epistréphein*). And to my fellow-oppressors I must preach our common need for "conversion" of this kind.

A sign of my repentance will be my development of an ascesis, which expresses and promotes my own release from the grip of materialistic values. The true Christian "possesses" this world's goods "as though he did not possess them" (*hōs mē*, 1 Cor. 7:29-31; see also Matt. 6:19-21, 24-34; and the parable of the rich fool, Luke 12:13-21). Fasting, for instance, is an exercise of freedom which prevents one's proper bodily appetites from passing into greed; sacrificial giving prevents the laying up of treasures on earth—it is an entry into the movement of him who, though he was rich, yet for our sake became poor (2 Cor. 8:9; Paul introduces this christological remark while talking of the collection for the needy in Jerusalem). Such a true ascesis, if undertaken by all Christians who have the opportunity to do so, could help in the revolutionary redistribution of the earth's resources which is necessary if the "fast" of many other human beings is to become the voluntary renunciation of available food rather than the enforced lack of any food at all. Starvation can be no proper part of either the order of preservation or the order of salvation.

Christian ascesis is possible only in a life of communion with God. The revolutionary power of *prayer* is not to be overlooked. Archbishop Anthony Bloom goes so far as to say that "the act of prayer . . . is a more essential, final act of rebellion against slavery than taking up arms."[26] By seeking God's will in prayer, the Christian may both join in the spiritual fight against the forces of evil in the world and find guidance (for prayer clarifies vision) for his or her own loving intervention on behalf of the victims of evil.[27] There is no love of God without love of the human brother or sister (1 John 3:17; 4:20; see also the parable of the rich man and Lazarus, Luke 16:19-31). Worship is empty when it is offered by the perpetrators of injustice and oppression (Isa. 1:13-17; Amos 5:21-24)[28]: Camilo Torres abandoned his cultic priesthood and "gave himself to the revolution" because "the Christian community cannot worship in an authentic way unless it has first effectively put into practice the precept of love for fellow man"—"I have ceased to say mass in order to practice love for my fellow man in the temporal, economic and social spheres. When my fellow man has nothing against me, when he has carried out the revolution, then I will return to offering mass, God permitting."[29] I would, however, suggest that, in order to be true to the unarmed love of Jesus, the Christian should seek a *quiet* revolution.

2. Quiet revolution

An Oxfam gift-envelope expresses very well one way in which the well-to-do Christian (or any person of goodwill) may participate in the quiet revolution:

THE QUIET REVOLUTION
A peaceful way to radical change

The horrors of hunger, malnutrition and disease *can* be conquered. Poor communities all over the world are fighting to free themselves from desperate, grinding poverty. But theirs is a Quiet Revolution where the weapons are seeds and vaccines rather than bombs and bullets and where training is in how to save lives rather than take them. Please help through Oxfam. Just 1p, for example, has vaccinated a Brazilian child against polio and £1 has bought enough seed to plant an acre of rice in India. Another poor and hungry family could be taking part in this Quiet Revolution tomorrow. All they are waiting for is your help. Please be generous.

Large-scale generosity ("charity" in the best sense of self-giving love) on the part of individuals and Churches could make an enormous contribution to the removal of economic injustice (and dismissal of "charity" as a mere palliative can be a mask for mere meanness). In the democracies of the West, Christians also have an opportunity to denounce existing injustice and oppression and to influence civil governments to act in favor of radical changes in the political and economic structures which, nationally and internationally, hold people in oppression and injustice. In a fine analysis of the scriptural vocabulary, G. Gutiérrez has shown how, in the Bible, material poverty is repudiated and combated as a degrading human situation, incompatible with the kingdom of God (Jesus pronounces the poor blessed "because the coming of the kingdom will *put an end* to their poverty"); and how spiritual poverty—which means "openness to God," "being a 'client' of Yahweh"—involves, on the "horizontal" level, a "commitment of solidarity and protest": a lifestyle of solidarity with those who suffer misery and injustice, a protest against their poverty . . . and a struggle to abolish it.

The Christian who finds, or places, himself or herself—in the name of freedom and justice—*within* a revolutionary movement has the specific duty of bearing witness to the practice of forgiveness and reconciliation. He or she must hope thereby to save the potentially violent revolutionaries from their own violence. For violence dehumanizes its perpetrators. In the words of Vergniaud, the Girondin: "The revolution may devour its own children." In the words of Jesus: "All who take the sword will perish by the sword."

CONCLUSION

Some words of the Czech theologian J. M. Lochman will illustrate how the "human face" in politics is the face of Jesus: "There will be no doubt about the 'trend' of our social discipleship: the maintenance of non-violent love is clearly the first essential in our political diakonia. . . . At the same time, however, the "pacifist" is warned: the testimony of non-violent love is not true if it is understood quietistically or ideologically (as a luxury-attitude in which the *beati possidentes* can indulge); it is true only if it is expressed in serious Christian testimony, i.e. in a revolutionary way, attacking the inhuman, godless structures of the world in the light of God's Kingdom. It is only through ecumenical solidarity with the hungry, oppressed peoples in the developing countries, that the privileged Christians of Europe today can make a testimony of non-violent love which will carry any conviction."[30]

X
MARY AND METHODISM

The figure of Mary, the role dogma ascribes to her in the mystery of salvation, the place she occupies in liturgical and private piety: this is still perhaps what most obviously distinguishes Roman Catholicism from Protestantism. And it is not just a matter of Mary herself, as an individual—as though she simply came on to the stage more often in the Catholic than in the Protestant version of the same play. The play itself may be qualitatively different, depending on the nature and importance of Mary's part. Questions may arise as to whether in fact it is the same play in the two cases and ultimately, perhaps, whether the same author could possibly have been responsible for both. To speak plainly: such an eminent Catholic theologian as Edward Schillebeeckx once saw in their respective attitudes toward Mary an indication that Catholicism and Protestantism have two different dogmatic views of Christ, of the Incarnation, and of the relation between God and humanity.[1]

But is Methodism Protestant? The Belgian Franciscan writer Maximin Piette considered that original Methodism marked a "reaction" within the evolution of Protestantism,[2] and this "reaction" brought Wesley in some ways closer to Catholicism: "The justification by faith which Wesley preached was nearer to the doctrine of the Council of Trent than to what he contemptuously called Luther's crazy solafidianism. Similarly, his unswerving Arminianism puts him in direct opposition to Genevan predestination."[3] Continental Lutheran and Calvinist theologians have seen Wesley as reneging on some of the fundamental principles of the Protestant Reformation.[4] Even within eighteenth-century England, John Wesley and his Methodists were accused of "Popery."[5]

If Methodism truly marked a reaction in the direction of

Catholicism, and if the Roman Catholic attitude toward Mary is a key to the specific nature of Catholicism, then it may be that there exists within Methodism the potential of an attitude toward Mary that could be regarded by Catholics as giving to Mary more of her due than is ordinarily the case within Protestantism. I say "potential," because in fact Methodism has until now shown little awareness of Mary.[6] This may mean that we have not, in this matter, given enough room to our own Catholic tendency. On the other hand, the reason may at least partly lie in the fact that Methodism remains firmly enough attached to some of the principles of Protestantism for the Roman Catholic attitude toward Mary to appear to Methodist eyes as in some directions excessive. It may be that these apparent excesses of Catholicism have frightened Methodists from developing a more positive appreciation of Mary.

The plan of my exposition is as follows. In the first and longest part, I shall look in turn at six of the doctrinal or spiritual emphases characteristic of Methodism. In each case I shall first explain the Methodist emphasis, then look for the nearest corresponding feature in the Roman Catholic attitude toward Mary, and lastly consider how far Methodism can accept that Catholic feature. In a second part, I shall draw together the fundamental theological reasons why, at some points, Methodism is unable—as things are at present understood on each side—fully to share the Roman Catholic attitude toward Mary. In the third and final part, I shall mark out the ground on which Methodists and Catholics might work together toward a closer common understanding of the person and place of Mary. In all this, I do not believe that I am being disloyal to John Wesley's sermon "Catholic Spirit" and his "Letter to a Roman Catholic."[7]

I. SIX METHODIST EMPHASES AND THEIR RELATION TO CATHOLIC MARIOLOGY

1. Faith as active receptivity

(a) Contrary to Luther's doctrine of the "servile will" and the Calvinist doctrine of irresistible special grace, Methodism holds that all people have the capacity, when they hear the

gospel, freely to accept it, and that some of them do in fact
freely believe the gospel. Although he did not deny the existence of "exempt cases" in which "the overwhelming power
of saving grace" fell upon a person, Wesley did not consider
this to be "God's general manner of working."[8] But Methodist optimism here is not of a Pelagian kind, as though
humanity had a natural freedom in its fallen state: it is an
"optimism of grace" (the phrase was, I think, first given a
Methodist application by Dr. Gordon Rupp in his *Principalities and Powers*), the grace being first of all a *universal*
grace[9] which, in virtue of Christ's universally *redemptive*
work, sets the whole human race in a position freely to receive and accept the preaching of the gospel; and then, too,
faith is a gift to each individual, but it is not received in
entire passivity: it is—with God's noncoercive "assis-
tance"[10]—a free decision and act of the will, an active consent of God's saving of us.

(b) The nearest correspondence is the stress which Roman
Catholicism puts on Mary's *fiat* at the Annunciation. To the
message brought from God by Gabriel, Mary replied, "Be it
unto me according to thy word" (Luke 1:38); and Elizabeth
called Mary blessed because she had *believed* (Luke 1:45).
Fide concepit, said St. Augustine: "she conceived by faith."[11]
Non concubuit et concepit, sed credidit et concepit: "She
did not lie with a man and conceive, rather she *believed* and
conceived."[12] Or, in the words of Leo the Great, *prius concepit mente quam corpore:* "she conceived in her heart before she conceived in her body."[13] E. Schillebeeckx says of
Mary's *fiat:* "It was the first case of explicit and free consent
to the specifically Christian plan of redemption. . . . She was
active conception in the bodily sense and active receptivity
in the spiritual sense. . . . She allowed the Redeemer to give
himself to her, and consequently allowed redemption also
to be bestowed on her. Redemption always demands cooperation with, free consent to, and full acceptance of, the
gift of the God-man, who, by his very calling, is the Redeemer" (pp. 91, 93). Although Mary is unique by virtue of
her physical conception of Christ, she is also, by virtue of
her active consent of the will, the model for all Christian
belief.

(c) The danger comes when human "co-operation" is

understood in such a strong sense that talk turns to "co-redemption." Although no dogmatic definition has been made, Roman Catholics have without official discouragement talked of Mary as co-redemptrix. True, they deny any intention to detract from the uniqueness of Christ's work. But, as Schillebeeckx admits, if one took the strictest sense of the word co-redemptrix, Mary would be "a principle in addition to Christ," "she would take over those essential saving functions which in fact belong to Christ's humanity" (p. 124). Because of this danger, is it not better to avoid all talk of "co-redemption," even in a loose sense? There should be no maximizing of the Irenaean idea that "by her obedience, Mary became a *cause* of salvation for herself and for the whole human race"[14]—or of the Augustinian notion of Mary's *cooperatio caritatis*.[15]

The danger becomes greater when we move from the Hail Mary to the *Stabat mater*. Roman Catholic theologians see a deep theological implication in the fact that Mary stood at the foot of the Cross (John 19:25). Thus Schillebeeckx, who is by no means an extremist, writes of "the sacrifice of the Cross, accomplished by Christ himself and co-accomplished in a maternal manner by Mary" (p. 163). As his mother, Mary "enjoys the most intimate human communion" with Jesus (p. 148), and at the Cross we have the climax of "Mary's maternal self-identification with Christ's work of salvation" (see p. 162). Schillebeeckx can even say: "As a mother, her suffering *was* Christ's suffering" (p. 115, my italics). Now we can understand and accept this statement at the affective level, in the sense of sym-pathy and com-passion; and there is also, as we shall see, a "sacramental" sense in which all Christians suffer and die with Christ. But in its strictest sense, Schillebeeckx's statement will not pass, either anthropologically or theologically. Anthropologically: a person dies *alone*. Theologically: it is Christ *alone* who died for our sins (Rom. 5:8; 1 Cor. 15:3; 2 Cor. 5:14f.; 1 Thess. 5:9f.; 1 Pet. 3:18). Scripture nowhere says that Mary "surrendered" Jesus, but rather "*God* gave up his own Son" (Rom. 8:32; see also John 3:16). In order to *be born*, Christ "needed" a mother; but he *gave himself* up to death (Mark 10:45; Gal. 1:4; 2:20; Eph. 5:2, 25).[16]

Let us move back again from the particular case of Mary to the general case of Christians. Schillebeeckx suggests that the cause of Protestant "misunderstanding of Mary's true greatness and sublime place in the event of the incarnation" is that Protestants "deny man's personal, meritorious cooperation in his salvation" (pp. 149f.). Now all Protestants admit that Christians "suffer with Christ" (Rom. 8:17; 1 Pet. 4:13) and "die with him" (Rom. 6:1-11; Gal. 2:20; Phil. 3:10; 2 Tim. 2:11). This happens through faith, of which baptism is the sacrament. Methodists admit that faith is free and active. But along with all Protestants we should deny that faith is "meritorious." Faith is the *condition* of our salvation, but in no sense its efficient *cause*. If our "cooperative" faith is not the *cause* of our salvation, then we cannot *merit* our salvation. The notion of human *merit*, in the Catholic sense, is in fact foreign to all Protestant theology, except in the sense that Christ alone "merited" our salvation (if we are using an Anselmian picture of the atonement). "Works of supererogation" is an impossible idea for Protestants, because God requires *total* service from all; in that he or she has once sinned, a person can never *merit*, in the strict sense, his or her own salvation, let alone acquire a surplus of merit that may be credited to others. Neither Methodism nor Wesley himself could understand in a *meritorious* sense the Augustinian tag which Wesley frequently quoted: *Qui fecit nos sine nobis, non salvabit nos sine nobis*, "He that made us without ourselves, will not save us without ourselves."[17] The author of our salvation is God himself, its "cause" is the redemptive work of Christ, and our active acceptance is its simple, though necessary, condition. Neither for ourselves nor for Mary would we desire the title co-redeemer. Such a title shifts the accent away from the primary fact that we, with Mary, are the *objects* of redemption. *That* is why we stop the language of "cooperation" short of the language of "co-redemption." Our active faith, like Mary's, remains *reception* of a divine gift.

2. Entire sanctification

(a) The second doctrinal emphasis of Methodism falls on "entire sanctification," which may also be termed "Scriptural holiness," "Christian perfection," or "perfect love."[18] John Wesley believed that the great twofold commandment of the Lord Jesus, love of God and love of the neighbor (Mark 12:28-31), was far from being simply an instrument to convict us of our shortcoming or an inspiring but unattainable ideal. With the help of the Holy Spirit, perfect love was to be prayed for and aimed at, accepted and achieved. In the *prima facie* negative expression Wesley sometimes used, perfect love meant the absence of all voluntary and deliberate sin, freedom from evil thoughts and tempers. Wesley's "perfection," once "achieved," had always still to be progressed in. Nowadays, there is perhaps more awareness, through depth psychology, of the influence of the unconscious on all our motives and actions—and so Methodists hesitate to preach perfect love, even in the sense of the absence of voluntary and deliberate sin. But we still retain a measure of the old conviction that Christ frees us not only from the *guilt* of sin, but also from the *power* of sin; and so we keep our distance from the Lutheran tag that speaks of the Christian as *simul justus et peccator*, especially when the theme is propounded in its extreme dialectical form of *totaliter justus et totaliter peccator*. We expect the Christian to "grow in grace." Many of Charles Wesley's hymns express a prayer for entire sanctification. For example (from *The Methodist Hymn Book*, no. 550):

O for a heart to praise my God,
A heart from sin set free,
A heart that always feels Thy blood
So freely spilt for me:

A humble, lowly, contrite heart,
Believing, true, and clean;
Which neither life nor death can part
From Him that dwells within:

A heart in every thought renewed,
And full of love divine;
Perfect, and right, and pure, and good,
A copy, Lord, of Thine.

Or again (from *The Methodist Hymn Book*, no. 562):

> Purge me from every evil blot;
> My idols all be cast aside;
> Cleanse me from every sinful thought,
> From all the filth of self and pride.

> Give me a new, a perfect heart,
> From doubt, and fear, and sorrow free;
> The mind which was in Christ impart,
> And let my spirit cleave to Thee.

(b) The nearest correspondence in Roman Catholic Mariology to the Methodist stress on entire sanctification is found in the twin dogmas of Mary's immaculate conception and her assumption, according to which Mary was kept free from sin from the moment of her conception in her mother's womb and was at the end of her earthly life directly lifted, body and soul, to heaven.

(c) Methodists can appreciate the work of the Holy Spirit in the human person, and we can understand what Roman Catholics mean by "created grace," even though we do not use that phrase. But even if Mary were to be presented as a special and singular case of "entire sanctification," Methodists would still share a number of common Protestant objections to the idea of Mary's immaculate conception and bodily assumption. Leaving aside for the moment the problems posed in regard to the sources of revelation and the seat of doctrinal authority by the act of the Roman magisterium in 1854 and 1950 in proclaiming the immaculate conception and the bodily assumption precisely as *dogmas,* the very idea of Mary's immaculate conception and bodily assumption raises problems for Protestants. When Mary rejoiced in God *her Savior* (Luke 1:47), we find it hard to admit that her salvation, uniquely, was a salvation *by exemption*[19] and a salvation that would be *totally complete* ("soul and body") at her "falling asleep." Guided by the Pauline view of the relation of Christ to humanity and the relation between what Christ has already accomplished and what he still has to do, we hold that only the obedient Christ has reversed the trespass of Adam (Rom. 5:12-21; Phil. 2:5-8), that otherwise "there is none righteous, no, not one" (Rom. 3:10), that Christ alone is the firstfruits of them that have fallen asleep (1 Cor. 15:20-23), and that the general resurrection is reversed for the day of Christ's coming (1 Cor. 15:23; 1 Thess. 4:16). In short, the dogma of Mary's immaculate conception seems to us to deny that "all people need to be saved" on account of sin "in Adam," and the dogma of Mary's assumption seems to us a case of overrealized eschatology. In Charles Wesley's Ascension hymns, it is in heart and mind that we ascend, while "our bodies continue below."

3. Assurance[20]

(a) John Wesley insisted upon the text Romans 8:15f.: Sermons IX, X, and XLV in Sugden's edition expound this passage. It matters little for our purpose whether his interpretation of *symmartyrei tō pneúmati hēmṓn* as "bears witness *with* our spirit" will stand up against the exegesis that favors "bears witness *to* our spirit."[21] The important thing is Wesley's stress on the Spirit-given assurance to believers that they are God's adopted children. Protestant anti-Pietists sometimes deride this Methodist emphasis as "justification by feeling." That is unfair; for the assurance of salvation is given, Wesley teaches, precisely to *believers,* and it is therefore grounded *extra nos* in Christ and his work and is the gift *in nobis* of the Holy Spirit. Assurance, on the subjective side, brings out the fact that Christian faith includes the dimension of trust and confidence, *fides* has a touch of *fiducia* about it. Take, for instance, Charles Wesley's hymn (*The Methodist Hymn Book*, no. 363):

> Spirit of faith, come down,
> Reveal the things of God. . . .
>
> No man can truly say
> That Jesus is the Lord,
> Unless Thou take the veil away,
> And breathe the living word;
> Then, only then, we feel
> Our interest in His blood,
> And cry, with joy unspeakable:
> Thou art my Lord, my God!

Inspire the living faith,
Which whoso'er receives,
The witness in himself he hath,
And consciously believes. . . .

And again (*The Methodist Hymn Book*, no. 368):

With confidence I now draw nigh,
And Father, Abba, Father! cry.

At the psychological level, assurance may express itself in a sense of warmth and comfort. Again we may take Charles Wesley's words (*The Methodist Hymn Book*, no. 406):

My God, I am Thine;
What a comfort divine,
What a blessing to know that my Jesus is mine!
In the heavenly Lamb
Thrice happy I am,
And my heart it doth dance at the sound of His name.

(b) A Catholic equivalent, at the psychological level and even at the theological level, may perhaps be found in Mary's role as mediatrix. Psychologically, she brings warmth and comfort and the sense of "being her children."[22] Moreover, she is held to do this in a theologically significant way as mediatrix *of grace*.

(c) Methodists feel a common Protestant unease when Mary's part in the bringing of assurance shifts from the psychological to the theological plane. Perhaps most Catholics today would endorse R. Laurentin's repudiation of what he calls "a dangerous gangrene": "There is one last myth which has been like a dangerous gangrene in a whole stream of Marian devotion. This has set masculine brutality against the unfailing tenderness of the mother who protects her children against the anger of the male. It is almost incredible that such a myth could have been shamelessly applied to Christ and Mary. And yet it is a fact that there is a school of iconography (which has now disappeared) in which Jesus is depicted armed with a bow or a thunderbolt which he brandishes in anger against sinners, while Mary intercedes for them, baring her maternal breast to move him to pity. It is just as alarming to find that a seventeenth century author

with an otherwise good reputation should have let himself
go so far as to write: 'Jesus wishes to condemn, Mary to save'.
Whatever the good intentions, such a statement is objec-
tively blasphemous. The mercy of Mary is nothing but a
sharing in the mercy of God. She herself comes from God's
mercy. She is a particularly sensitive sign of it that he himself
has made for us. Mary's intercession makes no sense except
when seen in this light."[23] But is there not a danger, albeit
much more subtle, when E. Schillebeeckx talks of Mary as
representing in her person the maternal aspect of God's
love?[24] Schillebeeckx writes: "In this sense, Mary's state of
being Christ's and our mother explicates something of Christ's
redemption, an element which is not explicated itself in
Christ's act of redemption and which even cannot be explicated in this act. This is the feminine and maternal quality
of goodness. . . . This maternal quality of mildness, this particularly feminine tenderness, this *quid nesciam* which is
the special mark of the mother cannot, however, be explicated as such in the man Jesus. It can only become explicit
in a mother who is a woman. God chose Mary so that this
maternal aspect of his love might be represented in her person. At the deepest level this would seem to be the basic
reason why a woman, a mother, should have a role in the
Redemption" (pp. 141f.). To Protestant ears, this sounds,
whatever the disclaimer, like a threat to the sufficiency of
the Christ who himself said: "O Jerusalem, Jerusalem . . .
how often would I have gathered your children together as
a hen gathers her brood under her wings, and you would
not!" (Matt. 23:37). A Protestant finds it hard to understand
how a Roman Catholic may claim that his or her talk of
Mary's mediation does not infringe the central affirmation
expressed in 1 Timothy 2:5: "There is one God, and there is
one mediator between God and men, the man Christ Jesus."

4. The universal offer of the gospel

(a) 1 Timothy 2:4 speaks of God's desire that all people
should be saved and come to the knowledge of the truth.
Against all Calvinist talk of double predestination and limited atonement, Arminian Methodism proclaims the universal scope of Christ's redemptive death and seeks to offer the

gospel to all and sundry. This rings out in Charles Wesley's hymn (*The Methodist Hymn Book,* no. 75):

Father, whose everlasting love
Thy only Son for sinners gave,
Whose grace to all did freely move,
And sent Him down the world to save:

Help us Thy mercy to extol,
Immense, unfathomed, unconfined;
To praise the Lamb who died for all,
The general Saviour of mankind.

Thy undistinguishing regard
Was cast on Adam's fallen race;
For all Thou hast in Christ prepared
Sufficient, sovereign, saving grace.

The world He suffered to redeem,
For all He hath the atonement made,
For those that will not come to Him
The ransom of His life was paid.

Arise, O God, maintain Thy cause!
The fullness of the Gentiles call;
Lift up the standard of Thy cross,
And all shall own Thou diedst for all.

John Wesley said: "I look upon all the world as my parish."[25] Every member of the British Methodist Church is *ipso facto* a member of the Methodist Missionary Society, and Methodism has a long and strong tradition of overseas missionary work in Asia, Africa, and the Caribbean.

(b) The closest correspondence in Roman Catholic Mariology would seem to lie in the idea of Mary as the Mother of humankind. Schillebeeckx (pp. 105ff., 147f., 165) grounds Mary's universal motherhood in the fact that she is the mother of the representative Head of humankind; as mother of the Redeemer, she is the spiritual mother of the whole of redeemed humanity.

(c) The problem here for a Protestant is the exact sense of the passage from Christ's universal status and role to a universal status and role for his earthly mother. Methodists might rejoice in Mary's universal motherhood insofar as it is a sign of the universality of God's grace; but they would share the common Protestant unease about Mary's universal motherhood insofar as it is associated with the idea of Mary as the personal mediatrix of all grace. Protestants feel bound to reject that refinement of ecclesiological imagery—approved even by Schillebeeckx (p. 122)—which makes of Mary the neck joining Chris* the Head to his body. "Through Mary to Christ" is not a slogan which commends itself to Protestants whose theology and spirituality depend on the *direct* relation between Christ and the believer who is "in Christ" and in whom Christ is (see Gal. 2:20).[26]

5. The social implications of the gospel

(a) Already in his early Oxford days, John Wesley was zealous in his evangelistic and charitable work among prisoners. When in April 1739 he first "submitted to be more vile" and preached in the open air, his text for the sermon in a Bristol brickyard was Luke 4:18f., with its "gospel for the poor." And in the tale of his long ministry a significant place is held by his opening of medical dispensaries for the poor and his educational enterprises, by his orphanage and his home for aged widows; he supported the campaign against slavery; he pleaded for government action to deal with unemployment and the high cost of food; he wrote pamphlets against smuggling, bribery at elections, and intemperance; one of his standard sermons is entitled "The Use of Money."[27] John Wesley held that "Christianity is essentially a social religion" and that there is "no holiness but social holiness."[28] In the *Hymns for the Use of the People called Methodists*, there was a verse which unfortunately showed scant regard for the contemplative life (this has always been a weakness in Methodism) but which finely expressed the social concern of Christianity:

> Not in the tomb we pine to dwell,
> Not in the dark monastic cell,
> By vows and grates confined;
> Freely to all ourselves we give,
> Constrained by Jesu's love to live
> The servants of mankind.

In the nineteenth century, city-center mission halls began an important social work, and the distinguished Wesleyan Hugh Price Hughes became a spokesman of the Nonconformist conscience. In our century, John Scott Lidgett was for many years a London councillor and alderman as well as a Methodist minister and warden of the Bermondsey settlement; and the "Christian citizenship department," which has now become the "division of social responsibility," has played a significant advisory part not only in the life of the Church but also in government circles. These are all expressions of the Methodist sense that "faith works by love" (see Gal. 5:6).

(b) In his apostolic exhortation *Marialis cultus,* Pope Paul VI has stressed what might be called the "social and political clauses" of Mary's Magnificat:

> He hath put down the mighty from their seat:
> and hath exalted the humble and meek.
> He hath filled the hungry with good things:
> and the rich he hath sent empty away.

The pope calls Mary "a woman of strength, who experienced poverty and suffering, flight and exile" and goes on to say: "These are situations that cannot escape the attention of those who wish to support, with the Gospel spirit, the liberating energies of man and of society" (para. 37).

(c) Methodism, too, can look to Mary's song for inspiration and guidance as she seeks to align herself with God's action in human society.

6. The communion of saints

(a) The early Methodists experienced close earthly fellowship through their structures of Society, Class, and Band. This helped them to the sense that Christian fellowship cannot be broken by death. Listen to Charles Wesley's words on the unity between the Church militant and the Church triumphant (*The Methodist Hymn Book,* no. 824):

> Let all the saints terrestrial sing,
> With those to glory gone;
> For all the servants of our King,
> In earth and heaven, are one.

> One family we dwell in Him,
> One Church, above, beneath,
> Though now divided by the stream,
> The narrow stream of death:
>
> One army of the living God,
> To His command we bow;
> Part of His host have crossed the flood,
> And part are crossing now.

If a person has not joined in the singing of this hymn of Charles Wesley's at a Methodist funeral, he or she will not have fully appreciated Methodist spirituality.

(b) A recurrent title of Christ in Charles Wesley's hymns is "King of saints." Could we accept that Mary is their queen?

(c) I think that Methodists might well see in Mary "the perfect model of the disciple of the Lord,"[29] a woman of prayer and attentive to the word of God. Her example we ought to be willing to follow. But what of her intercession for us? Again, the associated notion of *merit* makes us suspicious of Roman Catholic talk of the prayers of the saints. But if, without that, Mary may be seen as part of the "one family," then we ought to be glad for her prayers.

II. UNDERLYING THEOLOGICAL DIFFERENCES

If I may now draw together the fundamental theological reasons which would prevent Methodists, as things are at present understood on each side, from fully sharing the Roman Catholic view of Mary, then I may arrange them under two headings: 1. Scripture and tradition; 2. God and humanity.

1. Scripture and tradition

It must be said quite frankly that few Protestants find in Scripture, either explicitly or implicitly, any basis for certain Roman Catholic tenets concerning Mary, and particularly the dogmas of her immaculate conception and her assumption and any future dogma concerning her as co-redemptrix. We find it hard to accept that her immaculate conception should be read out of the word *kecharitōménē* at Luke 1:28 and that her assumption should be read out of the *mulier amicta sole* at Revelation 12:1. Yet the bulls *Ineffabilis Deus* (1854) and *Munificentissimus Deus* (1950) make appeal to these texts. Historically, there is no "evidence" for Mary's assumption before the fourth century, and belief in her immaculate conception results from a particular combination of popular piety and theological speculation which did not antedate the twelfth century.[30] Since Newman, no thinking Christian can deny that historical development has in fact taken place in Christian doctrine, and that *some kind* of development, or at least "structuration" in different conceptual forms, was necessary and inevitable. But Protestants hold that the course of development, or the structure of doctrine at any particular time and place, must always be subject to critical control by Scripture, since Scripture, though it is itself no *absolute* authority (for it needs *some kind* of interpretation), is the *sufficient primary witness* to the words and deeds of the saving revelation focused in Jesus of Nazareth.[31] As to the *interpretation* of Scripture, Protestants do not accept the *sensus plenior* approach which finds mariological meaning in Old Testament texts concerning, for instance, Wisdom or the ark of the covenant or the daughter of Zion, but where the New Testament writers, with a few possible exceptions, found no typological reference to Mary. We are therefore not immediately persuaded that Marian doctrines and devotion are scriptural when Pope Paul VI's exhortation on Mary, in reference to the new Lectionary of the Roman rite, says: "The Lectionary contains a larger number of Old and New Testament readings concerning the Blessed Virgin. This numerical increase has not however been based on random choice: only those readings have been accepted which in different ways and degrees can be considered Marian, either from the evidence of their content or from the results of careful exegesis, supported by the teachings of the Magisterium or by solid tradition" (*Marialis cultus*, 12). Or again: "In its wonderful presentation of God's plan for man's salvation, the Bible is replete with the mystery of the Savior, and *from Genesis to the Book of Revelation also contains clear reference to her who was the Mother and Associate of the Saviour*" (ibid., 30).

2. The relation and distinction between God and humanity

E. Schillebeeckx argued that the inadequacy of the Protestant attitude toward Mary is fundamentally due to the inadequacy of the Protestant doctrine of the Incarnation: "The basic reason for the difference between the Protestant and the Catholic attitudes towards Mary in the sphere of worship is undoubtedly to be found in the different dogmatic views of Christ and in the fact that we, as Catholics, do not hesitate to call our Lady the mother of the redeeming God in humanity. Our Protestant brothers in faith, on the other hand, do not appear to grasp the deep and fundamental meaning of this great reality, 'God in humanity', and consequently fail to fathom the full depths of Mary's motherhood" (p. 149). I am not sure how far Methodists fall under this condemnation as regards the doctrine of the Incarnation.[32] It would be hard to find a stronger expression of the christological doctrine of the Council of Ephesus than this couplet from one of Charles Wesley's great Christmas hymns (*The Methodist Hymn Book*, no. 134):

> Being's source begins to be,
> And God Himself is born.

Or again, consider the view of divine incarnation and human destiny expressed in *The Methodist Hymn Book*, no. 142:

> Let earth and heaven combine,
> Angels and men agree,
> To praise in songs divine
> The incarnate Deity,
> Our God contracted to a span,
> Incomprehensibly made man.
>
> He deigns in flesh to appear,
> Widest extremes to join;
> To bring our vileness near,
> And make us all divine:
> And we the life of God shall know,
> For God is manifest below.
>
> Made perfect first in love,
> And sanctified by grace,

We shall from earth remove,
And see his glorious face:
Then shall His love be fully showed,
And man shall then be lost in God.

As Methodists we sing our faith in the Incarnation and our hope for humanity's final beatitude;[33] but our awareness of God as the transcendent redeemer of sinful human beings means that we must accept Schillebeeckx's reproach that we, as Protestants, "deny man's personal *meritorious* coopera- tion in his salvation" (pp. 149f., my italics). And if that denial be, as Schillebeeckx suggests, a cause of our "misunder- standing of Mary's true greatness and sublime place in the event of the Incarnation," then I fear that as long as we remain within the Protestant tradition we shall continue to misunderstand Mary's "true greatness." There is a sense— and it is highlighted by the question of "merit"—in which we must, if we are to remain true to "the fundamental prin- ciples of the Protestant Reformation" (as our British Meth- odist Deed of Union declares we do), hold fast in the matter of our redemption to the principle of *Deus solus*[34]—and this without falling into the false "competitive thinking" (*Kon- kurrenz-Denken*) of which Catholics sometimes accuse Prot- estants, whereby it is thought that whatever is attributed to humanity is thereby detracted from God.

III. FUTURE EXPLORATION AND COLLABORATION

Having indicated the limits of agreement and potential agreement between Methodists and Roman Catholics, *as things now stand,* on the subject of Mary, let me now mark out three areas in which future exploration and collaboration might lead to greater accord.

1. Common study of Scripture

In an attempt to study *together* what Scripture has to say about Mary, it would be best to begin with those texts which we already understand, from the *christological* angle, in sim-

ilar ways and whose depths we might plumb together. I
mean the passages which tell of the birth of Jesus. Remembering that it is as *Theotokos* that Orthodox Christians predominantly think of Mary, we might here widen the
ecumenical scope of the study. Methodist interpretation could
suitably be guided by a verse of Charles Wesley:

> Who gave all things to be,
> What a wonder to see
> Him born of His creature and nursed on her knee![35]

After this, we might pass on to the gospel passages in which
Mary appears during the ministry of Jesus. It would be important not to balk at those texts which Protestants have often
thought "anti-marian" and which Catholics have seen as ex-
tolling Mary. This kind of issue is pinpointed by some sentences in *Marialis cultus* (para. 39): "When the children of
the Church unite their voices with the voice of the unknown
woman in the Gospel and glorify the Mother of Jesus by
saying to him: 'Blessed is the womb that bore you and the
breasts that you sucked' (Luke 11:27) they will be led to
ponder the divine Master's serious reply: 'Blessed rather are
those who hear the word of God and keep it!' (Luke 11:28).
While it is true that this reply is in itself lively praise of
Mary, as various Fathers of the Church interpret it and the
Second Vatican Council has confirmed, it is also an admo-
nition to us to live our lives in accordance with God's com-
mandments." Finally, the question of the mariological
interpretation of biblical texts that do not overtly mention
Mary would have to be faced.

2. Mary as an "active model" of the Church

The phrase "active model" is from Schillebeeckx. In an ecumenically intended article, Dr. Lukas Vischer, then director
of Faith and Order in the WCC, pointed out the close relation, at varying periods in history, between the Church's
image of itself and its image of Mary: he suggests that the
Church today could well find inspiration in the picture of
Mary as the humble handmaid of the Lord and servant of
humanity.[36] This would probably be the picture of Mary that

Protestants found easiest to accept, and it would help *all* the Churches to remember the quality of their own proper role and to avoid the dangers of triumphalism. It would be good for the Churches, individually and together, to model themselves on the woman of prayer (Acts 1:14), who pondered the word of God (Luke 2:19, 51) and who aligned herself with God's poor (Luke 1:46-55).[37]

3. Prayer

It is rumored that a book written by a Methodist minister has been responsible for a revival of the rosary among some English Roman Catholics. I am referring to Neville Ward's *Five for Sorrow, Ten for Joy* (1971). It is just possible that this firmly Christocentric "consideration of the rosary" may also cause some Methodists to explore this pattern of prayer. If Methodists and Catholics met at *that* level, then increased understanding at the doctrinal level might result.

CONCLUSION

For Catholics and Methodists to come to fuller agreement on the subject of Mary, some changes would have to take place. On the Methodist side, there would have to be willingness to explore a whole stream of Christian tradition hitherto foreign to us.[38] On the Roman Catholic side, René Laurentin has admitted the existence of a Marian crisis due to the development of two opposed tendencies which may roughly be characterized as maximalist and minimalist, christotypical and ecclesiotypical, devotional and critical.[39] Paul VI's "apostolic exhortation" saw itself as following Vatican II in denouncing "both the exaggeration of content and form which even falsifies doctrine and likewise the small-mindedness which obscures the figure and mission of Mary" (*Marialis cultus*, 38); the same document says that "everything that is obviously legendary or false must be eliminated" (ibid.). If Catholics and Methodists could join together in a search for the truth concerning Mary, surprises might happen on both sides. Meanwhile, here is a prayer that we could all pray together:[40]

Thou who didst so greatly stoop
To a poor virgin's womb,
Here Thy mean abode take up:
To me, my Saviour, come!
Come, and Satan's works destroy,
And let me all Thy Godhead prove,
Filled with peace, and heavenly joy,
And pure eternal love.

XI
ECCLESIAL LOCATION AND
ECUMENICAL VOCATION

I. SCHISM AND PLURALISM

When, in the teaching of fundamental theology, I come to
the Church and tradition, I begin, tongue-in-cheek, with a
rapid sketch of ecclesiastical history. It shows how, in the
fifth century, the non-Chalcedonians split from the hitherto
undivided Church. Then the Byzantine East broke away in
1054. The unreformed Roman Catholics were left behind in
the sixteenth century, while the continental Protestants had
the misfortune of being foreigners. In the eighteenth century, even the Church of England refused Wesley's mission,
so that finally only Methodists remained in the body of Christ.
At this point in the recital, general laughter occurs. Closer
inspection of the emotions released reveals that English
Methodist students usually experience a little *Schaden-
freude* at seeing the tables turned in this way; but they retain
after all a certain guilt at the responsibility of their forebears
in the separation from the Church of England and, while
being forced by historical circumstances to reject the ecclesiological model ironically employed in the sketch, they cannot quite be content with an alternative understanding that
renders all divisions innocuous. On the other hand, Roman
Catholic students are sometimes shamed into awareness that
their instinctively Cyprianic view is not entirely satisfactory
either, when it takes all schism to be schism *from* the Church
and rejects the "other party" into an ecclesiological void.
Anglican students are caught in the middle, marooned on
their bridge. In contrast to the English, American students
of all ecclesiastical stripes tend to be surprised that one should
begin thus diachronically at all, rather than synchronically

189

with the existing state of denominational pluralism; and to this contrast between the two approaches I will return in a moment.

But first a paragraph about the theological seriousness of the strictly ecclesiological question in the Christian faith, particularly with reference to recent ecumenical discussion. The decade following the 1952 Lund Conference brought a welcome christological concentration into the work of Faith and Order as well as the explicit introduction of the Holy Trinity into the membership basis of the World Council of Churches. Attention should never stray from the divine center of the message which is being proposed for the world's belief and salvation. But it was a mistake to suppose that the earlier concerns of "comparative ecclesiology" had then been surpassed. It is no accident that "the Church" figures among the realities confessed in the classical creeds. The official entry of the Roman Catholic Church into the modern ecumenical movement, and then the bilateral conversations which followed on Vatican II, probably did most to recall the fundamental importance of the ecclesiological question for the ecumenical movement as its very *raison d'être*. At stake in the understanding of unity and schism, of continuity and discontinuity, of integrity and fragmentation, is precisely the *identity of the Church* and therewith the nature and substance of *truth* and the conditions of its *authoritative expression*. To seek and confess the ecclesiological location of one's community is an act of discerning and proclaiming the gospel itself. There is no preaching and living of the gospel without at least an implicit ecclesiological claim being made.[1]

Now to return to the diachronic and synchronic approaches to the matter of Christian unity. From his observations of the United States in the 1930s Dietrich Bonhoeffer drew a contrast between a European sense of a unity once given and now sundered and an American sense of a given pluralism which might perhaps, though not certainly, call for the construction of an eschatological unity.[2] On the European side, Bonhoeffer's own preferred emphasis on the divine gift of unity may have derived as much from a Constantinian nostalgia as from the once-and-for-all redemption recorded in the New Testament. On the American side, the varied escapes from Europe, the hard-won development of internal tolerance, and the effort of building one nation from the many peoples have all contributed to a semicompetitive, semicooperative denominationalism whose strongly voluntaristic character is seen as an acquisition not lightly to be set at risk for the sake of a unity that might mean restrictive uniformity. In the republic of God, pluralism rules O. K. Individual crossovers from one denomination to another are achieved fairly easily, while the denominational structures remain intact. To the European churchman with a diachronic sense of schism, American Christianity may appear as too ready a synchronic acquiescence in an existing fragmentation whose murkier historical and theological origins are best not inquired into. Something of this contrast underlies the well-known tension between British and American Methodists in their understandings of ecumenism; and one result which may be hoped for from the work of the Oxford Institute of Methodist Theological Studies is increased mutual understanding and correction on these issues. The contrast between the British-diachronic and the American-synchronic is not, of course, absolute. American scholars such as Albert Outler, John Deschner, and, I think, William Cannon have placed their loyal investigation of Wesleyan origins and the Methodist tradition in the context and service of historic Christianity and its search for full unity; while the dearest desire of some British Methodists at present seems to be the further dilution of the Wesleyan content in the principal vehicle of our tradition (namely, the hymn-book), though they yet remain content with a denominational life thus largely deprived of its distinction.

In the final section of this chapter I will return to the fundamental ecclesiological question concerning necessary unity and legitimate diversity. The intervening six sections will particularize the Methodist application. Sections II, III, and IV will be largely diachronic in method. Their purpose is to illuminate the way in which we have reached the present situation and so to help show what factors will shape our choices if we are to be recognizably Methodist in face of our synchronic options as set out in section V, VI, and VII.

II. A PART, NOT THE WHOLE

The notion of "a part, but not the whole" was recurrently employed by Wesley in ecclesiological controversy. Thus in reply to Bishop Richard Challoner's *The Grounds of the Old Religion* he notes: "In the first thirty pages the author heaps up scriptures concerning the privileges of the Church. But all this is beating the air till he proves the Romanists to be the Church, that is, that a part is the whole."[3] Conversely, in response to the same Roman Catholic bishop's *Caveat against Methodists* Wesley claims that all sinners converted to God by preachers and teachers of the faith once delivered to the saints, even if they be Methodists or any other kind of Protestant, "although they are not the whole 'people of God', yet are they an undeniable part of his people."[4] As far as Methodism is concerned, our question must be: *What kind* of part did, does, and might Methodism constitute in *what kind* of whole? Let me give one answer that is phenomenologically certain, another that is historically speculative, a third that is scripturally indefensible, and a fourth that is eschatologically possible.

1. A society within the Church of England

That Methodism began as a society within the Church of England is certain, whether one think of the Holy Club at Oxford[5] or of "the rise of the United Society, first at London [The Foundery] and then in other places."[6] A minor complication stems from the fact that some who were admitted to membership—upon the sole condition of their "desire to flee from the wrath to come, to be saved from their sins"—were not Anglicans but belonged to Dissenting bodies. Wesley no more desired them to interrupt their old allegiance than he would countenance the withdrawal of Methodists from the Church of England. Internal pressures for "separation" from the Church of England arose early in the Methodist movement, but Wesley resisted them at successive Conferences.[7] Neither the early violence of the mobs, nor the persistent hostility of the parochial clergy, nor the recurrent rebuffs of the bishops could weaken John Wesley's self-understanding as "a Church of England man."[8] He rejected his disappointed brother Charles' acceptance that "ordination was separation";[9] and it is true that not even Wesley's ordination of men for America, Scotland, and finally England brought forth an official explusion from the Church of England. Yet there is no doubt that a certain "unstitching" (the image is Wesley's own)[10] had already begun during Wesley's lifetime; and his death soon removed the final reticence from his English followers,[11] so that on the ground plan which he himself had drawn—notably in the Deed of Declaration of 1784—an ecclesiastical structure was quickly built. The process is usually called the transition "from Society to Church."[12] Certainly by 1795 the Plan of Pacification was allowing Methodist worship at the times of Church services (Wesley's discouragement of this liturgical "competition" had been a key element in his resistance to separation[13]), and the Methodist people were being permitted to receive the sacrament at the hands of their own preacher-pastors. As distinct from those nineteenth-century Methodist bodies with less direct origins in Wesley's work, the Wesleyan Methodists for longer saw themselves as retaining certain links with the Church of England, such as occasional communion and the use of "Mr Wesley's Abridgement" or even the *Book of Common Prayer* itself. But the growth of Methodist "self-confidence,"[14] coupled with a perceived Romeward drift of the Church of England,[15] had by the middle of the nineteenth century undeniably put an end to any but the most romantic idea of English Methodism's *continuing* as a society within the Established Church. That option was closed; but the sense of our partial character remains with us from our origins.

2. A province of the Anglican communion?

The adaptation which sticks closest to our original position was put forward some years ago in the brilliant hypothesis of a non-Methodist historian of Methodism to a Strasbourg colloquium on "Aspects de l'Anglicanisme." Writing at the time of the Anglican-Methodist unity scheme in England, C. J. Bertrand suggested that Methodism might be viewed and treated as a hitherto "unrecognized province of the Anglican communion."[16] Bertrand showed how Methodism was the first body—with the possible exception of the Scottish Episcopalians?—to display an ensemble of characteristics which later came to mark the various ecclesiastical "provinces" that developed beyond England but remained in communion with Canterbury and one another: a doctrinal kernel well within the limits of Anglican "comprehensiveness," an independent liturgy but with family resemblances to the Prayer Book, a spirituality and a ministry adapted to the people, an autonomous administration, and withal a certain *je ne sais quoi* which can only be called Englishness. Interestingly, Bertrand recalls the proposal, made by Fletcher of Madeley to John Wesley at the Conference of 1775, that Methodism should become an independent denomination— the Methodist Church of England—in close association with the Church of England itself: article 1 of his plan suggested that "the growing body of the Methodists in Great Britain, Ireland, and America be formed into a general society—a daughter church of our holy mother," with article 5 "asking the protection of the Church of England, begging that this step might not be considered as a schism."[17]

Bertrand's hypothesis deliberately left out of account American Methodism, which at least since the War of Independence has enjoyed little "special relationship," whether real or imagined, with Anglicanism. It remains questionable how far even English Anglicans, at least since the latter part of the nineteenth century, have viewed Methodism with any greater affection than they have the other Free Churches. The biggest obstacle in the way of Bertrand's proposal has proved to be a very legalistic understanding by Anglicans of their claimed episcopal succession which was shared neither by Wesley nor by many other Anglicans before the Oxford Movement.[18] British Methodism has repeatedly declared its willingness to accept an episcopal ordering of the Church, but English plans for unity were blocked in 1969 and 1972 and again in 1982 by Anglican doubts concerning the generation of living Methodist or other ministers who would not have received ordination from a bishop meeting Anglican approval. It grieves me to say it, but I think that Bertrand's kind of ecclesiological interpretation and the consequent possibilities for a relatively easy (re)integration of Methodism into the Anglican communion have now been killed stone dead.

3. A Church within the Church catholic?

As early as the Christmas Conference at Baltimore in 1784, American Methodism declared itself the Methodist Episcopal Church; and its nineteenth-century historian Abel Stevens had little hesitation in writing of the "catholicity of Methodism."[19] In England, Wesleyan Methodism took a century longer before officially calling itself a Church—as part, no doubt, of its late nineteenth-century assimilation to the "Free Churches"; but then H. B. Workman showed little doubt as to Methodism's churchliness when he wrote his celebrated essay *The Place of Methodism in the Catholic Church.*[20] In 1932, the Methodist Church in Great Britian declared at the start of the doctrinal article in its Deed of Union: "The Methodist Church claims and cherishes its place in the Holy Catholic Church which is the Body of Christ."[21] The problem with such formulations is that all *denominational* claims to the word *church*, for example, "The Methodist Church," run counter to the New Testament. The 1937 British statement *The Nature of the Church according to the Teaching of the Methodists* was being a little self-sparing when it said that "The Church today is gathered for the most part in certain denominations or 'churches.' These form but a partial and imperfect embodiment of the New Testament ideal."[22] As Wesley rightly recognized in his sermon "Of the Church" (1786), the New Testament writers mean by Church either the Church universal or a local church, whether its size be that of a family, a city, or a country. The nearest things to denominations get short shrift from the apostle Paul: "Each one of you says, 'I belong to Paul', or 'I belong to Apollos', or 'I belong to Cephas', or 'I belong to Christ'. Is Christ divided? Was Paul crucified for you? Or were you baptized in the name of Paul?" The existence of *denominations*—which so far in history always implies *divisions*—calls into question the reality of *the Church*. As Howard Snyder has recently observed concerning certain paradoxes in Wesley's own ecclesiology: "The paradoxical nature of the church in a sinful world . . . makes a totally consistent, systematic theory of the church difficult, if not impossible, from a human standpoint."[23] But it is not simply a matter of theology in a pejorative sense: the very power of the gospel is at stake if it fails to unite those who claim to respond to it.[24]

The question is: What is the *Ecclesia* in which Methodist writers sometimes rather too cozily claim for Methodism the status of an *ecclesiola*?[25] A befitting tentativeness in respect both of the *Ecclesia* and of the *ecclesiola* marked the words of the English Wesleyan Methodist J. E. Rattenbury in *Wesley's Legacy to the World* (1927):

> The struggle of Methodism to remain a mere Society within the Church of England, when she had no longer association with a Church of which she could be called a Society, lingered on till our days. It was one hundred years before [Wesley's] society called itself a Church. ... Methodism seems to be standing at the crossways. Much of her distinctive denominational life has gone, and she is feeling, perhaps subconsciously, after Catholicity.

Colin Williams used that text thirty years later to illustrate his description of Methodism as "a society in search of the Church."[26] Retain the tentativeness and shift the model from "society" to "order," and I think we may even today find the direction for a dynamic self-understanding with which to share in the ecumenical task and pursue the ecumenical goal.

4. An order within the Una Sancta?

In his contribution "Methodism and the Catholic Tradition," made to the 1933 volume *Northern Catholicism*,[27] R. N. Flew observed that "from Southey onward, the biographers of Wesley have compared him to the founders of great orders in the Church of Rome. His genius for organization ensured discipline in his 'societies'." But Flew himself drew no broader ecclesiological consequences from this observation. Albert Outler once described Wesley as "rather like the superior-general of an evangelical order within a regional division of the church catholic";[28] and elsewhere he has proposed a Methodist ecclesiology consonant with this view of

Methodism's founder. In a paper given to the Oxford Institute of twenty years ago,[29] Outler showed how reluctantly Methodism became a denominational Church, always retaining a memory of its *ad interim* beginnings:

> [Methodism] has never developed—on its own and for itself—the full panoply of bell, book, and candle that goes with being a "proper" church properly self-understood. This makes us *une église manquée*, theoretically and actually. . . . One of our difficulties, I suggest, is that Methodism's unique ecclesiological pattern was really designed to function best *within* an encompassing environment of *catholicity* (by which I mean what the word meant originally: the effectual and universal Christian *community*). . . . We need a catholic church within which to function as a proper evangelical order of witness and worship, discipline and nurture. Yet, it is plain to most of us that none of the existing unilateral options are suitable alternatives to our existing situation. The way to catholicism—i.e., Christian unity—is *forward*—toward the *renewal* of catholicity rather than in *return* to something that has lost its true status as truly catholic.

As a sympathetic Roman Catholic writing before Vatican II, John M. Todd held John Wesley's inspiration and faith to be consonant with Catholic doctrine and considered that "for that very reason [they] could only find [their] proper fulfilment in the Catholic Church."[30] Much more recently, Francis Frost, author of the substantial article "Méthodisme" in the encyclopedia *Catholicisme*,[31] recognizes the fundamental unity of Methodism in its spiritual heritage, and again the image of the religious order suggests itself: "Le méthodisme moderne doit en premier lieu cet héritage à John Wesley, tout comme, dans l'Église catholique romaine, un ordre religieux ou une famille spirituelle tient son esprit d'un fondateur." In a most accurate and appreciative essay, Frost treats Methodism as "une confession chrétienne autonome" and recognizes the institutional part already played by Methodism within the comprehensive ecumenical movement in which the Roman Catholic Church now also shares. But Frost's conclusion may be even more significant:

Les efforts de rapprochment entre les Églises sur les plans doctrinal et institutionnel doivent s'enraciner dans l'oecuménisme spirituel. La division entre les chrétiens est un péché; autrement dit, elle est fruit d'un refroidissement de la vie théologale. Ce sont l'obéissance et l'humilité qui conduisent à l'unité, parce qu'elles rendent possible à nouveau l'épanouissement de l'amour. Ne fait-il pas partie intégrante de l'héritage spirituel du méthodisme de témoigner de ces vérités?

Whereas H. B. Workman regarded "experience" as the governing "Idea" of Methodism and considered "assurance," as its primary corollary, to be "the fundamental contribution of Methodism to the life and thought of the Church" (and John Todd vigorously defended Wesley against the charges brought against him in Ronald Knox's *Enthusiasm* on these scores), the more recent consensus—represented by writers as diverse as Todd, John Kent, and Reginald Kissack—has in fact returned to seeing the original inspiration, the motive force, and the abiding goal of Wesley and of Methodism as residing rather in *HOLINESS*. The early Methodists understood that their providential call was to "spread scriptural holiness through the land,"[32] and for this purpose Wesley was ready to "look upon all the world as [his] parish."[33] The proclamation and pursuit of holiness reached as far as "entire sanctification," "perfect love" of God and neighbor. The traditional Methodist doctrine of Christian perfection can in fact be extended into the realm of ecumenism. The prayer of Jesus was that his disciples might be "perfected into one" (John 17:23: *hína ôsin teteleiôménoi eis hén*), and the apostle's vision was that the Church might grow into "the unity of the faith and of the knowledge of the Son of God, to mature manhood, to the measure of the stature of the fulness of Christ" (Eph. 4:11-16). These texts were seized upon a century ago by the English Wesleyan Methodist Benjamin Gregory in his Fernley Lecture of 1873, *The Holy Catholic Church, the Communion of Saints*. Gregory recognized that "the unity of the Church and the spirituality of the Church must progress together equably"; it is encouraging that the contemporary Roman Catholic Francis Frost should think that Methodism might

have a special part to play in precisely that process. Reginald
Kissack, whose great merit it was to recall attention to Benjamin Gregory, comments:[34]

> The "original" unity of the Church is a logical concept,
> existing first in the mind of God and the will of Christ.
> It enters into history in the prayer of Jesus, and has had
> an imperative force as great as the call to holiness. . . .
> History has so far known only original sin among men,
> and original disunity in the Church. . . . The Methodist
> uses of Church unity the words Wesley uses of Chris-
> tian Perfection. He "goes on to it." It is one of his
> "oughts" that is yet to be realized in history.

The relation between the "already" and the "not yet" might
be differently phrased, but the eschatological tension toward
unity and holiness is definitely a dynamic mark of the Una
Sancta. A Methodism true to itself would engage in the common pursuit; and if Methodist holiness has sometimes taken
such problematic forms as those of revivalism, the nonconformist conscience, or liberal activism, we should hope that
while it may serve as a "leaven" (one of Wesley's favorite
images in connection with the spread of holiness) in the ecumenical movement, a more catholic environment will in turn
restore to it the sacramental dimension which the Wesleys'
teaching and practice never lacked. The visibility of the
Church and of its unity is at stake. The alternative to visible
unity is not spiritual unity but visible disunity; and that is
a counter-testimony to the gospel.

III. OUR OWN HISTORY

In one of his more triumphalist utterances, Gordon Rupp
told the 1959 Oxford Institute: "What is distinctive about us
is not our faith, for that we share with the whole catholic
Church, but our history. The way that God has led us and
what He has said and done among us—that really is our very
own."[35] As to our official doctrines, I too would be fairly
optimistic concerning their catholicity; but there is something rather divisive in this use of "our history." Even worse,
Dr. Rupp went on to talk about our "painless extraction"

from within the Church of England: "Call it separation, call it schism, there has never been a break as thoroughgoing and yet as undamaging on either side in the history of the Church." Can it be that our most eminent historian had forgotten Wesley's sermon "On Schism"?[36] A "causeless separation from a body of living Christians" is "evil in itself," being "a grievous breach of the law of love" ("The pretences for separation may be innumerable but want of love is always the real cause"); such a separation is also "productive of mischievous consequences," bringing forth in ourselves and in others "unkind tempers," "bitter words," "ungodly and unrighteous actions." "The love of many will wax cold," and they will be led astray from the way of peace into everlasting perdition. And as to the effect on nonbelievers:

> What a grievous stumbling-block must these things be to those who are without, to those who are strangers to religion, who have neither the form nor the power of godliness! How will they triumph over these once eminent Christians! How boldly ask, "What are they better than us?" How will they harden their hearts more and more against the truth, and bless themselves in their wickedness! from which, possibly, the example of the Christians might have reclaimed them, had they continued unblamable in their behaviour.

There can be no doubt of Wesley's loyalty to what later Methodists called "the fundamental principles of the Protestant Reformation," at least as they were expressed in the Anglican *Homilies;* but he chastised Luther and Calvin for some unnecessary provocativeness in their "open separation from the Church":

> When the Reformation began, what mountainous offences lay in the way of even the sincere members of the Church of Rome! They saw such failings in those great men, Luther and Calvin! Their vehement tenaciousness of their own opinions; their bitterness towards all who differed from them; their impatience of contradiction, and utter want of forbearance, even with their own brethren.
> But the grand stumbling-block of all was their open, avowed separation from the Church; their rejecting so

many of the doctrines and practices, which the others accounted most sacred; and their continual invectives against the Church they separated from, so much sharper than Michael's reproof of Satan.

Were there fewer stumbling-blocks attending the Reformation in England? Surely no: for what was Henry the Eighth? Consider either his character, his motives to the work, or his manner of pursuing it! . . . The main stumbling-block also still remained, namely, open separation from the Church.

As early as the very first Conference in 1744, Wesley and his preachers faced the question: "Do you not entail a schism in the Church? That is, Is it not probable that your hearers, after your death, will be scattered into all sects and parties, or that they will form themselves into a distinct sect?" The answer they gave was: "We do, and will do, all we can to prevent those consequences which are supposed likely to happen after our death." Yet despite Wesley's lifelong efforts, Methodism did separate from the Church of England; and, worse still, the sixty or seventy years after his death witnessed, both in England and in the United States, a further fragmentation of the Methodist movement. Does Dr. Rupp believe that Methodist fissiparity in the first half of the nineteenth century did not result at least in part from our original separation from the Church of England? And was not our loss of sacramental sense at least partly due to our absence from a Church whose own Tractarian revival we might have been able to moderate in such a way as to prevent the excesses and intransigencies of Anglo-Catholicism? And who can calculate the loss to Anglicanism of that Methodism which, in the judgment of such an outside observer as C. J. Betrand, was best organized in both Britian and America to meet the needs and opportunities of evangelism?

We must face up to that nineteenth-century fissiparity. Outler describes it thus:

The British Methodists experienced five years of turmoil after Wesley's death before their first schism broke wide open. Thereafter in America and England, schism followed schism in controversy after controversy over a bewildering variety of issues: ecclesiastical authority, racial equality, lay representation, slavery, the status of the episcopacy, the doctrine of holiness, and many another. When the first "Ecumenical Methodist Conference" was held in London in 1881, there were ten separate denominations from the British side, eighteen from America—all Methodists![38]

Yet the Ecumenical Methodist Conference was positively significant, for it helped to begin that series of reunions which has brought so much of sundered Methodism together again at the national level in the twentieth century: first in Australia (1902), then in Britian and its missionary areas with the United Methodist Church of 1907 and the subsequent union of that body with the Wesleyans and the Primitives to form the Methodist Church in Great Britian in 1932, and finally in the United States with the reunion of the Methodist Episcopal Church, the Methodist Episcopal Church, South, and the Methodist Protestant Church in 1939 and the formation of the United Methodist Church as a result of the merger of the Methodist Church with the Evangelical United Brethren in 1968. These reunions within the Methodist family demonstrate that, for all the early fissiparity, "fellowship" is more than an invisibilist sentiment for Methodists and is rather grounded in the

> Christ, from whom all blessings flow,
> Perfecting the saints below,

and in whom

> Love, like death, hath all destroyed,
> Rendered all distinctions void.
> Names and sects and parties fall:
> Thou, O Christ, art all in all.

It is no accident that it should be the Methodist Outler who powerfully interpreted the WCC as a recovered *koinonia* in whose ambit the members press on to fuller unity.[39] Outler insists that it is important for all to reappropriate "our *common Christian* history," and he himself has greatly helped to render "our" history as Methodists accessible to others, so that the possessive pronoun may acquire an inclusive rather than an exclusive sense.[40]

Individual Methodists have in fact made prominent contributions to the modern ecumenical movement from the early days of John R. Mott, the roving American, and Sir Henry Lunn, the British travel agent. In Faith and Order there have been Ivan Lee Holt, Clarence Tucker Craig, the unforgettable Robert Newton Flew, Albert Outler himself (so important in the Montreal agreement on Scripture and Tradition), J. Robert Nelson, and A. Raymond George. Philip Potter, the present general secretary of the WCC, is unmistakably Methodist.

Methodist Churches have been members of the WCC from its inception. They have also engaged in various official bilateral dialogues in the different countries, notably with Roman Catholics and Lutherans; and it is with these that the World Methodist Council has engaged in conversations at the "world confessional" level. By this stage of the ecumenical movement, however, the crucial test must be that of Methodist participation in concrete transconfessional unions. First in Canada and then in Australia the Methodists have joined with the Congregationalists and the majority of Presbyterians to form, respectively, the United Church of Canada (1925) and the Uniting Church in Australia (1977). In 1938 most of the French Methodists entered the Église Réformée de France. The more difficult, and perhaps therefore more exciting, unions have issued in the Church of South India, which in 1947 brought Methodists, Presbyterians, and Congregationalists together with Anglicans in an episcopally ordered Church, and the Church of North India (1970), which included Baptists and Brethren in addition to the others. The "American" Methodists remain outside the two Indian churches; and one gathers that the reasons are more financial than theological. Apart from their forcible inclusion in the rather unsatisfactory unions contrived by the secular authorities in Japan (1940) and Zaïre (1970), "American" Methodists have—in comparison with the "British" achievement in India and the rather thwarted promises in Sri Lanka and several African countries—a somewhat poor record of participation in unity schemes.[41] Financial reasons apart, one may wonder whether the contrasting perceptions indicated in our first section have not also played a part in the attitudes fostered among those who have received the gospel from American and British missions respectively. That makes all the more crucial the outcome of participation by the United Methodist Church, and indeed the three "black" Methodist Churches, in the U.S. Consultation on Church Union as it seeks to move, by way of some form of mutual recognition, toward a Church of Christ Uniting. In Britain, the Methodist Church was twice jilted at the altar by the Church of England, in 1969 and 1972. And more recently a somewhat looser covenant arrangement has been rejected by most Baptists, by the Roman Catholic Bishops' Conference, and at the last minute by a sufficient spoiling minority of the house of clergy in the Church of England synod. It seems unlikely that the Methodists, the United Reformed, and the Moravians will proceed into the episcopally ordered relationship that the covenant envisaged as a step toward fuller unity. In 1979, the Methodist Synod in Scotland turned down a union with the Church of Scotland despite the fact that the latter staunchly Calvinist body, while retaining its inveterate opposition to the very name of "superintendent" and rejecting the stationing implications of connectionalism, had been willing to accept a statement of faith that was all an Evangelical Arminian could desire. This experience with the difficulties of a tiny minority-church in relation to the national Church of Scotland should give British Methodists as a whole some fellow feeling with the small Methodist churches in the midst of the *Volkskirchen* of Germany and Scandinavia. What two very small minority churches can do together is illustrated by the "integrazione" (1979) of the Methodists and the Waldensians in Italy, where the governing synod is united while the scattered local congregations retain their traditional name and flavor.

One final aspect of "our history" needs to be mentioned in the present connection. Wesley's stand on the universal offer of the gospel naturally led Methodism to play a leading role in the great missionary expansion of the nineteenth and early twentieth centuries. It is a fact of abiding ecclesiological significance that membership in the British Methodist

Church has carried with it automatic membership in the Methodist Missionary Society: the mission is recognized to be part of the Church's very being. Yet historically, as Outler once again notes, "the very success of denominational missions served to expose the anomaly of a divided Christianity trying to carry the Gospel message to every creature";[42] and we recall that the modern ecumenical movement is conventionally dated from the Edinburgh Missionary Conference of 1910. If "the mission is one," a divided Christianity is no more tolerable "at home" than it is "overseas": the being of the Church and the credibility of its message are everywhere called into question by division.

IV. THE EPONYMOUS HERO IN THE COMMUNION OF THE SAINTS

It may not be superfluous to admit and explain that Wesley's name has already been, and will again be, invoked in this essay with an intention that goes beyond the historical into the theological and even into the spiritual. For Albert Outler, John Wesley is both the "eponymous hero of [our] particular denomination" and an "ecumenical theologian."[43] For Colin Williams, it is by sympathetically and critically "analyzing the Methodist tradition at the point of its origin," namely *John Wesley's Theology*, that we shall be enabled to make an authentically Methodist contribution to the changed ecumenical situation of *today*.[44] As already mentioned, Francis Frost recognizes the theologically and spiritually decisive imprint of Wesley on the whole of Methodism; and the other Roman Catholic, John Todd, not only recognizes the continuing historical influence of an inimitably great man but ends up confessing: "As I have come to know Wesley I have believed him to be [in heaven] and have prayed to God through him—not publicly as the Church prays through those declared to be saints—but privately as I pray for and to those who have been close to me."[45] The Wesley brothers figure in the new Anglican calendars in both England and the United States and in the calendar of the new North American *Lutheran Book of Worship*. Should Methodists be less open to the Wesleyan presence, in person, words, and deeds?

A few catchwords removed from their context have sometimes been used to make out that Wesley was an ecclesiological laxist, particularly in matters with a doctrinal import.
But in his sermon "Catholic Spirit," he gives a full credal,
experiential, and practical content to "Is thine heart right, as
my heart is with thy heart?" before he will say "Give me
thine hand";[46] and in the third part of the sermon, Wesley
expressly denies any charges of "speculative latitudinarian-
ism ("A catholic spirit . . . is not indifference to *all* opinions.
. . . A man of a truly catholic spirit . . . is as fixed as the sun
in his judgment concerning the main branches of Christian
doctrine") or of "practical latitudinarism" whether in worship ("The man of a truly catholic spirit . . . is clearly con-
vinced that [his] manner of worshipping God is both scriptural
and rational") or in ecclesical allegiance ("A man of a truly
catholic spirit is fixed in his congregation as well as his principles"). In other words: while "a difference in opinions or
modes of worship may prevent an entire external union," the
"union in affection" which it need not prevent is limited to
those who are recognizably Christian, "brother[s] in Christ,"
"joint heir[s] of his glory." Again, when in *The Character of
a Methodist* it is stated that "we think and let think," this
magnanimity is limited to "opinions which do not strike at
the root of Christianity."[47] And when Wesley writes in the
Letter to a Roman Catholic that "if we cannot as yet think
alike in all things, at least we may love alike," he has already
expressed the faith of "a true Protestant" through an ampli-
fied version of the Nicene Creed that is set in a context of
worship and Christian practice.[48] An unfortunate phrase in
A Plain Account of the People Called Methodists—that "orthodoxy, or right opinions, is at best a slender part of religion,
if it can be allowed to be any part at all"[49]—is best understood along the lines of St. James' refusal of saving efficacy
to the devil's impeccable monotheism.

Nor may Wesley's exegetical point in his sermon "On
Schism"—that Paul's usage of the word *schisma* in
1 Corinthians refers to divisions within a religious community which continues outwardly united—fairly be used to
father on him the view that renders Christian disunity as we
know it relatively innocuous by talk of the Church as being

in a state of internal schism.[50] Internal disunion was already
bad enough in Wesley's eyes, but we have earlier heard his
even fiercer description—in the latter part of that same sermon—of the nature and consequence of visible separation;
and *that* is what the ecumenical problem is about. Wesley's
position on Christian disunity and the unity of the Church
is in fact rather complex. Taken as a whole, it is not directly
applicable to our situation two hundred years on—with
Methodism having become "an autonomous Christian
confession," the modern ecumenical movement having grown
and developed the way it has, and the possibilities for institutional relationships with the Roman Catholic Church having opened up in a manner quite unforeseeable in the
eighteenth and indeed the nineteenth and early twentieth
centuries; but there are elements in Wesley's historically
conditioned position that may help us toward a characteristically Methodist perspective on the present form of some
apparently perennial issues.

To the Roman Catholic bishop Challoner, Wesley[51] defined "the Catholic Church" as "the whole body of men,
endued with faith working by love, dispersed over the whole
earth, in Europe, Asia, Africa, and America. And this Church
is 'ever one' [the quotations are from Challoner]; in all ages
and nations it is the one body of Christ. It is 'ever holy'; for
no unholy man can possibly be a member of it. It is 'ever
orthodox'; so is every holy man, in all things necessary to
salvation; 'secured against error,' in things essential, 'by the
perpetual presence of Christ and ever directed by the Spirit
of Truth', in the truth which is after godliness." To the Baptist
minister Gilbert Boyce, Wesley wrote: "I do not think either
the Church of England, or the people called Methodists, or
any other particular society under heaven to be the *True
Church of Christ*. For that Church is but one, and contains
all the true believers on earth. But I conceive every society
of true believers to be a branch of the one true Church of
Christ."[52] How far this insistence on "true believers" and on
holiness is removed from invisibilism or from Donatism will
appear in a moment. Meanwhile we note, on the one hand,
the practical generosity which flows from this attitude. The
Anglican Wesley refuses to damn Quakers.[53] The words of

the sermon "Catholic Spirit" concerning congregational loyalty—matched by Wesley's practical advice to all his hearers and followers not to separate from the ecclesial body in which they found themselves—imply an unwillingness on the part of the mature Wesley to unchurch the Dissenting bodies.[54] Wesley also followed the hitherto traditional Anglican recognition of continental Protestant churches even though they lacked the preferred form of episcopal government.[55] At times he appears to hold that Roman Catholics could be Christians only in spite of their Church.[56] Thus he says to Boyce: "If I were in the Church of Rome, I would conform to all her doctrines and practices as far as they were not contrary to plain Scripture."[57] But that limitation would surely have presented difficulties for one who, say, shared the view of the Anglican Articles on Roman eucharistic doctrines and practices. Wesley, in fact, points to much "error," "superstition," and even "idolatry" in the Roman Catholic Church.[58] But his attitude even on doctrinally more significant matters appears to have been in line with his remarks on the miracles at the grave of a certain French *abbé:* "The 'times of ignorance' God does 'wink at' still; and bless the faith notwithstanding the superstition."[59] Wesley aims not only at popular but also at official credulity when he calls Roman Catholics "volunteers in faith," "believing more than God has revealed."[60] Yet, he says, "it cannot be denied that they believe all which God has revealed as necessary to salvation. In this we rejoice on their behalf." And "we are glad that none of those new articles, which they added at the Council of Trent to the 'faith once delivered to the saints' does so materially contradict any of the ancient articles, as to render them of no effect." What, we may wonder, would Wesley have said of the subsequent Marian dogmas and, more fundamentally, that metadogma of 1870 which qualifies all the others, namely papal infallibility?

If Wesley's position on "true believers" and on "holiness" allows in some directions a certain ecclesiological generosity, it also permits him to be more restrictive on other scores. In his *Letter to a Roman Catholic,* he denies the name of "true Protestant" to "all common swearers, Sabbath-breakers, drunkards, all whoremongers, liars, cheats, extortioners—in a word, all that live in open sin. These are no Protestants; they are not Christians at all. Give them their own name: they are open heathens. They are the curse of the nation, the bane of society, the shame of mankind, the scum of the earth." Wesley was no Donatist in the technical sense, for he maintained the Roman and Anglican position that the unworthiness of the minister does not hinder the grace of the sacrament.[61] But he certainly held that holiness belonged to the essence of Christianity and was indeed the realization of the human vocation: "That course of life tends most to the glory of God wherein we can most promote holiness in ourselves and others."[62] Holiness is thus the key to all Wesley's ecclesiology, theoretical and practical. But the broad terms of admission to the Methodist societies ("a desire to flee from the wrath to come, to be saved from their sins")—coupled with fruits evidencing the desire of salvation as a condition for continuing in membership—show that the holiness is one of aspiration before it is one of achievement.[63] Methodism cannot fairly be accused of being a perfectionist sect, as long as its members consider perfection as a goal to be pressed on toward (Phil. 3). Nor can Wesley properly be charged with invisibilism, when one notes his insistence—over against Moravian quietism—on the use of the instituted means of grace even by seekers, let alone by those who have already received the new birth. Wesley's teaching and practice of the Lord's Supper are firmly sacramentalist. Nor would an antiinstitutionalist have devoted such attention as Wesley did to questions of church order.

The historical context and chief practical problem of Wesley's preaching of a New Testament holiness Christianity were of course provided by the large number of purely nominal Christians in the Church of England. The qualitative tension of growth in holiness that marks all original and authentic Christianity had been turned into a daunting quantitative discrepancy between the vast number of the baptized and the much smaller "congregation of English believers."[64] The gap between the "multitudinous" and the "gathered" conceptions of the Church is one of the problems bequeathed by what Wesley called "that evil hour, when Constantine the Great called himself a Christian."[65]

The relics of Constantinianism remain a major though rarely named issue in contemporary ecumenism. They affect in yet another way the question of a national church. In his sermon "Of the Church," Wesley finds some New Testament justification for the use of "church" to refer to the Christian congregations dispersed throughout a civil province or country. But Constantinianism meant legal Establishment—what Wesley calls "a mere political institution";[66] and even the Reformation retained *cuius regio eius religio.* Already by the time of the 1749 sermon "Catholic Spirit," Wesley was confessing the abatement of his earlier zeal for the view that "the place of our birth fixes the church to which we ought to belong; that one, for instance, who is born in England ought to be a member of that which is styled the Church of England and, consequently, to worship God in the particular manner which is prescribed by that church." He realized that on those principles "there could have been no reformation from popery." Wesley in fact respected the laws of the Church of England only to the point where conscience or evangelistic need obliged him to "vary." If he loved its liturgy and preferred its episcopal constitution, it was on account of their consonance with Scripture rather than for their Englishness. The test remained the Primitive Church; and it is interesting that from first to last, Wesley considered "America" a place where those pristine conditions might be approximated, away from the constraints of England. A line leads from his attempt to restore supposedly apostolic rites and disciplines in Georgia in the 1730s[67] to the closing statement in his letter to "Our Brethren in America" of September 10, 1784: "As our American brethren are now totally disentangled both from the state and from the English hierarchy, we dare not entangle them again either with the one or the other. They are now at full liberty simply to follow the Scriptures and the primitive church. And we judge it best that they should stand fast in that liberty wherewith God has so strangely made them free."

This section may be closed, and the next prepared, by briefly noting the specific views of Wesley on some questions of faith and order. Wesley held the creedal truths concerning the Trinity, the Incarnation, and the Atonement; and he viewed Arians, Semi-arians, Socinians, and Deists as having departed from the Christian faith.[68] Their heart was not right with his heart, and he did not offer them his hand as brothers and sisters in Christ. For collaboration in preaching to non-believers Wesley demanded agreement—as, for instance, his "Letter to Various Clergymen" reveals[69]—on the articles of "original sin, justification by faith, and holiness of heart and life." Granted this unity in evangelistic witness, Wesley was willing to allow that differences over predestination or perfection—which "are important in the nurture of Christians," as Colin Williams says, "rather than in the missionary proclamation of the gospel"[70]—should not be church-dividing, though they would be apparent in the distinction between his own societies and, say, Whitefield's. In its more official sense also, the ordering of the Church was strictly subservient to the conversion of sinners and their edification in that holiness without which no one shall see the Lord:

> What is the end of all ecclesiastical order? Is it not to bring souls from the power of Satan to God; and to build them up in his fear and love? Order, then, is so far valuable, as it answers these ends; and if it answers them not, it is nothing worth.[71]

With that, we are structurally at the mid-point in this chapter. The second half will, however, be shorter. The diachronic lines drawn in the first half still allow a vector of choices on various issues in our present ecumenical situation. I will in each case simply indicate my own preferences within the authentically Methodist range. Section V—on Faith and Order—links up with section IV on Wesley. Section VI—on choice of partners—corresponds back to section III on our institutional history. Section VII—on Methodism's ecumenical contribution—matches section II on the parts and the whole. The opening section on schism and pluralism finds its pendant in the concluding section on reconciled diversity and costly unity.

V. FAITH AND ORDER

The most important ecumenical document before the Churches at the moment is the Lima text *Baptism, Eucharist and Ministry* (1982), a fruit of fifty-five years' work in Faith and Order. Under the mandate given by the WCC's Fifth Assembly at Nairobi in 1975 and renewed by its Central Committee at Dresden in 1981, the Faith and Order Commission "now respectfully invites all churches to prepare an official response to this text at the highest appropriate level of authority, whether it be a council, synod, conference, assembly or other body." Having worked closely for the past several years on the final stages of its production, I am persuaded that this document can be received from a Methodist standpoint as stating "the faith of the Church through the ages." The ecumenical question then becomes that of "the consequences your church can draw from this text for its relations and dialogues with other churches, particularly with those churches which also recognize the text as an expression of the apostolic faith."

The treatment of infant and believers' baptism perfectly reflects the persistent tension in Wesley—which he himself never clearly thematized theologically—between a baptismal regeneration in infants and the necessity of a subsequent spiritual rebirth.[72] The statement on the eucharist might well have served as the text for the Wesleys' *Hymns on the Lord's Supper,* and Dean Brevint himself would have been pleased with it; it is actually the fruit of the recent biblical, patristic, and liturgical renewal. The knottiest problems in ministry are those concerning the priesthood and the episcopal succession. While the relation of ministerial priesthood to the general priesthood is directly addressed only in section 17, the whole document presents a description of the ordained ministry within the whole Church which is fully in line with the emergent consensus expressed by three such different voices as the following. First, the British Methodist *Statement on Ordination* of 1974:

> As a perpetual reminder of this calling [of the whole people of God to be the body of Christ] and as a means of being obedient to it, the Church sets apart men and women, specially called, in ordination. In their office the calling of the whole Church is focused and represented, and it is their responsibility as representative persons to lead the people to share with them in that

calling. In this sense they are the sign of the presence and ministry of Christ in the Church, and through the Church to the world.

Second, the seventh chapter of the text of the Consultation on Church Union in the United States, *In Quest of a Church of Christ Uniting* (1980):

Their ordination marks them as persons who represent to the Church its own identity and mission in Jesus Christ.

Third, David N. Power, a leading Roman Catholic theologian on orders and ministry:

The needs of the church and of its mission are what determine ministry. . . . The office-holder, through the service of supervision and presidency, represents back to the Church that which in the faith of the ordination ceremony it has expressed about itself. . . . Because [the eucharistic president] is empowered to represent the church in this vital action, to represent to it its own very ground of being, we say that he is empowered to represent Christ. . . . The role of the ordained minister is to represent in the midst of this community its work for the kingdom, its eschatological nature, and its relationship to Christ. . . . The validity of ministry, to use the word loosely, is not assessed on the ground of its ecclesiastical provenance, but on the ground of its benefit to the church.[73]

Wesley had no difficulty in defining the ministerial office in priestly terms.[74] He also believed the bishop and the three-fold order to be scriptural and apostolic, though not exclusively prescribed for all times;[75] and he valued continuity in ministry highly, while denying the provability of an uninterrupted episcopal succession.[76] This is consonant with the Faith and Order text on ministry—which suggests that all should now adopt the existing episcopal succession as a *sign* ("though not a guarantee") of continuity in that apostolic tradition whose *substance* may be recognized beyond the episcopal churches, which themselves need to "regain their lost unity." Granted Wesley's views on the historical variability of church order[77] and its subservience to evangelical needs,

Methodists may without disloyalty now themselves accept
an historic episcopate for the sake of a unity whose absence
is a counter-testimony to the gospel.

The work of Faith and Order on *Baptism, Eucharist and
Ministry,* together with a more limited study, *How does the
Church teach authoritatively today?,*[78] will be taken up into
the next big project, entitled "Towards the Common Expression of the Apostolic Faith Today." I know of no more ecumenically acceptable description of the interdependence of
authoritative functions than that provided by the thoroughly
Wesleyan statement on doctrine and doctrinal standards included in the 1972 *Discipline* of the United Methodist
Church: it speaks of "a 'marrow' of Christian truth that can
be identified and that must be conserved. This living core
. . . stands revealed in Scripture, illumined by tradition, viv-
ified in personal experience, and confirmed by reason."[79]
And the Lima decision to take the Nicene Creed as the determinative foundation for the project on "the common
expression of the apostolic faith today" follows exactly the
procedures of Wesley's own confession in his "Letter to a
Roman Catholic."[80]

VI. CHOICE OF PARTNERS

I have concentrated on WCC Faith and Order work because—whatever other denominations may believe concerning their own achievements in bilateral conversations—those
multilateral WCC statements, in whose elaboration Methodists and indeed Roman Catholics have strongly participated, are doctrinally much further advanced than anything
yet produced by Methodist bilateral dialogues with the Roman Catholics or, more recently, the Lutherans. At least since
Vatican II, considerable tensions of procedure and emphasis
have run through the ecumenical movement: multilateral
versus bilateral, local versus worldwide, organic versus federal. People tend to opt consistently for either the first or the
second term in the series of pairs, so that the multilateral,
the local, and the organic line up against the bilateral, the
worldwide, and the federal. At the Lima meeting of Faith
and Order in January 1982, Fr. Jean Tillard suggested that

local "unions" among non-Catholics should see themselves
as a rather loose "communion de groupes" which did not
prejudice the particular denominational constituents in their
respective worldwide confessional relations, notably with
the Roman Catholic Church. Granted that any entry into
communion with Rome would be a great step for another
confession or denomination to take, might we not look for a
concomitant stride by Rome which would in fact reverse
Tillard's emphasis? Could not Rome—in bold application of
its own principle of subsidiarity[81]—permit Catholic Bishops'
Conferences to enter into local unions with other churches
in ways that did not impair their own relationship with the
Roman see but rather invited the other local participants to
join them in it? The most significant version for Methodists
of the general tension concerning "choice of partners" is put
in the very title of Gerald Moede's article in the *Journal of
Ecumenical Studies:* "Methodist participation in church
union negotiations and united churches: possible implications for Methodist–Roman Catholic dialogue."[82]

In ecumenical relations, much depends on the partners
one chooses or gets chosen by. If the partners are Lutheran,
one deals with a denomination which—in the Lutheran World
Federation—has a strongly developed world confessional
structure, in which the dominant model for ecumenical unity
is one of "reconciled diversity" among the continuing
confessions. If the Roman Catholics are the partners, one is
dealing with a Church which is organically united throughout the world; and the model nearest to hand for integrating
other traditions is a kind of uniatism in the Roman obedience; though that existing model itself includes the problem
of geographically overlapping jurisdictions among the various "rites."

Whatever the complexities of interpreting "place" when
the New Delhi definition speaks of "all in each place," unity
must first or last find a *local* embodiment;[83] for it is locally
that the scandal of disunity is most obvious, and it is locally
that the day-to-day need arises for united worship, mission,
and decision-making. That is doubtless why the World Methodist Conference in 1951 declared that it could only rejoice
to see Methodism giving up its denominational existence in

order to find new life in the wider community of the United
Church of Canada and the Church of South India.[84] And that
is what British Methodists have realized from the earliest
days of modern ecumenism. It explains their positive response to the Archbishop of Canterbury's sermon in 1946;
and had the Anglican-Methodist scheme succeeded in 1969
or 1972, it would have created in two stages an organic union
with the possibility of an interesting modification of the Constantinian pattern, so that the new Church's national responsibilities would have been fulfilled in its mission to the
peoples of Britain (which is not an un-Wesleyan thought).
Later on, the British Methodists joined with several other
bodies to explore an invitation from the United Reformed
Church. With the adverse decision of the Church of England's Synod in July 1982, the heart has gone out of the
ensuing covenant proposals; for full ecumenism in England
cannot get on without Anglican participation. These disap-
pointments are serious, not only nationally but also in their
international repercussions. Of the Anglican refusal of union
with the Methodists the Roman Catholic writer Francis Frost
has observed that "cet événement douloureux a contribué à
une baisse sensible de l'influence des Églises britanniques
non-catholiques romaines sur l'ensemble du mouvement
oecuménique."[85] The effect of the 1982 collapse of the English convenanting proposals on the Consultation on Church
Union in the United States remains to be seen. Unity in England, where several of the now universal confessions took
their origin in whole or in part, could still have a powerful
effect for good elsewhere in the world.

That unions at the national level need not cut churches
off from the wider world is shown by the newly developing
relationships of united churches among themselves within
the context of the WCC. Internationalism will also be fur-
thered by the world confessional bodies, as long as they ex-
ist; and by whatever universal structures emerge from a
process in which the special position of the Bishop of Rome
is recognized more and more widely. That is why it may
now be the moment for British Methodists—without giving
up their concern for unity at the national level, and without
turning their backs on the historically close Moravians or the
United Reformed Church with which they now have

hundreds of joint local congregations in one shape or another, or indeed on those Anglican friends who have desired unity with us—for British Methodists (I say) to abandon the reticence of the last generation toward the World Methodist Council and find in it an organ of international ecclesial fellowship and a valuable instrument in carrying on negotiations with the Roman Catholic Church in particular, but also with the Lutherans and with any others who are willing. In his last letter to America, written to Ezekiel Cooper on February 1, 1791, John Wesley summoned American Methodists to "see that you never give place to one thought of separating from your brethren in Europe. Lose no opportunity of declaring to all men that the Methodists are one people in all the world." Perhaps that same summons, *mutatis mutandis*, will now be heard by the British brothers and sisters. Their commitment to the WCC need in no wise be impaired.

VII. METHODISM'S ECUMENICAL CONTRIBUTION

It has become rather unfashionable to envision the denominations bringing their separate treasures into the service of the coming great Church. Perhaps we have all become aware that our partners do not always see our gifts as we ourselves see them but sometimes even look upon them as an embarrassing and unwanted offering. Certainly we need to be aware of the temptation to compare our ideal self-image with the unpolished actuality of others' conditions. With all due tentativeness we must, however, state the values we would like others to share for the sake of the gospel. Let me briefly risk it for Methodism. Two points will suffice.

First, I consider that Methodism holds what Wesley called the "proportion of the faith."[86] I find it typically expressed in the liturgical corpus of the Wesleyan hymns. What I mean is the connected, coherent, and balanced configuration of the great doctrinal truths of Christianity held with a real assent as the content of a living relationship with the God confessed. At the level of theology, it is remarkable how often writers refer to what Howard Snyder calls "the Wesleyan synthesis." Colin Williams sees Wesley's theology as enabling the combination of traditional Catholic, classical Protestant, and Free Church Protestant concerns. Albert Outler

manages to see Wesley's "evangelical catholicism" as vitally
fusing such eclectic elements as "Macarius the Egyptian"
and Jonathan Edwards—a "conjunctive theology" indeed.[87]
The spiritual integrity of the Wesleyan synthesis—important
both for its own substance and as an example of method—is
evident even to some observers outside of Methodism, particularly Roman Catholics. Maximin Piette's brave thesis in
the 1920s—that Wesley represented a Catholic "reaction" to
the Protestant extremes of Luther and Calvin[88]—was followed by John Todd's recognition in the 1950s of "Wesley's
genius to combine two commonly separated Christian truths,
the truth of the divine call to every man to surrender himself,
totally, to God, and the truth of the Church established for
the purpose of enabling each man to respond in the fullest
possible way to the call."[89] Recently there has been the most
perceptive and generous article, already several times referred to, of Francis Frost in the encyclopedia *Catholicisme:*
Methodism there appears as a unified spiritual heritage with
a precious witness to bear in the reconciliation of divided
Christianity.

The second value is the drive for holiness which characterized Wesley's manhood, ministry, and mission, and which
has never entirely disappeared from Methodism, however
serious our mistakes and failings. It is a comprehensive thrust,
embracing the person, the Church, and the world, and linking the present age with the age to come. At the moment it
is finding expression in the often transconfessional search for
patterns of spirituality, in Methodist participation in the liturgical movement for an ecumenical renewal of worship,
and in those widely desired connections between sanctification and liberation to which the Oxford Institute gave special attention in 1977.[90]

There is a third Methodist contribution to ecumenism
which I will reserve for the last paragraph of the concluding
section.

VIII. RECONCILED DIVERSITY AND COSTLY UNITY

Hints have already been dropped concerning the differences
between "reconciled diversity" and "organic union" as

models of church unity. But signs of a rapprochement are
not lacking. One mediating category may perhaps be found
in the idea of "conciliarity" developed in Faith and Order
from the Salamanca consultation in 1973. That notion was
not intended to present an alternative to "local churches
which are themselves truly united." "Conciliar fellowship"
was meant to designate the structure of "sustained and sustaining relationships" to be maintained among such churches,
which would allow the calling of councils whenever needed
to make decisions affecting all. But some supporters of "reconciled diversity" happily appear to have found the notion
of conciliarity to allay some of their fears about organic unity.
In a positive move from his side, Harding Meyer—the leading Lutheran proponent of reconciled diversity—has allowed that reconciled diversity may in some circumstances
appropriately extend to organic union.[91]

At the time of the English unity scheme between Anglicans and Methodists, Reginald Kissack argued strongly for
federalism as a "left-wing" alternative to the "catholic" model
of organic union.[92] Kissack appeared to think federalism de-
sirable in itself, but with an advocate's skill he allowed that
it would not exclude a more organic pattern in the longer
run. Such a concession was needed if Kissack was to dodge
the full force of John Kent's trenchant critique: "Christ is
more than the President of a Federal Republic of Christian
Associations; He is the Head of the Body which is His
Church."[93] We might put the point sacramentally by saying
that something more than federalism is required to bring to
an end the situation in which it is possible, and sometimes
even necessary, to ask whether baptism and confirmation
initiate a person into a denomination or into the Christian
Church, whether the eucharistic celebration is that of a particular communion or of the Body of Christ, whether ordination admits a person to official ministry in a conventicle
or in the Church of God.

At one point[94] Kissack contemplated the possibility that
"scriptural holiness can keep alight and be spread abroad by
a company of Christians if they make themselves an Order
inside a Church, but not if they make themselves a self-
sufficient Church. . . . Does holiness become significant again
in the new ecumenical context, in the sense that nostalgia

for its traditional function should encourage Methodism to unmake itself as a Church, but to remake itself as an Order inside a new Church in England?" About the same period C. J. Bertrand was suggesting that the reintegration of Methodism into the Anglican communion would make of Methodism the unique historical phenomenon of a "province in time" rather than a province in space.[95] To accept temporal limitations, the Christian might say, is to be ready to die in the hope of resurrection to a more glorious life.

To universalize the scene, let us listen one more time to Albert Outler. He visualizes for the future "a united Christian community really united in *communicatio in sacris* (in membership, ministry, and sacraments) in which the distinctive witness of divers denominations, functioning as 'orders', 'societies', or 'movements' under their own self-appointed heads, will be conserved within a wider catholic perimeter, organized constitutionally on some collegial and conciliar pattern."[96] That that vision entails more than reconciled diversity is made clear by Outler's ensuing sentences:

> Who should know better than we [Methodists] that denominations may be justified in their existence for this "time being" or that, but not forever? We were commissioned by the Spirit of God "for the time being" to carry out an extraordinary mission of witness and service, for just so long as our life apart is effective in the economy of God's providence. We are, or ought to be, prepared to risk our life as a separate church and to face death as a denomination in the sure and lively hope of our resurrection in the true community of the whole people of God. . . . The price of true catholicity may very well be the death and resurrection of the churches that we know—in the faith that God has greater things in store for his people than we can remember or even imagine.[97]

It is because Dr. Outler is so firmly committed to the ecclesiological provisionality of Methodism that I am willing to reappropriate the words with which he closed his lecture at the Oxford Institute in 1962,[98] in order to close my essay some twenty years later: "Every denomination in a divided and broken Christendom is an *ecclesiola in via*, but Methodists have a peculiar heritage that might make the transitive character of our ecclesiastical existence not only tolerable but positively proleptic."

NOTES

CHAPTER ONE

1. For the "analogical" relation between the ecclesial and the civic, see K. Barth, *Christengemeinde und Bürgergemeinde* (1946; ET in *Against the Stream* [1954]). See further, pp. 130, 138, 153.

2. Not that such an august authority is needed in demonstration of the point, but Pope John Paul II prayed thus at the opening in Passiontide of the Roman Holy Year of 1983-84: "Grant, O Lord, that this Holy Year of your redemption may also become an appeal to the modern world, which sees justice and peace on the horizon of its desires—and yet yields ever more to sin and lives, day after day, in the midst of mounting tensions and threats, and seems to be travelling in a direction perilous for all."

3. On Mott, see C. H. Hopkins, *John R. Mott 1865-1955* (1979).

4. For the early history of the modern ecumenical movement, see R. Rouse and S. C. Neill (eds.), *A History of the Ecumenical Movement*, Vol. I (2nd ed. 1968) and Vol. II (1970; ed. H. E. Fey).

5. See Commission on Faith and Order Lima 1982, *Towards Visible Unity*, I (Faith and Order Paper 112), 89-100, and II (Faith and Order Paper 113), 28-46.

6. The text was published by the WCC in 1982. Responses are requested by 1985.

7. The crystallizing text was the *Report on Traditions and traditions* (Faith and Order Paper 40 [1963]) presented to the Fourth World Conference on Faith and Order at Montreal in 1963; see also P. C. Rodger and L. Vischer (eds.), *The Fourth World Conference on Faith and Order* (Faith and Order Paper 42 [1964]), 50-61 ("Scripture, Tradition and traditions"). Contemporaneously, the important evolution of Vatican II's dogmatic constitution on Revelation, *Dei Verbum*, was taking place; see N. Lash, *Change in Focus* (1973).

8. See A. Schilson, *Theologie als Sakramententheologie: Die Mysterienlehre Odo Casels* (1982). Another important study is F. Eisenbach, *Die Gegenwart Jesu Christi im Gottesdienst* (1982).

9. J. Jeremias, *Die Abendmahlsworte Jesu* (3rd ed. 1960, pp. 229-46; ET *The Eucharistic Words of Jesus* [1966], pp. 237-55).

10. M. Thurian, *L'eucharistie: mémorial du Seigneur, sacrifice d'action de grâce et d'intercession* (1959; ET *The Eucharistic Memorial* [1960-61]).

11. For the historic differences between East and West and the need for an "Eastward correction," see R. Hotz, *Sakramente im Wechselspiel zwischen Ost und West* (1979).

12. From L. Vischer (ed.), *A Documentary History of the Faith and Order Movement 1927-1963* (1963), pp. 167-76 ("The Church, the Churches and the World Council of Churches").

13. See the interview with W. Pannenberg in *The Christian Century*, February 17, 1982.

14. See A. D. Falconer, "Contemporary attitudes to the Papacy: Protestant and Orthodox perspectives," in *The Furrow* 27 (1976), 3-19.

15. On catholicity—though the "Roman connection" will need expansion—see J. Ratzinger, *Theologische Prinzipienlehre: Bausteine zur Fundamentaltheologie* (1982), passim.

16. The participating denominations are: African Methodist Episcopal Church, African Methodist Episcopal Zion Church, Christian Church (Disciples of Christ), Christian Methodist Episcopal Church, Episcopal Church, National Council of Community Churches, Presbyterian Church in the U.S., United Church of Christ, United Methodist Church, United Presbyterian Church in the U.S.A. See particularly *In Quest of a Church of Christ Uniting* (revised ed. 1980).

17. A similar analysis and a similar vision, equally unafraid of putting hard questions to the denominations, is offered by Richard A. Norris, "What is 'Church Unity'?" in *One in Christ* 18 (1982), 117-30.

18. *In Quest of a Church of Christ Uniting* (as in note 16), p. 37.

19. From the Roman Catholic side, Avery Dulles writes this: "The Church, in its fundamental reality as sacramentally representing Christ, has a plenitude of apostolic authority that is prior to, and hence independent of, its own canonical regulations. By virtue of this 'pre-canonical' power *the Church can structure its own pastoral office in certain specific ways.* It is not absolutely essential that the Church call its highest office-holders by the title of bishop or that they be inducted into office by having other bishops impose hands on them. These canonical regulations, which currently have the force of law within the Roman Catholic Church, are not necessarily binding on all churches for all time. The question as to the conditions under which the Catholic or Orthodox Churches can partially or fully recognize the pastoral ministries in churches that lack the 'historic episcopate' is far too complicated to be treated in this essay. Much of the current literature maintains that the Church is not faced with a simple alternative between validity and invalidity. Any church or ecclesial community, to the extent that it participates in the reality of the Church of Christ, has a capacity to confer spiritual power on its own pastors, even though these pastors be not ordained by bishops. That

is not to claim, however, that all church polities are equally good or that all genuine Christian ministers have the same measure of ministerial power. According to a growing body of ecumenical opinion, the episcopal form of polity is to be esteemed as an efficacious sign of continuity and solidarity in the apostolic ministry." In this article "Successio apostolorum, successio prophetarum, successio doctorum," in *Concilium* §148 (October 1981), 61-67, Dulles appeals also to K. Rahner, *Vorfragen zu einem ökumenischen Amtsverständnis* (1974), and to C. Vagaggini, "Possibilità e limiti del riconoscimento dei ministeri non cattolici," in *Ministères et célébration de l'eucharistie* (Studia Anselmiana 61 [1973]).

20. For a recent summary, see the contributions of L. Scheffczyk, "Jesus Christus—Ursakrament der Erlösung" and "Die Kirche—das Ganzsakrament Jesu Christi," in H. Luthe (ed.), *Christusbegegnung in den Sakramenten* (1981), pp. 11-61, 63-120. See also A. Dulles, *Models of the Church* (1974), pp. 58-70, and *A Church to Believe In* (1982), pp. 41-52.

21. For a more detailed statement of my ethical perspective, see G. Wainwright, *Doxology* (1980), pp. 399-434; and for martyrdom, pp. 454-56.

22. See L. Vischer, "Confessio fidei in der ökumenischen Diskussion," in *Oekumenische Perspektiven* 11 (1982), 137-54.

23. See G. H. Williams, *The Mind of John Paul II* (1981), pp. 279-84.

24. See J. M. R. Tillard, "Sensus fidelium," in *One in Christ* 11 (1975), 2-29. Tillard writes of the proper complementarity but frequent tension between "popular faith" and "educated faith." On the one hand, "the non-essential is necessary," if the faith is meant to take concrete form in the whole human *humus.* On the other hand, spontaneous movements have to be tested for their "genuineness" in relation to "the data of Revelation." It is just this testing that is involved in the Marian question.

25. T. A. Langford, *Practical Divinity: Theology in the Wesleyan Tradition* (1983), pp. 162-69.

26. In the Soviet Union, a couple of years ago, I was interviewed by a Tass correspondent on the subject of peace. I began by pointing out the Christian belief that when human beings fall away from the living God, they write death into their destiny; the gospel tells of a reconciliation of the world to God, into which people are invited to enter with consequences for their relations on the human plane. On the whole, the Russian Orthodox Church is witnessing to that gospel. At Odessa cathedral we were shown the baptistery where, in the previous year, 4,000 infants had been baptized and, even more significantly, 150 believing adults. That is taking place in a country where the Church is forbidden to evangelize and atheism is taught in the schools.

27. See Eusebius, *Historia Ecclesiastica* 5, 1, 3ff.

CHAPTER TWO

1. In the earliest evidence for creeds, there is some tension between threefoldness and fivefoldness, although the ecclesiological and eschatological references usually find themselves integrated in one way or another into the pneumatological "third article." Explaining the five loaves of the feeding miracle, the second-century *Epistula Apostolorum* states that Christian belief is in the Father, in Jesus Christ, in the Holy Spirit, in the holy Church, and in the forgiveness of sins. The third baptismal question in the Latin version of *The Apostolic Tradition* reads "Credis in Spiritu sancto et sanctam ecclesiam et carnis resurrectionem?" Cyprian testifies to the baptismal interrogation "Do you believe in remission of sins and life eternal through the holy Church?" (*Epistle* 69, 7, ed. Harkel, p. 756). The creed in the Dêr Balyzeh papyrus should be similarly construed: "and in the Holy Spirit, and in the resurrection of the flesh in the holy catholic church." Note, finally, P. Nautin, *Je crois à l'Esprit saint dans la sainte Église pour la résurrection de la chair* (1947). On the whole question of the early structures and forms, see the opening chapters of J. N. D. Kelly, *Early Christian Creeds* (5th ed. 1977).

2. For the equivalence of Western *sanctificatio* and Eastern *théōsis* see J. Meyendorff and J. McLelland (eds.), *The New Man: An Orthodox and Reformed Dialogue* (1973), especially the chapters by J. W. Beardslee III and R. G. Stephanopoulos.

3. See, for instance, the *Letters* of St. Athanasius to Serapion, against the Tropici; and the treatise of St. Basil, *On the Holy Spirit*, against the Macedonians.

4. Karl Rahner speaks of the "axiomatic unity of the 'economic' and 'immanent' Trinity": "The 'economic' Trinity is the 'immanent' Trinity and the 'immanent' Trinity is the 'economic' Trinity" (in *The Trinity* [1970]; ET of "Der dreifaltige Gott als transzendenter Urgrund der Heilsgeschichte," from *Mysterium Salutis*, Vol. II [1967]).

5. Pentecost hymn from the Byzantine liturgy.

6. St. Basil, *On the Holy Spirit*, especially paras. 16, 63, and 68.

7. For New Testament prophets see Acts 11:27; 13:1; 15:32; Romans 12:6; 1 Corinthians 11–14; Ephesians 3:5; 4:11. But see also 1 Peter 1:10-12.

8. See, for instance, Augustine's *De dono perseverantiae* 23, 63-65 (*PL* 45, 1031-33) and his *Epistle* 217 (*PL* 33, 978-89), where appeal is made to the *lex orandi* fact of the Church's prayer for the conversion of unbelievers.

9. See A. C. Outler, *John Wesley* (1964), pp. 9f., 14.

10. Something is said about the sacrament of penance in note 21.

11. English translation from E. C. Whitaker, *Documents of the Baptismal Liturgy* (2nd ed. 1970), pp. 80f.

12. Quoted from *The Methodist Hymn Book* (1933), no. 363. Almost half the hymns in this British hymnal stem from the Wesleys, and it is from this source that Wesleyan hymns are usually quoted in the rest of the present book.

13. Chapter 31, 2 in the edition by G. Dix and H. Chadwick (1968), p. 58 ("ad ecclesiam ubi floret Spiritus").

14. *The Book of Common Prayer*, "collect for purity."

15. Thus, for instance, the anaphora of *St. John Chrysostom*: "We offer you also this reasonable and bloodless service, and we beseech and pray and entreat you, send down your Holy Spirit on us and on these gifts set forth; and make this bread the precious body of your Christ, and that which is in the cup the precious blood of your Christ, changing them by your Holy Spirit; so that they may become to those who partake for vigilance of soul, for forgiveness of sins, for fellowship of your Holy Spirit, for the fulness of the kingdom of heaven, for boldness towards you, not for judgment or condemnation."

16. Note especially J.-J. von Allmen, "Le Saint-Esprit et le culte," in *Prophétisme sacramentel* (1964), pp. 287-311.

17. The Faith and Order texts on *One Baptism, One Eucharist, and A Mutually Recognized Ministry* were sent by the Nairobi Assembly in 1975 to the churches for study and response. After revision, they reached their final form at Lima in 1982, under the title *Baptism, Eucharist, and Ministry*.

18. The text of the *Hymns on the Lord's Supper*, together with a study of them, is found in J. E. Rattenbury, *The Eucharistic Hymns of John and Charles Wesley* (1948). The two hymns quoted are nos. 72 and 16, which are respectively nos. 767 and 765 in *The Methodist Hymn Book*. The prayer from Apostolic Constitutions VIII reads as follows: "And we beseech you ... to send down your Holy Spirit upon this sacrifice, the witness of the sufferings of the Lord Jesus, that he may make this bread body of your Christ, and this cup blood of your Christ; that those who partake may be strengthened to piety, obtain forgiveness of sins, be delivered from the devil and his deceit, be filled with the Holy Spirit, become worthy of your Christ, and obtain eternal life, after reconciliation with you, almighty Lord."

19. For penetrating observations of American Protestant ecumenism, based on his visits to the United States in the 1930s, see already D. Bonhoeffer, *No Rusty Swords: Letters, Lectures and Notes 1928-1936* (1965), pp. 86-118.

20. In a fuller treatment, this would be the place at which to talk about the holiness brought to the Church by its heavenly members. For a positive Protestant view of the communion of the saints, see my *Doxology* (1980), pp. 109-12 (also pp. 444-62).

21. Excommunication is the recognition that the Holy Spirit has departed from a sinner. Penance is the sacramental sign of the

Spirit's return and of the person's restoration to the fellowship of the Church.

22. N. A. Nissiotis, "Die qualitative Bedeutung der Katholizität," in *Die Theologie der Ostkirche im oekumenischen Dialog* (1968), pp. 86-104.

23. For Cappadocian teaching on the Trinity, see in summary J. N. D. Kelly, *Early Christian Doctrines* (5th ed. 1977), pp. 258-69.

24. See note 17 for the reference to the text on *Ministry*.

25. *Methodist Hymn Book*, no. 814. There is no need to take Wesley's phraseology in a filioquist sense. For evidence of recent ecumenical progress on the *filioque* question, see the WCC Faith and Order study, *Spirit of God, Spirit of Christ* (1981).

26. Irenaeus, *Adversus omnes haereses* 5, 1, 3; 5, 5, 1; 5, 6, 1; *Demonstratio* 11.

27. So in the Greek *St. James* and in the Alexandrian *St. Mark*.

28. For the *sobria ebrietas*, see for example St. Ambrose, *De sacramentis* 5, 3, 17; and the treatment by P. Lebeau, *Le vin nouveau du Royaume* (1966). The *Westminster Shorter Catechism* of 1647-48 declared that man's chief end is "to glorify God, and to *enjoy* him for ever."

29. See E. Käsemann, "Der gottesdienstliche Schrei nach Freiheit," in *Paulinische Perspektiven* (1969), pp. 211-36.

30. *Methodist Hymn Book*, no. 431: "Love divine, all loves excelling."

31. For a more developed treatment of our principal theme by an Orthodox author, and at about the same level of technicality as my main text, see T. Hopko, *The Spirit of God* (1976).

CHAPTER THREE

1. Texts from L. Vischer (ed.), *A Documentary History of the Faith and Order Movement 1927-1963* (1963), pp. 27-39, in particular p. 39.

2. From Vischer, *Documentary History*, pp. 40-74, in particular p. 56.

3. The Orthodox note reads:

Validity. As regards the validity of sacraments the Orthodox delegates would like to confine themselves only to the following statement: According to the Orthodox doctrine valid sacraments are only those which are (1) administered by a canonically ordained and instituted minister and (2) rightly performed according to the sacramental order of the Church. They regard it therefore as unnecessary to accept any other document on this matter presented by the Conference.

As late as the Bangalore meeting of the Faith and Order Commission in 1978, the Orthodox Church of Greece was ready to withdraw from the study of baptism, eucharist, and ministry, on the grounds that baptism, let alone the eucharist, depended on its celebration by a minister in the apostolic succession as defined by the Greeks. Happily, G. Konidaris, the veteran Greek ecumenist, was able to vote in favor of the Lima text in 1982.

4. J. E. Skoglund and J. R. Nelson, *Fifty Years of Faith and Order* (1963), p. 99.

5. *One Lord, One Baptism* (Faith and Order Paper 29) (1960).

6. P. C. Rodger and L. Vischer (eds.), *The Fourth World Conference on Faith and Order Montreal 1963* (Faith and Order Paper 42) (1964), p. 72, §111.

7. Ibid., §112.

8. *Faith and Order Louvain 1971* (Faith and Order Paper 59) (1971), pp. 35-49.

9. Text also in Faith and Order Paper 59, pp. 49-53.

10. The Crêt-Bérard report appeared as Faith and Order Paper 84 (1977).

11. Commission on Faith and Order Bangalore 1978, *Sharing in One Hope* (Faith and Order Paper 92), pp. 247-56.

12. *Louisville Consultation on Baptism* (Faith and Order Paper 97). This appeared as the Winter 1980 number of *Review and Expositor*. The papers presented at the consultation are followed, on pp. 101-08, by the report.

13. The minutes appear in the Commission on Faith and Order Lima 1982, *Towards Visible Unity*, I (Faith and Order Paper 112). The "Lima text" itself—*Baptism, Eucharist, and Ministry*—was published in 1982 in Geneva by the WCC. In the interests of wide discussion within and among the Churches it has been translated into many languages, and the English text has been reprinted in several places (for example, *One in Christ* 18 [1982], 348-84).

14. These two books were published by the WCC in Geneva in 1983.

15. See R. Hotz, *Sakramente im Wechselspiel zwischen Ost und West* (1979).

16. See T. F. Torrance, *Theology in Reconciliation: Essays towards Evangelical and Catholic Unity in East and West* (1975), pp. 82-105.

17. In chapter IV of *Doxology* (1980), I have discussed the relations between baptism and ecclesiology. It is a question of the boundaries of the Church. As an individual theologian, my preference is for the baptism of believers; but given the inconclusiveness of Scripture on the point and the preponderance of tradition in favor of the baptism of infants, I cannot see the Church as a whole renouncing infant baptism. There is much to be said for limiting it to children brought by believing and communicant parents or guardians. Even better would be the admission of such infants to the catechumenate in the hope of their future baptism upon profession of faith: "As far as the 'boundaries' of the Church are concerned, I would rather have the 'positive' indefiniteness brought by the idea of a provisional place for the children of be-

lievers than the 'negative' penumbra of baptized unbelievers resulting from the failure of many millions baptized in infancy to arrive at personal commitment. In other words, any fringe had better be composed of those hopefully 'on their way in' than of those apparently 'on their way out' " (p. 141).

18. I have several times appealed to exegetical difficulties and to the variety of social and cultural circumstances in which the Church historically finds itself, in order to justify a variety of initiation practice. The advocates and practitioners of the various patterns can be relied on to bring out the positive values of each; but they must be brought together in a tense though tolerable unity. See G. Wainwright, *Christian Initiation* (1969); "The rites and ceremonies of Christian initiation: developments in the past," in *Studia Liturgica* 10 (1974), 2-24; and "Christian initiation: development, dismemberment, reintegration," in D. C. Brockopp (ed.), *Christian Initiation: Reborn of Water and the Spirit* (1981), pp. 31-57.

19. For the theological problems involved, see G. Wainwright, *Christian Initiation* (1969), pp. 66-69.

20. See L. H. Stookey, *Baptism, Christ's Act in the Church* (1982), pp. 198-200, and R. W. Jenson, *The Triune Identity* (1982), especially pp. 1-20.

21. A valuable select bibliography on Christian initiation is provided by the publication of the Murphy Center for Liturgical Research at the University of Notre Dame, *Made, Not Born* (1976), pp. 168-78.

CHAPTER FOUR

1. Some recent scholars have detected a hymn at the basis of Ephesians 2:11-22: so G. Schille, *Frühchristliche Hymnen* (1962), pp. 24-31; J. T. Sanders, "Hymnic Elements in Ephesians 1-3," in *Zeitschrift für die neutestamentliche Wissenschaft* 56 (1965), 214-32; J. Gnilka, "Christus unser Friede—ein Friedens-Erlöserlied in Eph. 2, 14-17," in *Die Zeit Jesu* (Schlier Festschrift) (1970), pp. 190-207; but not R. Deichgräber, *Gotteshymnus und Christushymnus in der frühen Christenheit* (1967), pp. 165-67. Certainly the passage corresponds to an early recurrent pattern of experience and expression in Christian worship.

2. Origen, *De oratione*. This is not to say that the precise way in which Origen worked out this principle is identical with later orthodoxy. See the discussion in J. Lebreton, "Le désaccord de la foi populaire et de la théologie savante dans l'Eglise chrétienne du IIIe siècle," in *Revue d'Histoire Ecclésiastique* 19 (1923), 481-506, and 20 (1924), 5-37, in particular 19ff.

3. See J. A. Jungmann, *Die Stellung Christi im liturgischen Gebet* (1925, 1962²).

4. Some see the solution in a rich understanding of the verb

"to re(-)present," with or without the hyphen; this is exploited in the Les Dombes agreement on the eucharist between French Catholics and Protestants (1972). Others see in the term "re(-)presentation" an ambiguity which masks the real problem; the Anglican-Roman Catholic Agreed Statement on the eucharist of 1971 manages to avoid the term and speaks rather of the "effective proclamation" of Christ's atoning work. If it be said that Calvary and the eucharist are the *same* sacrifice, the latter being identical with the former but in sacramental mode, then there is this difficulty: both Calvary and the eucharist belong, in their *essence* or deepest reality, not only to the transcendent realm but also to *history*, and it is therefore hard to escape some notion of *repetition*; and a second occurrence threatens the sufficiency of the first. For further effects toward clarity, see my *Doxology* (1980), pp. 271-74. In this connection, Edmund Schlink has lately called attention to the divine sovereignty over the very structures of time: see "Struktur und Rangordnung der dogmatischen Aussagen über das Herrenmahl," in K. Lehmann and E. Schlink (eds.), *Das Opfer Jesu Christi und seine Gegenwart in der Kirche: Klärungen zum Opfercharakter des Herrenmahls* (1983), pp. 138-75.

5. *Catechesis Mystagogica* 5, 4: *échein en ouranō tēn kardían prós tón philánthrōpon Theón.*

6. Matthew 14:19; Mark 6:41; Luke 9:16; see also John 11:41; 17:1.

7. See also *Apostolic Constitutions* VIII, 12, 36, Greek *St. James*, Alexandrian *St. Mark*, Coptic *St. Cyril*, Ethopian *Anaphora of the Apostles*. The texts are in Brightman, *Liturgies Eastern and Western*, pp. 20, 51, 132, 176, 232, and in Hänggi-Pahl, *Prex Eucharistica*, pp. 92, 246, 112, 136, 148. Ambrose, *De sacramentis* 4, 5, 21f., gives the text: *respexit ad caelum ad te.*

8. See, for example, in the litany at the Inclination in *Apostolic Constitutions* VIII, 13, 3: "We pray on behalf of the gift offered to the Lord God that the good God may receive it through the mediation of his Christ on his heavenly altar for a sweet-smelling savour" (Brightman, p. 23); and in the intercessions within the canon of the liturgy of *St. Mark*: "Accept, O God, the sacrifices, oblations and thank-offerings of the offerers upon thy holy and heavenly and rational altar in the highest heaven through the ministry of thy archangels" (Brightman, p. 129; Hänggi-Pahl, p. 108).

9. See H. Lietzmann on the "Weihrauchgebete," in *Messe und Herrenmahl* (3rd ed. 1955), pp. 86-93.

10. Some Gallican and Mozarabic eucharistic prayers contained a pneumatological epiclesis (see E. G. C. F. Atchley, *On the Epiclesis of the Eucharistic Liturgy* . . . [1935], pp. 145-70); the English Prayer Book of 1549 invoked "thy holy spirite and worde." It does not matter for our present purpose whether it is in connection with the elements, the people, the fruits of communion, or any combination of these, that the Holy Spirit is invoked in the various ancient and modern rites.

11. M. Black has recently linked *maranatha* with *élthen Ký-rios* of Jude 14 and suggested that both represent a prophetic *perfectum futuri* ("The Maranatha invocation and Jude 14, 15 [1 Enoch 1:9]," in *Christ and Spirit in the New Testament* [Moule Festschrift] [1973], pp. 189-96). Philologically, it remains possible to analyze *maranatha* as an imperative: "Our Lord, come!"

12. "Adesto quaesumus, Domine Jesu Christe, medius inter servulos huius cenae convivii editor . . ." (M. Férotin [ed.], *Liber Sacramentorum*, col. 239); "Adesto, adesto, Jesu, bone pontifex, in medio nostri, sicut fuisti in medio discipulorum tuorum . . ." (*Missale mixtum* [PL 85, 116, 124, and 550]).

13. See J. M. Hanssens, *Institutiones liturgicae de ritibus orientalibus*, II (1930), 24-34.

14. So, for example, the Church of South India; the British Methodist 1968/74; the American Methodist 1972; the United Reformed Church in England and Wales 1974; the Church of England *Alternative Service Book* (1980).

15. The Pauline text is quoted at the Fraction in the eucharistic rite of the Taizé community and in the Church of England's *Alternative Service Book*.

16. Augustine, *Sermo* 57, 7 (*PL* 38, 389); *Sermo* 227 (*PL* 38, 1099-1101); *Sermo* 272 (*PL* 38, 1247f.). See already Cyprian, *Epistle* 69, 5 (ed. Harkel, pp. 753f.); *Epistle* 63, 13 (p. 712).

17. Modern liturgical scholars have sometimes reintroduced this motif from the *Didache* and Serapion when composing eucharistic rites: W. E. Orchard, in *Divine Service* (1919), p. 128 (see *A Free Church Book of Common Prayer* [1929], p. 114); A. van der Mensbrugghe, *La liturgie orthodoxe de rit occidental: essai de restauration* (1948), 40f.; M. Thurian, in *Eucharistie à Taizé* (1963), p. 45.

18. On the inclusive meaning of *hoi polloí*, see J. Jeremias, *Die Abendmahlsworte Jesu* (3rd ed. 1960), pp. 171-74, 218-23.

19. For evidence of this practice, see the references given in J. H. Srawley, *The Early History of the Liturgy* (2nd ed. 1947), p. 234 (see also pp. 124, 155).

20. N. Afanassieff, "Le sacrement de l'assemblée," in *Internationale kirchliche Zeitschrift* 46 (1956), 200-13. For the eucharist as a sign particularly of *local* unity, see M. F. Wiles, "Sacramental Unity in the Early Church," in J. Kent and R. Murray (eds.), *Church Membership and Intercommunion* (1973), pp. 35-49.

21. G. Wainwright, *Eucharist and Eschatology* (1971; expanded ed. 1981), pp. 135-46, and "L'intercommunion, signe et issue de l'impasse oecuménique," in *Nouvelle Revue Théologique* 92 (1970), 1037-54.

22. Brightman, pp. 436f., 515; Hänggi-Pahl, pp. 321, 402.

23. Theodore of Mopsuestia, *Homélies catéchétiques* (eds. R. Tonneau and R. Devreesse) XVI, 17-20, 25-26. M. Schmaus, "Die Eucharistie als Bürgin der Auferstehung," in *Pro Mundi Vita: Festschrift zum eucharistischen Weltkongress* (1960), pp. 256-79;

Schmaus safeguards the "objective" value of the elements by saying that as in ordinary human relations bodily proximity has value
as "Ausdruckgestalt und Intensivierungsmedium der Begeg-
nung," similarly in the eucharist the reception of the sacramentally present body and blood of Christ offers "besondere Chancen
für die Christusbegegnung" (p. 274).

24. ... obsecrantes ut infundere digneris spiritum tuum sanc-
tum edentibus nobis vitam aeternam regnumque perpetuum con-
latura potantibus (Missale Gothicum, prayer no. 527, ed. L. C.
Mohlberg [1961], p. 120).

25. Brightman, p. 287; Hänggi-Pahl, p. 380.

26. See Hilary, De trinitate VIII, 12-17 (PL 10, 244-49); Cyril
of Alexandria, In Iohannis evangelium XI, 12 (PG 74, 561-65).

27. These phrases come respectively from the new Roman Eucharistic Prayers III and IV.

28. ... ut per hoc ad perpetuum diem et ipsam Christi perven-
iamus ad mensam, ut unde hic gustum sumpsimus, inde ibi plen-
itudinem totasque satietates capiamus (Sermo 68 [PL 52, 395]).

29. ... ut cujus laetamur gustu, renovemur effectu (no. 39, 3;
H. Lietzmann, Das Sacramentum Gregorianum nach dem Aache-
ner Urexemplar [1921]).

30. Justin, Dialogus contra Tryphonem 138 (PG 6, 793).

31. Luke 24:28-35; 24:36-43; John 21:13; Acts 10:41.

32. Matthew 5:6 = Luke 6:21; Matthew 8:11 = Luke 13:29;
Luke 12:37; Matthew 22:1-10; Matthew 22:11-13; Matthew 25:1-13;
Matthew 25:21, 23; Mark 14:25 = Matthew 26:29 = Luke 22:15-18,
29-30; Revelation 19:7-9. For the interpretation of these and related texts, see Wainwright, Eucharist and Eschatology, pp. 18-42.

33. 1 Corinthians 7:31b; 2 Peter 3:13; Revelation 21:1, 5.

34. On the "cosmic" dimension of the eucharist, see A.
Schmemann, For the Life of the World (1963) (= Sacraments and
Orthodoxy [1965]).

CHAPTER FIVE

1. The New Delhi Report, pp. 116-22.

2. The Uppsala Report 1968, p. 17. See L. Vischer, " 'A genuinely universal council . . .'?" in The Ecumenical Review 22 (1970),
97-106.

3. The Ecumenical Review 26 (1974), 291-98. The link between
Uppsala and Salamanca was provided by Committee IV of the
Faith and Order Commission meeting at Louvain in 1971.

4. For further consideration of "local churches truly united,"
see In Each Place: Towards a Fellowship of Local Churches Truly
United (WCC 1977).

5. Breaking Barriers: Nairobi 1975, pp. 59-61, 69.

6. Breaking Barriers: Nairobi 1975, pp. 317f.

7. See the "Toronto Statement" of 1950: The Church, the
Churches and the World Council of Churches—The Ecclesiological
Significance of the World Council of Churches. Also W. A. Visser 't

Hooft, "The Super-Church and the Ecumenical Movement," in *The Ecumenical Review* 10 (1957-58), 365-85.

8. See already *The Fourth World Conference on Faith and Order: Montreal 1963*, pp. 48f. And thereto W. A. Visser 't Hooft, "Die Bedeutung der Mitgliedschaft im Oekumenischen Rat der Kirchen," in *Oekumenische Rundschau* 12 (1963), 229-36, and H. H. Wolf, "Oekumenische Erneuerung im Verständnis des Oekumenischen Rates und der römisch-katholischen Kirche," in *Materialdienst des Konfessionskundlichen Instituts* 15 (1964), 61-65.

9. For a personal view, see G. Wainwright, "L'intercommunion, signe et issue de l'impasse oecuménique," in *Nouvelle Revue Théologique* 92 (1970), 1037-54. For a survey of the debate, see "Beyond intercommunion: on the way to communion in the Eucharist," in *Study Encounter* 5 (1969), 94-114, which was then taken up by the Louvain meeting of the Faith and Order Commission in 1971. The more recent tendency has been to remove the offensive particle "inter" altogether and rather conduct the dicussion in terms of "eucharistic sharing"; see already H. J. McSorley, "Eucharistic sharing: a new state of the question for Roman Catholics," *The Ecumenical Review* 22 (1970), 113-24.

10. G. Wainwright, "Christian Initiation in the Ecumenical Movement," in *Studia Liturgica* 12 (1977); see chapter III above, where it is shown that these features persist into the final text of Lima in 1982.

11. The Orthodox theologian Oliver Clément sees time as the God-given possibility for God's creation to learn to love: *Transfigurer le temps* (1959).

12. For evidence that Paul's letters were intended to be read in the liturgical assembly, see G. J. Cuming, "Service-endings in the Epistles," in *New Testament Studies* 22 (1975-76), 110-13.

13. See P. C. Bori, *Koinonia: l'idea della communione nell'ecclesiologia recente e nel Nuovo Testamento* (1972).

14. See K. F. Nickle, *The Collection* (1966).

15. See Bori (note 13).

16. See the Vatican II Decree on the Eastern Churches (*Orientalium ecclesiarum*, November 21, 1964); and then the following: the Ecumenical Directory (*Ad totam ecclesiam*, May 14, 1967); the Declaration on the Position of the Catholic Church on the Celebration of the Eucharist in Common by Christians of Different Confessions (*Dans ces derniers temps*, January 7, 1970); the Instruction on Admitting Other Christians to Eucharistic Communion in the Catholic Church (*In quibus rerum circumstantiis*, June 1, 1972), and the Note interpreting the "Instruction on Admitting Other Christians to Eucharistic Communion under Certain Circumstances" (*Dopo la pubblicazione*, October 17, 1973). All these texts are to be found in A. Flannery (ed.), *Vatican Council II: the conciliar and postconciliar documents* (1975).

17. Hefele and Leclercq, *Histoire des Conciles*, I (1907), 293.

18. At this point in particular I am indebted to M. F. Wiles, "Sacramental unity in the early Church," in J. Kent and R. Murray (eds.), *Church Membership and Intercommunion* (1973), pp. 35-49.

19. For this interpretation, which makes the sending a matter internal to Rome, see G. La Piana, "The Roman Church at the end of the second century," in *Harvard Theological Review* 18 (1925), 201-77. La Piana gives a strongly "jurisdictional" flavor to the practice; Irenaeus' account, however, does not bear this sinister complexion—at least on the surface.

20. L. Duchesne, *Le "Liber Pontificalis,"* I (1886), 168f., 216.

21. Innocent, *Epistle* 25, 7 (*PL* 20, 556). The phrase *maxime illa die* suggests that it is *Easter* Sunday which is being referred to, and one manuscript supplies the heading *de fermento in die sancto paschae*. . . .

22. See J. A. Jungmann, *Missarum Sollemnia*, part IV, chap. III, para. 5.

23. Hefele and Leclercq, I, 1006f., 1016.

24. *De sacro altaris mysterio* 4, 36 (*PL* 217, 879).

25. See G. Wainwright, *Eucharist and Eschatology*, pp. 115-17.

26. Augustine, *Sermo* 57 (*PL* 38, 389), 227 (*PL* 38, 1099-1101), and 272 (*PL* 38, 1247f.).

27. The eucharist may be seen as a "projection" of the Parousia in two senses: it is a "throwing forward" from the future; it is also, in a "cartographical" sense, the representation of a large reality by means of a set of comprehensible symbols (see G. Wainwright, *Eucharist and Eschatology*, pp. 92f.).

28. See G. Wainwright, "The Eucharist as an ecumenical sacrament of reconciliation and renewal," in *Studia Liturgica* 11 (1976), 1-18, or chapter IV above.

29. See my chapter "The ecclesiological significance of interchurch marriage," in M. Hurley (ed.), *Beyond Tolerance* (1975), pp. 104-109.

30. In connection with eucharistic sharing J. C. Hoekendijk powerfully argued that Christians are *always* in an emergency situation; the "urgent" is the "normal" for the Christian. See the chapter "Safety last" in his *The Church Inside Out* (1967), pp. 148-66.

31. The theme of "qualitative catholicity" has been much developed by N. A. Nissiotis; see especially "Die qualitative Bedeutung der Katholizität," in his *Die Theologie der Ostkirche im ökumenischen Dialog* (1968), pp. 86-104.

32. N. Afanassieff, "Le sacrement de l'assemblée," in *Internationale kirchliche Zeitschrift* 46 (1956), 200-13.

33. J.-J. von Allmen, *Essai sur le repas du Seigneur* (1966), pp. 111-16, 120.

CHAPTER SIX

1. H. B. Porter, Jr., *The Ordination Prayers of the Ancient West-ern Churches* (1967). Hippolytus also gives prayers for the ordi-nation of presbyters and deacons.

2. *The Apostolic Ministry: Essays on the History and the Doc-trine of Episcopacy* (1946), prepared under the direction of Ken-neth E. Kirk, Bishop of Oxford. Other Anglican works of interest are: K. M. Carey (ed.), *The Historic Episcopate in the Fullness of the Church* (1954); A. G. Hebert, *Apostle and Bishop: A Study of the Gospel, the Ministry and the Church-community* (1963); R. C. Moberly, *Ministerial Priesthood* (repr. 1969); R. P. C. Hanson, *Christian Priesthood Examined* (1979).

3. See especially the dogmatic constitution on the Church: *Lumen Gentium* 22.

4. See P. M. Gy, "Remarques sur le vocabulaire antique du sacerdoce chrétien," in B. Botte and others, *Etudes sur le sacre-ment de l'ordre* (1957; ET *The Sacrament of Holy Orders* [1962], pp. 98-115). It is well known that the New Testament reserves the name of priest(s) for Christ and for the entire Christian people. The (temporary) need for a distinction over against Judaism is sometimes alleged as the reason for early avoidance of any sug-gestion of a "priestly class" within the Church, while later adop-tion of sacerdotal terminology may have been apologetically motivated by the desire to prove, over against paganism, that Christianity was after all a "real religion." Presidency and other functions at the eucharist will have been an important factor in the growth of priestly language around the special ministry. While sacrificial dimensions inevitably attach to the eucharist as the memorial of Christ's death (and note also, historically, the anti-gnostic insistence in Irenaeus on offering the good gifts of creation), it will be remembered that St. Paul chose to use liturgical and priestly vocabulary in connection with evangelism and ethics rather than with the cult. Theologically, of course, evangelism, ethics, and cult can be shown to comprise a single whole, but differences in emphasis remain significant ecumenically. (On eucharistic presidency, see H. M. Legrand, "La présidence de l'eucharistie selon la tradition ancienne," in *Spiritus* 69 [1977], 409-31 [ET in *Worship* 53 (1979), 413-38]; and A. E. Harvey, *Priest or President?* [1975].)

5. "Quapropter infirmitati quoque nostrae, domine, quaesu-mus, haec adiumenta largire, qui quanto magis fragiliores sumus, tanto his pluribus indigemus. Da, quaesumus, pater, in hos fa-mulos tuos presbyterii dignitatem. Innova in visceribus eorum spiritum sanctitatis. Acceptum a te, deus, secundi meriti munus obtineant, censuramque morum exemplo suae conversationis in-sinuent. Sint probi cooperatores ordinis nostri. . . ." Text from H. B. Porter (as in note 1), pp. 26-29.

6. The particular text I have in mind in Jerome is his letter to

Evangelus (*Epistle* 146 [*PL* 22, 1192-95]), where he assimilates the presbyter to the bishop in order to distinguish him from the deacon. It is, however, well known that Jerome defended the presbyter not only on the diaconal front but also on the episcopal; see, for instance, T. G. Jalland in K. E. Kirk (ed.), *The Apostolic Ministry* (as in note 2), pp. 325-30.

7. So W. Telfer, "The episcopal succession in Egypt," in *Journal of Ecclesiastical History* 3 (1952), 1-13. Telfer is also the author of *The Office of a Bishop* (1962). For a general critique of Telfer on the practice in Alexandria, see J. Lécuyer, "Le problème des consécrations épiscopales dans l'église d'Alexandrie," in *Bulletin de littérature ecclésiastique* 65 (1964), 241-57, and "La succession des évêques d'Alexandrie aux premiers siècles," ibid., 70 (1969), 80-99.

8. G. Dix's interpretation of the particular phrase *hetérōn ellogímōn andrōn* is eccentric; see *The Apostolic Ministry* (as in note 2), pp. 253-66. In general, and rather more convincingly, Dix was espousing a view rejected by J. B. Lightfoot in his classic dissertation, "The Christian Ministry": "If bishop was at first used as a synonym for presbyter and afterwards came to designate the higher officer under whom the presbyters served, the episcopate properly so called would seem to have been developed from the subordinate office. In other words, the episcopate was formed not out of the apostolic order by localisation but out of the presbyteral by elevation: and the title, which was originally common to all, came at length to be appropriated to the chief among them" (*Saint Paul's Epistle to the Philippians* [7th ed. 1883], p. 196). Historically, *both* processes may have contributed to the formation of the classical episcopate, as Dix argues (pp. 266-74).

9. The recovery of the strictly "episcopal" strand in the tradition at Vatican II was facilitated by the work of such theologians as Rahner, Ratzinger, and Congar; but the book of D. N. Power, *Ministers of Christ and his Church: The Theology of the Priesthood* (1969), marks something of a "presbyteral" reaction. For the liturgical history Power is indebted, as all must be, to B. Kleinheyer, *Die Priesterweihe im römischen Ritus: eine liturgiehistorische Studie* (1962).

10. Thus Leo I attributes the *dignitas officii sacerdotalis* not only to bishops but also to presbyters and even to deacons (*Epistle* 6, 6 [*PL* 54, 620]).

11. See M. Andrieu, "La carrière ecclésiastique des papes et les documents liturgiques du moyen âge," in *Revue des sciences religieuses* 21 (1947), 90-120.

12. The key passage in the 1974 statement is as follows: "As a perpetual reminder of this calling [of the whole people of God to be the body of Christ] and as a means of being obedient to it, the Church sets apart men and women, specially called, in ordination. In their office the calling of the whole Church is focused

and represented, and it is their responsibility as representative persons to lead the people to share with them in that calling. In this sense they are the sign of the presence and ministry of Christ in the Church, and through the Church to the world." Historical and theological studies of ordination and ministry within Methodism are these: J. L. Nuelsen, *Die Ordination im Methodismus: ein Beitrag zur Entstehungsgeschichte der kirchlichen Selbständigkeit der Methodistenkirche* (1935); E. W. Thompson, *Wesley, Apostolic Man: Some Reflections on Wesley's Consecration of Dr. Thomas Coke* (1957); A. B. Lawson, *John Wesley and the Christian Ministry* (1963); J. Stacey, *About the Ministry* (1967); J. C. Bowmer, *Pastor and People: a study of Church and ministry in Wesleyan Methodism from the death of John Wesley (1791) to the death of Jabez Bunting (1858)* (1975); A. R. George, "Ordination," in R. E. Davies, A. R. George, and E. G. Rupp (eds.), *A History of the Methodist Church in Great Britain*, II (1978), 143-60. American Methodism is episcopally ordered but with no claim to the "historic succession" in a "catholic" sense; see G. F. Moede, *The Office of Bishop in Methodism: its history and development* (1965).

13. *One Baptism, One Eucharist, and A Mutually Recognized Ministry* (Faith and Order Paper No. 73) (1975).

14. Compare Numbers 11:29.

15. Implicit here, purpose, plan, or design *(boulé)* becomes explicit in the model eucharistic prayer provided by Hippolytus for the new bishop.

16. As we shall see, it is "gentleness and a pure heart" which "smell sweetly," an odor agreeable to God.

17. B. Cooke makes clear the importance of one's view of Providence in this connection: "To ask the question 'What is *de iure divino?*' in the sense of 'What did God himself will the church to be?' seems to be based on the notion of a conceptualized divine decree. What seems more acceptable theologically than this divine 'prevision' and predetermination of the church's history is a view that sees God working through the secondary casuality of human history, with the incarnate Word working *ab intra* in this history as the risen Christ, and the Christian community responding in freedom to the transforming presence of God in the risen Christ and his Spirit. In other words, the view one has of 'Providence' seems quite clearly to control the view one has of notions such as 'divine institution,' *'de iure divino'* " (*Ministry to Word and Sacraments* [1976], p. 51).

18. The "translation" offered by the Roman Catholic ICEL (International Commission on English in the Liturgy) is: "By your gracious word you have established the plan of your Church." The prayer in the American *Book of Common Prayer* "omits" the phrase altogether.

19. H. B. Porter (as in note 1), pp. 19, 25-27, 33. The Latin runs respectively: "Deus honorum omnium, deus omnium dignitatum

quae gloriae tuae sacratis famulantur ordinibus ..." (p. 18); "Domine sancte pater omnipotens aeterne deus, honorum omnium et omnium dignitatum quae tibi militant distributor, per quem proficiunt universa, per quem cuncta firmantur, amplificatis semper in melius naturae rationabilis incrementis per ordinem congrua ratione dispositum ..." (p. 24); "Adesto, quaesumus, omnipotens deus, honorum dator, ordinum distributor, officiorumque dispositor; qui in te manens innovas omnia, et cuncta disponis per verbum, virtutem sapientiamque tuam Jesum Christum filium tuum dominum nostrum, sempiterna providentia praeparas et singulis quibusque temporibus aptanda dispensas ..." (p. 32). Notice also two Eastern prayers quoted by P. M. Gy, "La théologie des prières anciennes pour l'ordination des évêques et des prêtres," in *Revue des sciences philosophiques et théologiques* 58 (1974), 599-617. First, the Byzantine prayer for the ordination of a bishop, from the Barberini euchologion: "Sovereign Lord, our God, who by thine illustrious apostle Paul hast established the hierarchy *(táxin)* of degrees and orders *(báthmōn kaí tagmátōn)* for the service of thy venerable and pure mysteries at thy holy altar—first apostles, then prophets, then teachers. ..." Then a Palestinian prayer at the ordination of a presbyter: "Thou, Master, art worshipped by the heavenly powers, thousands and thousands worship thee. Thou hast established the liturgy on earth by giving presbyters to thy people. ..."

20. For Augustine and pseudo-Denys, see B. Cooke (as in note 17), pp. 77, 97, 99, 265, 557, 577. For the general idea, see A. O. Lovejoy, *The Great Chain of Being* (1936).

21. See P. M. Gy (as in note 4); and P. van Beneden, *Aux origines d'une terminologie sacramentelle: "ordo", "ordinare", "ordinatio" dans la littérature chrétienne avant 313* (1974).

22. P. M. Gy (as in note 4), p. 104, shows that the expression *ordo laicalis* was common from the Carolingian era until the end of scholasticism, and that the terminology of *ordo laicorum* was reinstated by Pope Pius XII.

23. In the deutero-Paulines, the body image is of course used differently: *Christ* is the *Head* (Col. 1:18; 2:19; Eph. 1:22f.; 4:15f.; 5:23).

24. On the associated vocabulary, see G. Dix, in *The Apostolic Ministry* (as in note 2), pp. 284f.; P. Gy (as in note 4), pp. 100f.; D. N. Power (as in note 9), pp. 61-67.

25. For the christological titles and functions, see O. Cullmann, *Die Christologie des Neuen Testaments* (1957; ET *The Christology of the New Testament* [1959]).

26. *Dominus/Deus regnavit a ligno* is an old reading of Psalm 95(96):10, found as early as Justin (*Dialogue with Trypho* 73) and Tertullian (*Against Marcion* 3, 19). It was inevitably exploited christologically.

27. Thomas Aquinas, *Summa theologiae* III, 63, 3.

28. The shepherd motif is found in Gallican and English texts (Porter, pp. 42f., 74f.), and with explicitly self-sacrificial resonances in the Barberini euchologion: "Do thou, Lord, make him who has been established as a steward of high-priestly grace to be thine imitator, of thee the true Shepherd, giving his life for thy sheep . . ." (quoted by Gy, as in note 19).

29. Augustine, *Tractatus in Ioannis Evangelium* 6, 7 (*PL* 35, 1428).

30. John Chrysostom, *Second Baptismal Instruction* 26.

31. See B. Cooke (as in note 17), p. 560.

32. Constitution on the Sacred Liturgy 7. The formulations might be rather different in other confessions, but the main point remains ecumenically acceptable.

33. R. E. Reynolds, *The Ordinals of Christ from their origins to the twelfth century* (1978).

34. *Akoloutheō* is to follow.

35. See the previous discussion of the relationship between the two. Reynolds even suggests that the emergence of the acolyte, combined with the desire to maintain a septenary of orders, may have been responsible for the loss of distinction in order between presbyter and bishop (as in note 33), pp. 162f. I think it unlikely that such a small consideration should have played any significant part in such a weighty theological matter. Contrariwise, the general loss of distinction in order between presbyter and bishop may conveniently have left room for the acolyte to find a place among the seven orders.

36. See, more generally, J. Lécuyer, "The mystery of Pentecost and the apostolic mission of the Church," in B. Botte and others, *The Sacrament of Holy Orders* (as in note 4), pp. 131-62.

37. Isidore of Seville, *De ecclesiasticis officiis* 2, 5, 8 (*PL* 83, 782). Note also Jerome, *Adversus Jovinianum* 1, 34 (*PL* 23, 270): "Episcopus et presbyter et diaconus non sunt meritorum nomina, sed officiorum." And in the ordination prayer for a bishop in the Leofric Missal: "Sacerdotium ipsum opus esse existimet non dignitatem" (Porter, p. 76).

38. Note Mark 10:45: "The Son of Man came not to be ministered unto but to minister. . . ."

39. See earlier, note 28.

40. The phrase *cui servire regnare est* occurs in the prayer *Deus auctor pacis et amator*, found in the Gelasian and Gregorian sacramentaries.

41. P. M. Gy, as in note 19; also B. Botte, "Holy orders in the ordination prayers," in B. Botte and others, *The Sacrament of Holy Orders* (as in note 4), pp. 5-23.

42. The combination of Pauline and charismatic interests is found in J. D. G. Dunn's carefully nuanced study, *Jesus and the Spirit* (1975), pp. 199-300.

43. D. L. Gelpi, *Charism and Sacrament* (1976).

44. The French would allow a word-play between *discerner* and *décerner*.

45. The allusion is to the story of Matthias' appointment to the apostolic college (Acts 1:23-26). The point of the lottery is to entrust the choice to God. How else might the divine choice be indicated? It has been suggested that that designation may have been by inspired prophetic utterance (see 1 Tim. 1:18; 4:14). Later on, we know of a popular role in the election of bishops (see below, note 73). It is not clear who named elders or deacons. Our concluding discussion will show how important is the means of choice for the whole question of ministerial authority.

46. See B. Cooke (as in note 17), pp. 78, 85, 255f., 430. Notice the Gallican prayers at the ordination of bishops: "May their feet, by thine aid, be beautiful for bringing good tidings of peace, for bringing thy good tidings of good. Give them, O Lord, a ministry of reconciliation in word and in deeds and in power of signs and of wonders. Let their speech and preaching be not with enticing words of man's wisdom, but in demonstration of the Spirit and of power" (Porter, pp. 44f.).

47. A. T. Hanson, *The Pioneer Ministry* (1961). The author's "missionary" experience in South India is important.

48. See P. M. Gy, as in notes 4 and 19.

49. Anglican/Roman Catholic International Commission, *Authority in the Church* ("Venice 1976"), 6.

50. As one English liturgist put it: Apostolic succession is not so much a matter of hands on heads as of arses on seats. The ceremonial enthronement of the new bishop is at least as old as the fourth century; there is indirect evidence in Eusebius, *Historia Ecclesiastica* 6, 29, 3f., and direct evidence in *Canons of Hippolytus* (ed. Coquin, p. 354). Special seating for the bishop and presbyters in the regular assembly is known from Tertullian, *De exhortatione castitatis* 7 (*PL* 1, 922), and from Origen, *Comm. in Matt.* XVI, 22 on Matthew 21:12f. (ed. Klostermann, pp. 552f.). The episcopal chair became less that of the teacher and more that of the judge ("the power of the keys"). A special study is E. Stommel, "Die bischöfliche Kathedra im christlichen Altertum," in *Münchener Theologische Zeitschrift* 3 (1952), 17-32.

51. See studies in C. Vogel, *Ordinations inconsistantes et caractère inamissible* (1978).

52. See the WCC study *In Each Place: Towards a Fellowship of Local Churches Truly United* (1977).

53. M. McLuhan, *Understanding Media* (1964), chap. 10.

54. See B. Botte, "Imitatio," in *Archivum Latinitatis Medii Aevi* 16 (1942), 148-54. Since Vatican II the text reads: "Your ministry will perfect the spiritual sacrifice of the faithful by uniting it to Christ's sacrifice, the sacrifice which is offered sacramentally through your hands. Know what you are doing and imitate the mystery you celebrate. In the memorial of the Lord's death and

resurrection, make every effort to die to sin and to walk in the new life of Christ" (ICEL translation).

55. "Concede, quaesumus omnipotens Deus: ut paschalis perceptio sacramenti, continua in nostris mentibus perseveret" (postcommunion of Easter Tuesday); "Praesta . . . ut qui paschalia festa peregimus, haec, te largiente, moribus et vita teneamus" (collect of Sunday after Easter); "Da mentibus nostris, ut quod professione celebramus, imitemur effectu" (collect of Easter Friday). These are given in the wording and distribution found in the missal of Pius V; the material is redistributed in the missal of Paul VI.

56. Ignatius, *Letter to the Smyrnaeans* 8 (where it is also written: "Without the bishop, it is not permitted to baptize or to hold a lovefeast").

57. See B. Botte, "Collegiate character of the presbyterate and episcopate," in B. Botte and others, *The Sacrament of Holy Orders* (as in note 4), pp. 75-97.

58. Anglican/Roman Catholic International Commission, *Ministry and Ordination* ("Canterbury 1973"), 16.

59. See earlier, note 13.

60. This unofficial francophone ecumenical group published the text of *The Episcopal Ministry* in 1976 (ET in *One in Christ* 14 [1978], 267-88). Paragraphs 53-55 give the following "profile" of the *epískopos:* "The *episcopos* is, then, a man who animates the life of the people of God, who watches over the birth and harmonious development of the different communities, and who makes possible the full expansion of the spiritual gifts which are given to every baptized Christian. The *episcopos* is a man who ensures that all the ministries grow together towards Christ, and apart from whom these ministries run the risk of scattering the Church instead of gathering her together and building her up in unity and peace. The *episcopos* is a man with the task of helping to preserve the Church's identity between Pentecost and the Parousia, and this makes of him a constitutive element of the Church's tradition."

61. After Vatican II, the joke was that to Vatican III the bishops would be bringing their wives, and that to Vatican IV the bishops *(episcopae?)* would be bringing their husbands. I wonder who will assume the active presidency of Vatican V.

62. M. Werner, *Die Entstehung des christlichen Dogmas* (1941).

63. Consider the "vigilance parables" in the synoptic Gospels; also Romans 13:11-14 and 1 Peter 5:8f.

64. Compare Ezekiel 3:16-21; 33:1-20.

65. The two Byzantine prayers are given by Gy, as in note 19.

66. H. B. Porter (as in note 1), pp. 28f., 68f.

67. The terminological discussion around the use of *cheirotonía* and *cheirothesía* in the early Church is not our immediate concern; see, for instance, C. Vogel, as in note 51. But the connection of *cheirotonía* with *voting* is interesting.

68. M. Thurian, *Sacerdoce et ministère: recherche oecumé-nique* (1970), pp. 223-40.

69. See, for instance, G. W. H. Lampe, *Some Aspects of the New Testament Ministry* (1949); R. E. Brown, *Priest and Bishop: Biblical Reflections* (1970); R. P. C. Hanson, *Groundwork for Unity: Plain Facts about Christian Ministry* (1971), and *Christian Priesthood Examined* (as in note 2); A. Lemaire, *Les ministères aux origines de l'Eglise, naissance de la triple hiérarchie: évêques, presbytres, diacres* (1971), and *Les ministères dans l'Eglise* (1974; ET *Ministry in the Church* [1977]).

70. See, for instance, R. E. Brown, K. P. Donfried, and J. Reumann (eds.), *Peter in the New Testament* (1973).

71. P. van Beneden (as in note 21) has shown that in the earliest Christian use, following secular Roman usage, *ordinare* and *ordinatio* meant nomination or designation to office. Their use for the imposition of hands as the sacrament of entry upon the office came later. See also C. Vogel, as in note 51.

72. In the ancient rites, the general movement of thought is that God has chosen the candidates for ordination and that "we" (the presiding bishop? the congregation? the Church?) are now presenting them to God for his blessing; see D. N. Power (as in note 9), pp. 60f., and, with nuances, P. M. Gy (as in note 19), p. 607. It is a recurrent idea that *God's* hand ordains. Thus John Chrysostom: "The man's hand is imposed, but God does all. In fact it is his hand which touches the head of the one being ordained when he is rightly ordained" (*Homilies on Acts* 14, 3 [*PG* 60, 116]). The Gallican ordination of a presbyter: "Author of all sanctification, of whom is true consecration, full benediction: do thou, O Lord, spread forth the hand of thy blessing upon this thy servant, N., whom we set apart with the honour of the presbyterate; so that he may show himself to be an elder by the dignity of his acts and the righteousness of his life . . ." (Porter, pp. 50-53). And the Leofric missal, at the ordination of a bishop: "Though the hand be ours, let thy blessing be upon him" (Porter, pp. 74f.).

73. B. Cooke writes (as in note 17): "During the fourth and fifth centuries the voice of the local community was truly determinative, though not self-sufficiently so, in the selection of their bishop. There are occasions of a choice by acclamation, in which the entire people participated; such was, of course, the situation with Ambrose. Appraently, however, the more common pattern was to have representatives of the church, both clergy and laity, carry on the actual process of choosing. Even in instances where the incumbent bishop wishes to groom a successor and have him become the next bishop, he wisely submitted him to the people in advance for their approval, as did Augustine" (pp. 429f.).

74. This was already the practice according to Hippolytus, *The Apostolic Tradition.*

75. See B. Botte (as in note 41), in particular pp. 10f., 14, 24f.

The ceremony is found at the turn of the fourth and fifth centuries in *Apostolic Constitutions* VIII, 4, 5, and amusingly in the dialogue of Palladius on John Chrysostom: because of the election of an unworthy bishop at Ephesus, the gospel-book had rested on shoulders which had carried chorus girls around the room at drinking parties (*PG* 47, 52f.). In the West, the imposition of the Gospels is found in the late fifth-century *Statuta Ecclesiae Antiqua* (see B. Botte, "Le rituel d'ordination des Statuta Ecclesiae antiqua," in *Recherches de théologie ancienne et médiévale* 11 [1939], 223-41), in the Gelasian sacramentary, and on into the pontificals.

76. Note also the Orthodox theologian N. Afanassieff, "Le sacrement de l'assemblée," in *Internationale kirchliche Zeitschrift* 46 (1956), 200-13.

77. B. Minchin, *Every Man in his Ministry* (1960); A. Triacca (ed.), *L'assemblée liturgique et les différents rôles dans l'assemblée* (1977; ET *Roles in the Liturgical Assembly* [1982]).

78. The picture of a eucharist concelebrated by the presbyters under the presidency of the bishop dates back to Hippolytus and *The Apostolic Tradition.* Can the fathers of Vatican II be accused of archeologism? The preponderant practice, ever since the division of the diocese into parishes, has been for presbyters to preside at the mass. We face again the problem of the mismatch between the theological/sacramental and the practical/sociological structures.

79. The quotation is from an ordination address by Archbishop Lefebvre on July 29, 1976. ET from Y. Congar, *Challenge to the Church: the case of Archbishop Lefebvre* (1977), pp. 29f. (original: *La crise dans l'Eglise et Mgr Lefebvre* [1976]).

80. Y. Congar, *Challenge to the Church,* pp. 30f. Congar himself has shown how strong the Tradition is—when it was not being anti-Protestant—on the exercise by the faithful of their baptismal priesthood: "L'"ecclesia' ou communauté chrétienne, sujet intégral de l'action liturgique," in J. P. Jossua and Y. Congar (eds.), *La liturgie après Vatican II* (1967), pp. 241-82.

81. N. Lash, *Voices of Authority* (1976), pp. 43-54.

CHAPTER SEVEN

1. Marcel Proust, *A la recherche du temps perdu* (1913-27).

2. T. F. Torrance, *Space, Time and Incarnation* (1969).

3. David Jones, *Epoch and Artist* (1959).

4. John and Charles Wesley, *Hymns on the Lord's Supper*, no. 72 (*Methodist Hymn Book*, no. 767).

5. O. Cullmann, "La signification de la sainte cène dans le christianisme primitif," in *Revue d'Histoire et de Philosophie religieuses* 16 (1936), pp. 1-22 (ET in O. Cullmann and F. J. Leenhardt, *Essays on the Lord's Supper* [1958]).

6. In the restricted sense, the *anamnesis* is that part of the

anaphora or great eucharistic prayer which picks up the theme of remembrance immediately after the institution narrative. See W. J. Grisbrooke, "Anaphora," in J. G. Davies (ed.), *A Dictionary of Liturgy and Worship* (1972), pp. 10-17.

7. J. Jeremias, *Die Abendmahlsworte Jesu* (3rd ed. 1960; ET *The Eucharistic Words of Jesus* [1966]).

8. In Hebrew, *zkr* is the memory root.

9. O. Casel, *Das christliche Kultmysterium* (4th ed. 1960; ET *The Mystery of Christian Worship* [1962]).

10. John and Charles Wesley, *Hymns on the Lord's Supper*, no. 93.

11. J.-J. von Allmen, *Prophétisme sacramentel* (1964).

12. John and Charles Wesley, *Hymns on the Lord's Supper*, no. 81 (*Methodist Hymn Book*, no. 761).

13. A "cult-legend" would make the institution narrative an invention of the primitive Church to account for its own liturgical practice.

14. L. Dussaut, *L'eucharistie, pâques de toute la vie* (1972).

15. Thomas Aquinas, *Commentary on 1 Corinthians*.

16. B. Hebblethwaite, in *Heythrop Journal* (Jan. 1979).

17. *Hymns on the Lord's Supper*, no. 16 (*Methodist Hymn Book*, no. 765).

18. O. Clément, *Transfigurer le temps* (1959).

19. F. W. Dillistone, *Christianity and Symbolism* (1955).

20. G. Bornkamm, "Herrenmahl und Kirche bei Paulus," in *Zeitschrift für Theologie und Kirche* 53 (1956), 312-49; C. F. D. Moule, "The judgment theme in the sacraments," in W. D. Davies and D. Daube (eds.), *The Background of the New Testament and its Eschatology* (1956), pp. 464-81.

21. E. Jüngel, *Gott als Geheimnis der Welt* (1977; ET *God as the Mystery of the World* [1983]).

22. R. Guardini, *Vom Geist der Liturgie* (1918; ET *The Spirit of the Liturgy* [1930]).

23. E. Jüngel, *Tod* (1971; ET *Death* [1975]).

24. See J. A. Jungmann, *Die Stellung Christi im liturgischen Gebet* (2nd ed. 1962, pp. 234-38; ET *The Place of Christ in Liturgical Prayer* [1965]).

25. *Hymns on the Lord's Supper*, no. 108.

26. For the "cathedral offices" as distinguished from the "monastic offices," see C. Jones, G. Wainwright, and E. Yarnold (eds.), *The Study of Liturgy* (1978), pp. 358-69.

27. G. Dix, *The Shape of the Liturgy* (1945), XI.

28. Justin Martyr, *Dialogue with Trypho* 138.

29. So Pseudo-Athanasius, *De sabbatis et circumcisione* (*PG* 28, 137f.).

30. *Epistle of Barnabas* 15.

31. Ignatius of Antioch, *Letter to the Ephesians* 20.

32. For Theodore and Schamus, see my *Eucharist and Escha-*

tology (1971; expanded ed. 1981), p. 113; and for Schillebeeckx, his *Christ the Sacrament of Encounter with God* (1963).

33. E. Käsemann, "Gottesdienst im Alltag der Welt," in his *Exegetische Versuche und Besinnungen*, II (1964), 198-204 (ET in *New Testament Questions of Today* [1969]).

34. K. Barth, *Christengemeinde und Bürgergemeinde* (1946; ET in *Against the Stream* [1954]).

35. W. Pannenberg, *Die Bestimmung des Menschen* (1978; ET *Human Nature, Election, and History* [1977]).

36. E. R. Norman, *Christianity and the World Order* (1979).

37. In the Biblical Theology movement, *chrónos* was taken as mere "clock-time," while *kairós* was "significant time." The same movement discerned, and probably overplayed, a distinction between "cyclical time," said to be characteristic of pagan religion, and "linear time," which was typical of the Bible.

38. O. Cullmann, *Christus und die Zeit* (1946; ET *Christ and Time* [1950]).

39. John and Charles Wesley, *Hymns on the Lord's Supper*, no. 93.

40. G. Wainwright, *Eucharist and Eschatology*, p. 147.

41. G. Wainwright, *Doxology* (1980).

CHAPTER EIGHT

1. For more detailed treatment of some of these questions, see my *Doxology* (1980), especially chaps. 11 and 12. Note the still classic work of A. G. Hebert, *Liturgy and Society* (1935). Further: K. Barth, *Church Dogmatics* IV/2 (original 1955; ET 1958), pp. 695-824 (ET pp. 614-726: "The Holy Spirit and the upbuilding of the Christian community"); B. Wicker, *Culture and Liturgy* (1963); J.-J. von Allmen, *Worship: its theology and practice* (1965), especially chaps. 1-5; A. Schmemann, *The World as Sacrament* (1966); J. G. Davies, *Worship and Mission* (1966).

2. N. A. Nissiotis, "Worship, eucharist and 'intercommunion': an Orthodox reflection," in *Studia Liturgica* 2 (1963), 193-222, in particular p. 201.

3. E. Jüngel, "Die Autorität des bittenden Christus," in *Unterwegs zur Sache* (1972), pp. 187f.

4. G. Gutiérrez, *A Theology of Liberation* (ET 1973), p. 137, see also pp. 262-65.

5. C. K. Barrett, *A Commentary on the Epistle to the Romans* (1957), pp. 23f.

6. L. Newbigin, *The Open Secret: Sketches for a Missionary Theology* (1978).

7. For nuances, see my *Eucharist and Eschatology* (1971; expanded ed. 1981), pp. 128-35.

8. J. H. Hick, *God and the Universe of Faiths* (1973).

9. H. Richard Niebuhr, *Christ and Culture* (1951). Serious reflection on our question is found in the Grove booklet by P. R.

Akehurst and R. W. F. Wootton, *Inter-faith Worship?* (1977). See also Bryan Spinks, "The Anaphora for India: Some Theological Objections to an attempt at Inculturation," in *Ephemerides Liturgicae* 95 (1981), 529-49.

10. E. Jüngel, "Erwägungen zur Grundlegung evangelischer Ethik," in *Unterwegs zur Sache* (see note 3), especially pp. 244f. Jüngel says that "to be condemned to pass away is thus in truth to be set free to become." It is from the Yes which God said to the world in Christ that the light of promise falls on every honorable yes which the world says to itself in love, peace, compassion, freedom, and justice.

11. For a full study, see G. P. Wiles, *Paul's Intercessory Prayers* (1974). Wiles summarizes thus: "Signs are present throughout the letters that Paul believed himself appointed a mediator between God and the churches in his care, charged with the priestly responsibility of presenting them blameless to God at the parousia. The indications are sufficiently clear and frequent to reveal a deep intercessory sense lying behind all his preaching, teaching, prophesying, and urgency. While such mediation was clearly only one aspect of his complex apostolate, yet it seemed to lie near the heart of his self-understanding, a basic consequence of the intercessory act of God in Christ, an extension of the intercessory ministry of the exalted Christ (Romans 8.34), and of the indwelling Spirit (Romans 8.15f, 23, 26f; Galatians 4.6)."

12. K. P. Nickle, *The Collection* (1966).

13. See (and use) *For all God's people* (1978). The theological background is supplied in L. Vischer, *Intercession* (1980 = Faith and Order Paper No. 95).

14. Plenty of examples can be found in P. de Clerck, *La "prière universelle" dans les liturgies latines anciennes* (1977).

15. In chapter 32 of his *Apology*, Tertullian says that it is Christian prayer for the emperor which holds back the final castastrophe. It became a commonplace to equate the continuance of the Roman empire—identified with the last of the kingdoms in Daniel 2:36ff.—with the continuance of the world. In *Christ and Time* (ET 1951), pp. 164-66, O. Cullmann cites Theodore of Mopsuestia, Theodoret, and Calvin for the view that the "restraining agents" in 2 Thessalonians 2:6f. are the Christian missionary preaching and preacher (see Matt. 24:14: "And this gospel of the kingdom will be preached throughout the whole world, as a testimony to all nations; and then the end will come").

16. On this passage, see E. Käsemann, *Perspectives on Paul* (ET 1971), pp. 122-37. Käsemann suggests that Paul was critically reinterpreting glossolalic prayer by letting it be, like the other groanings, a mark of the "not yet."

17. E. Käsemann, for instance, shows great ethical sensitivity in his essay on "divine service in the everyday world" yet cannot abide what he pejoratively calls "the cult"; see his exegesis of

Romans 12:1f. in *New Testament Questions of Today* (ET 1969), pp. 188-95.

CHAPTER NINE

1. Among the vast and growing literature, the following writings proved useful in various ways: K. Barth, *Christengemeinde und Bürgergemeinde* (1946; ET in *Against the Stream* [1954]); S. G. F. Brandon, *Jesus and the Zealots* (1967); British Council of Churches and Conference of British Missionary Societies working party, *Violence in Southern Africa: a Christian assessment* (1970); J. Comblin, *Théologie de la révolution* (1970); O. Cullmann, *The State in the New Testament* (1957) and *Jesus und die Revolutionären seiner Zeit* (1970; ET *Jesus and the Revolutionaries* [1970]); G. R. Edwards, *Jesus and the Politics of Violence* (1972); J. Ellul, *Violence* (1970); J. Ferguson, *The Politics of Love: The New Testament and Non-Violent Revolution* (n.d.); G. Gutiérrez, *Teología de la liberación* (1971; ET *A Theology of Liberation* [1973]); A. Hastings, "The moral choice of violent revolution," in *Mission and Ministry* (1971), pp. 59-68; A. Kee (ed.), *A Reader in Political Theology* (1974); P. Lehmann, *The Transfiguration of Politics* (1975); G. Lewy, *Religion and Revolution* (1974); J. M. Lochman, "Ecumenical Theology of Revolution," in *Scottish Journal of Theology* 21 (1968), 170-86; E. McDonagh, "Human violence: a question of ethics or salvation," in *Gift and Call* (1975), pp. 138-66; J. Moltmann, *Theologie der Hoffnung* (1964; ET *Theology of Hope* [1967]), *Religion, Revolution and the Future* (1969), and *Der gekreuzigte Gott* (1972; ET *The Crucified God* [1974]); G. Müller-Fahrenholz, *Heilsgeschichte zwischen Ideologie und Prophetie* (1974); A. Richardson, *The Political Christ* (1973); R. Shaull, "Revolutionary Change in Theological Perspective," in J. C. Bennett (ed.), *Christian Social Ethics in a Changing World* (1966), pp. 23-43; Camilo Torres, *Revolutionary Priest* (1971); J. Yoder, *The Politics of Jesus* (1972). A review of theories of revolution by a secular historian can be found in the first chapter of L. Stone, *The Causes of the English Revolution 1529-1642* (1972). Since the time of first writing, the literature has widened but not necessarily deepened.

2. See G. Gutiérrez, "Liberation Movements and Theology," in *Concilium* (March 1974), pp. 135-46; and the 1974/2 number of *Études théologiques et religieuses* (Montpellier), under the title "Recherches de théologie politique"—but also the important critique by V. Subilia in *Protestantesimo* 29 (1974), 93-100.

3. The *lex talionis* is intended to *limit* retaliation.

4. In his fine book *Krummes Holz—aufrechter Gang* (1970), H. Gollwitzer has argued that humanity's search for meaning in life cannot finally be satisfied unless there is hope in a permanent and social context on the other side of death. Leaving aside all speculation on an "intermediate state" between the individual's death and the universal consummation, we may say that the Chris-

tian notion of a definitive kingdom of God provides just such a context, both social and lasting. Believers will of course expect skeptics to charge them with "wishful thinking."

5. For Catholics the distinction is softened by (a) the theological principle that grace does not abolish but rather perfects "nature" and (b) the historical claims which spiritual rulers made over the temporal rulers. The Calvinist tendency to theocracy also softens the distinction.

6. See especially *Von weltlicher Obrigkeit* (1523).

7. See, for example, H. Schmid, *Zwinglis Lehre von der göttlichen und menschlichen Gerechtigkeit* (1959).

8. I am of course speaking only of the "probabilities" of a Christian's political alignment: Professor Norman Young reminds me that it is "possible to argue from a very sharp distinction between preservation and salvation and from a *pessimistic* view of the possibility of defeating sin to an advocacy of revolutionary activity on 'realistic' grounds, not in order to 'bring in the kingdom' but to bring about a social structure in which more rights of more people are preserved until God fulfils his purpose."

9. The Reformers looked for the "godly prince" to reform the *Church*, not to perform a "salvific" duty in the *State*.

10. See my article "Autour de la notion de civilisation chrétienne," in *Revue de Théologie et de Philosophie* 22 (1972), 413-30.

11. "If the Incarnation has a meaning it can only be that God came into the most abominable of places (and he did not, by his coming, either validate or change that place). The 'Lordship of Jesus Christ' does not mean that everything that happens, happens by the decision of the Lord" (p. 25).

12. Especially pp. 43-47.

13. See, briefly, S. Neill, *Men of Unity* (1960), pp. 35f.

14. More deeply, the German Reformed theologian J. Moltmann, in *The Crucified God*, shows how the Roman crucifixion of Jesus becomes—in a *theologia crucis*—the permanent *krisis* of any sacral and authoritarian State.

15. At an earlier date, see R. Eisler, *The Messiah Jesus and John the Baptist* (1931).

16. O. Cullmann, *The State in the New Testament* (1957), pp. 14-17.

17. For a discussion, see E. Trocmé, *Jésus de Nazareth vu par les témoins de sa vie* (1971), pp. 125-36. Trocmé rejects the "zealot" interpretation of an incident to which he himself nevertheless attaches considerable importance.

18. Luke 22:35-38 is difficult; but there are many reasons for taking the present text as a Lucan construction, perhaps based on an original metaphor. See the commentaries of J. M. Creed and G. B. Caird, ad loc., and A. Richardson, *The Political Christ* (1973), p. 48.

19. Psalms of Solomon 17:23-27: "Behold, O Lord, and raise

up their King, the son of David, at the time thou hast appointed, O God, to reign over Israel thy servant. Gird him with strength to shatter wicked rulers. Cleanse Jerusalem from the Gentiles who trample it and destroy. In wisdom, in justice, may he thrust out sinners from God's heritage, crush the arrogance of the sinner like a potter's crocks, crush his whole substance with an iron mace, blot out the lawless Gentiles with a word, put the Gentiles to flight with his threats."

20. *De corona militis* 11; see also *De idolatria* 19: "How shall the Christian wage war, no, how shall he even be a soldier in peacetime, without the sword which the Lord has taken away?" At the end of the third century, some Christians suffered martyrdom for contracting out of the army; one of them, Maximilian, made the famous declaration, "I cannot serve as a soldier; I cannot do evil; I am a Christian." The *Apostolic Tradition* stipulates: "if a catechumen or one of the faithful wishes to become a soldier (i.e. a volunteer), let him be rejected, for he has despised God." For other examples, and for some practical modifications to the principle, see J. Ferguson, *The Politics of Love*, pp. 55-67, and J. Ellul, *Violence*, pp. 10-12.

21. In *Summa Theologiae* II.ii.40.1, St. Thomas sets out three conditions of a just war: it must be declared by the competent authority; the cause must be just; the belligerents must have a right intention. From time to time, the theologians include other conditions: war must be only a last resort, after all peaceful means have been exhausted; the methods employed during the war must be just; the benefits that the war can reasonably be expected to produce must be greater than the evils brought by the war itself; there must be a good prospect of victory; the final peace must be just. For a critical discussion, see Ellul (note 20), pp. 5-9. See further now F. H. Russell, *The Just War in the Middle Ages* (1975).

22. Thomas Aquinas allows the right to resist tyrannical government, by which he means government that is directed not to the common welfare but to the private benefit of the ruler (*Summa Theologiae* II.ii.42.2).

23. Thus Adrian Hastings: "It is hard not to hold that many of the violent revolutions of history were, in christian judgment, right and proper. . . . Man cannot do other than attempt to embody the condemning judgment of God in revolutionary action just as he attempts to embody the enjoining judgment of God in his laws" (*Mission and Ministry,* pp. 56f.). Paul Lehmann considers revolutionary violence as necessary but never "justifiable": by assigning it to the category of "apocalyptic," he thinks to put it beyond the just and the unjust (*The Transfiguration of Politics*).

24. I am clearly rejecting as inadequate those views of the Sermon on the Mount which see it as an instrument to convict us of our shortcoming or as the setting up of an inspiring but impracticable ideal.

25. Adrian Hastings raises the case in which a Christian "encounters a child being beaten to death: he cannot save the child except by immediate violent intervention. I cannot see that he has other than an absolute duty so to intervene, which means that at times the christian has the duty to take part in physical violence. Here and now this, and this alone, can properly express christian faith and love" (*Mission and Ministry*, pp. 60f.). I should rather place this simple human duty within the order of preservation: in such an emergency situation of life and death, the one who intervenes on behalf of the third party is exceptionally assuming the function of the civil authority. Does such an emergency situation of life and death ever occur on the *institutional plane?* I should say that this is the only case in which "violent intervention" (which may perhaps be distinguished from violent *revolution*) may be justified.

26. A. Bloom, *Living Prayer* (1966), p. 23. On "militant" prayer for a righteous cause and against the forces of evil, see Origen, *Contra Celsum* 8, 73 (ed. H. Chadwick, p. 509).

27. For a "prophetic" understanding of "dialogue with God," see G. Müller-Fahrenholz, *Heilsgeschichte zwischen Ideologie und Prophetie* (1974), pp. 221-33.

28. Old Testament scholars agree that such prophetic passages are not a condemnation of the cultus as such, but only of a cultus that has no ethical counterpart.

29. *Revolutionary Priest: the complete writings and messages of Camilo Torres* (Pelican ed. 1973), pp. 334, 375.

30. *Scottish Journal of Theology* 21 (1968), 180.

CHAPTER TEN

1. E. Schillebeeckx, *Mary, Mother of the Redemption* (1964), pp. 149f. (ET of *Maria, Moeder van de verlossing* [1954/1963]). In what follows I have made much use of Schillebeeckx: not being a specialist mariologist but rather a systematic theologian in the broadest sense, he was less prone to exaggeration and more able to see Mary within the total pattern of Roman Catholic dogma, theology, and life.

2. His book *John Wesley in the Evolution of Protestantism* (1937) had borne the French title *John Wesley, sa réaction dans l'évolution du protestantisme* (1925).

3. ET p. 475. For a more "Lutheran" picture of Wesley, see F. Hildebrandt, *From Luther to Wesley* (1951), and (less technical) *Christianity according to the Wesleys* (1956). (H. Carter, *The Methodist Heritage* [1951], pp. 221-32, argued that if Wesley saw himself in opposition to Luther, it was on account of his too hasty reading of the Reformer's *Commentary on the Epistle to the Galatians*.) For a more "Calvinist" picture of Wesley, see G. C. Cell, *The Rediscovery of John Wesley* (1935). (The whole question of Reformation and Tridentine views of justification has been set in

a fresh light by H. Küng, *Justification: The Doctrine of Karl Barth and a Catholic Reflection* [1964]; ET of *Rechtfertigung: Die Lehre Karl Barths und eine katholische Besinnung* [1957].) Selections from John Wesley's writings, with excellent introductions and notes, may be found in A. C. Outler, *John Wesley* (1964), and in P. S. Watson, *The Message of the Wesleys* (1965). The work of the German historian M. Schmidt has now appeared in English translation in three volumes, *John Wesley: A Theological Biography* (1962, 1971, 1973). Directly theological studies of the thought of Wesley may be found in H. Bett, *The Spirit of Methodism* (1937), pp. 129-68; W. R. Cannon, *The Theology of John Wesley, with special reference to the doctrine of justification* (1946); H. Lindström, *Wesley and Sanctification: a study in the doctrine of salvation* (1946); C. W. Williams, *John Wesley's Theology Today* (1960); J. Deschner, *Wesley's Christology* (1960); R. E. Davies, in R. E. Davies and E. G. Rupp (eds.), *A History of the Methodist Church in Great Britain*, I (1965), 147-79. For the Wesleys' sacramental doctrine, see B. G. Holland, *Baptism in Early Methodism* (1970); J. C. Bowmer, *The Sacrament of the Lord's Supper in Early Methodism* (1951); J. R. Parris, *John Wesley's Doctrine of the Sacraments* (1963); O. E. Borgen, *John Wesley on the Sacraments* (1972). Hymns are particularly important in the expression and transmission of Methodist doctrine: studies may be found in J. E. Rattenbury, *The Evangelical Doctrines of Charles Wesley's Hymns* (1941) and *The Eucharistic Hymns of John and Charles Wesley* (1948).

4. This kind of charge is brought against Methodism by the Waldensian dogmatician V. Subilia in his *Tempo di confessione e di rivoluzione* (1968), pp. 147-51. Whereas Subilia regrets the loss of a Reformation "Either/Or" theology, the Methodist A. C. Outler rejoices in the "Both/And" character of Wesley's thinking: "Wesley had glimpsed the underlying unity of Christian truth in both the Catholic and Protestant traditions and had turned this recognition to the service of a great popular religious reform and renewal. In the name of a Christianity both Biblical and patristic, he managed to transcend the stark doctrinal disjunctions which had spilled so much ink and blood since Augsburg and Trent. In their stead, he proceeded to develop a theological fusion of faith and good works, Scripture and tradition, revelation and reason, God's sovereignty and human freedom, universal redemption and conditional election, Christian liberty and an ordered polity, the assurance of pardon and the risks of 'falling from grace', original sin and Christian perfection. In each of these conjunctions, as he insisted almost tediously, the initiative is with God, the response with man." To "this distinctive doctrinal perspective" Outler gives the name "evangelical catholicism" (*John Wesley*, p. viii).

5. See, for example, A. M. Lyles, *Methodism mocked: the satiric reaction to Methodism in the eighteenth century* (1960). Some *Methodist* writers have drawn comparisons with elements from

Francis of Assisi and Ignatius Loyola: for example, H. B. Workman, "The place of Methodism in the life and thought of the
Christian Church," in W. J. Townsend, H. B. Workman, and G. Eayrs
(eds.), *A New History of Methodism*, I (1909), in particular pp. 43-53.
In a sympathetic study entitled *John Wesley and the Catholic
Church* (1958), the *Roman Catholic* layman J. M. Todd drew a
sustained comparison between the spiritual experience of Wesley
and the mystical teaching of St. John of the Cross, and he emphasized the consonance (except in some aspects of ecclesiology) between Wesley's doctrines and "traditional Catholic doctrine." The
Methodist R. N. Flew contributed a chapter, "Methodism and the
Catholic tradition," to N. P. Williams and C. Harris (eds.), *Northern Catholicism* (1933), pp. 515-30.

6. Lectures by G. S. Wakefield ("The Methodist point of view")
and S. Denyer ("Magnificat") have appeared in the *Mother of Jesus*
pamphlets published by the Ecumenical Society of the Blessed
Virgin Mary. Mention will be made later of N. Ward's "consideration of the rosary," *Five for Sorrow, Ten for Joy* (1971).

7. The sermon "Catholic Spirit" is found in T. Jackson's
edition of Wesley's *Works*, V, 492ff., and in E. H. Sugden's edition
of the *Standard Sermons*, II, 126ff. The "Letter to a Roman Catholic" is found in Jackson's edition of Wesley's *Works*, X, 80ff., and
in J. Telford's edition of the *Letters*, III, 7ff.; it was reedited by
Michael Hurley in 1968.

8. Sermon "The General Spread of the Gospel," in Jackson
(ed.), *Works*, VI, 280f.

9. "Every man has a measure of free-will restored to him by
grace" (*Works*, X, 392).

10. *Works*, VI, 280.

11. *Sermo* (Denis) XXV, 7 (*PL*, 46, 937).

12. Augustine, *Sermo CCXXXIII*, 3, 4 (*PL* 38, 1114).

13. *Sermo I in Nativitate*, 1 (*PL* 54, 191).

14. *Obediens, et sibi et universo generi humano causa facta est
salutis* (*Adversus omnes haereses*, 3, 22, 4 [*PG* 7, 959]).

15. Augustine, *De virginitate* 6, 6 (*PL* 40, 399).

16. With quotation from the *Lumen Gentium* of Vatican II and
then appeal to Pius XII's *Mystici Corporis*, Paul VI's "apostolic
exhortation" of February 2, 1974 says: "This union of the Mother
and the Son in the work of redemption reaches its climax on Calvary, when Christ 'offers himself as the perfect sacrifice to God'
(Heb. 9:14) and when Mary stood by the Cross (cf. John 19:25),
'suffering grievously with her only-begotten Son. There she united
herself with a maternal heart to his sacrifice, and lovingly con-
sented to the immolation of this victim which she herself had
brought forth' and *also was offering to the eternal Father" (Marialis cultus*, 20; cited according to the Vatican translation, *To Honour Mary*).

17. Wesley quotes the sentence in, for example, his sermon

"The General Spread of the Gospel" (*Works*, VI, 281) and his sermon "On Working Out Our Own Salvation" (*Works*, VI, 513). Outler alleges the influence upon Wesley of the Eastern notion of *synthelesis*, humanity's willing one will with God (*John Wesley*, p. 14). In the Minutes of Wesley's Second Conference (1745), Question 23 asks: "Wherein may we come to the very edge of Calvinism?" And the Answer is: "(1) In ascribing all good to the free grace of God, (2) in denying all natural free will and all power antecedent to grace, and (3) in *excluding all merit from man, even for what he has or does by the grace of God*" (*Works*, VIII, 285).

18. See H. Lindström, *Wesley and Sanctification* (1946); R. N. Flew, *The Idea of Perfection in Christian Theology* (1934), pp. 313-41; and the perceptive introduction to *A Rapture of Praise*, hymns of John and Charles Wesley selected, arranged, and introduced by H. A. Hodges and A. M. Allchin (both Anglicans) (1966), in particular pp. 18-30. Wesley's *Plain Account of Christian Perfection* appears in his *Works*, XI, 366ff. Wesley said of "full sanctification": "This doctrine is the grand depositum which God has lodged with the people called Methodists; and for the sake of propagating this chiefly He appears to have raised us up" (Letter of September 15, 1790 to Robert Carr Brackenbury; *Letters*, ed. J. Telford, VIII, 238).

19. "Mary's immaculate state is a redemption by way of exception or immunity" (Schillebeeckx, p. 66).

20. The fullest study is A. S. Yates, *The Doctrine of Assurance, with special reference to John Wesley* (1952). Yates shows that while there may be exegetical difficulties with regard to the rare New Testament word *plērophoría*, "full assurance" (Col. 2:2; 1 Thess. 1:5; Heb. 6:11; 10:22), yet the substance of Wesley's teaching on assurance and the witness of the Spirit is scriptural. The *tone* of Wesley's doctrine of assurance is set by his own account of his "evangelical conversion": "In the evening I went very unwillingly to a society in Aldersgate Street, where one was reading Luther's preface to the *Epistle to the Romans*. About a quarter before nine, while he was describing the change which God works in the heart through faith in Christ, I felt my heart strangely warmed. I felt I did trust in Christ, Christ alone for my salvation; and an assurance was given me that He had taken away *my* sins, even *mine*, and saved *me* from the law of sin and death" (*Journal*, May 24, 1738; note the words "felt," "warmed," "trust," "assurance"). Wesley's assurance is of *present* salvation, and does not exclude "falling away."

21. Wesley distinguishes between the *direct* witness of the Holy Spirit within us and the *indirect* testimony which we may infer from the fruit of the Spirit in our lives and which expresses itself in a good conscience toward God.

22. "We feel a special confidence in her as our merciful Mother" (R. Laurentin, *Mary's Place in the Church* [1965], p. 148; ET of *La*

question mariale [1963]). Schillebeeckx talks of the persistent sense of being "children of Mary" and says "Mary is the *dulcedo*, the sweetness in Christianity" (pp. 142-44).

23. *Mary's Place in the Church*, pp. 75f.

24. For the "maternal" quality of God's love, Schillebeeckx quotes Jeremiah 31:3; Hosea 11:1f.; Isaiah 49:15f.

25. Letter to James Hervey, March 20, 1739 (*Letters*, ed. Telford, I, 286).

26. See Schillebeeckx, pp. 180-82, who uses approvingly of Mary the title "suppliant omnipotence."

27. See P. S. Watson, *The Message of the Wesleys*, pp. 57f.; H. Bett, *The Spirit of Methodism*, pp. 200-36; F. Baker, *A Charge to Keep* (1947), pp. 149-76.

28. *Works*, V, 296=*Standard Sermons*, ed. Sugden, I, 382; *Works*, XIV, 321=Preface to *Hymns and Sacred Poems* (1739).

29. The phrase is from *Marialis cultus*, 37.

30. See G. Miegge, *La Vergine Maria* (1950; ET *The Virgin Mary* [1955]).

31. The Reformers held that "Holy Scripture contains all things necessary to salvation." On the complicated question of the relations between Jesus, Scripture, tradition, the ecclesiastical magisterium, and the individual believer, see my articles "Scripture and tradition: a systematic sketch," in *Church Quarterly* 3 (1970-71), 17-28, and "The New Testament as canon," in *Scottish Journal of Theology* 28 (1975), 551-71.

32. The fullest study of Wesley's doctrine is J. Deschner, *Wesley's Christology* (1960).

33. At about five in the morning on the day of his conversion, Wesley opened the Scriptures at 2 Peter 1:4: "There are given unto us exceeding great and precious promises, even that ye should be partakers of the divine nature" (*Journal*, May 24, 1738).

34. R. Laurentin recognizes the link between this Reformation principle and the Protestant attitude toward Mary (*Mary's Place in the Church*, pp. 117-27).

35. *The Poetical Works of John and Charles Wesley*, ed. G. Osborn, VII, 81. The verse is used in J. A. Kay's excellent selection, *Wesley's Prayers and Praises* (1958).

36. "Maria—Typus der Kirche und Typus der Menschheit," in L. Vischer, *Ökumenische Skizzen* (1972), pp. 109-23.

37. I am here insisting that Mary should be seen "ecclesiotypically" rather than "christotypically." In Roman Catholic thought, the identification between Christ and the Church is often so close that the "christotypical" and the "ecclesiotypical" merge. In its understanding of the image of Christ as the Head, Protestantism distinguishes Christ from the Church as its Lord and Judge; and would want to keep Mary, with the Church, firmly on the side of the redeemed (as distinct from the Redeemer), the servant (as distinct from the Lord).

38. I do not think Methodists would show much sympathy with the following passage from Harvey Cox's *The Seduction of the Spirit: the use and misuse of people's religion* (1974): "One refreshing thing about Mariology is that learning from it takes us completely away from our obsession with true-or-false games. ... Mary is so obviously an aggregate of human fantasy, myth making, projection and all the rest that it seems beside the point to worry about whether she really was conceived immaculately, is Theotokos, or went bodily to heaven. When we talk about God, Christ, even the 'death of God', we are still often stuck at the level of what we can 'believe' or 'not believe'. But Mary, as always, is easier on us. ... Mary is myth *par excellence*. She permits us, therefore, in a way that Jesus cannot, to find a radically different *modus* for approaching her. With Mary we may, indeed *must*, become mythic and symbolic if we are to approach her, whereas with Christ the belief-unbelief axis still tempts us. Appreciating Marian piety forces us to shift into another religious epistemology; Mary allows us to plumb again, in ourselves and in our cultural unconscious, that psychic sector which lies dormant but not dead beneath our overdeveloped cognitive intelligence" (pp. 182-84).

39. *Mary's Place in the Church*, pp. 53-81.

40. *The Poetical Works of John and Charles Wesley*, XIII, 101=*A Collection of Hymns for the Use of the People called Methodists* (1780/1877), no. 413.

CHAPTER ELEVEN

1. On the practical tensions, despite the ideal correspondence, between truth and unity, see C. W. Williams, *John Wesley's Theology Today* (1960), pp. 207ff.

2. D. Bonhoeffer, *No Rusty Swords: Letters, Lectures and Notes 1928-1936* (1965), pp. 86-118.

3. Entry in John Wesley's *Journal* for March 25, 1743.

4. *Journal*, February 19, 1761.

5. In his Sermon CVII, "On God's Vineyard" (1787-89), Wesley refers to "the body of people commonly called Methodists" as "that Society ... which began at Oxford in the year 1729, and remains united at this day."

6. The "Rules of the United Societies" (1743)—from which come the quotation in the text and the next following it—define a society as "a company of men having the form and seeking the power of godliness, united in order to pray together, to receive the word of exhortation, and to watch over one another in love, that they may help each other to work out their salvation."

7. See A. C. Outler, "Do Methodists have a doctrine of the Church?" in D. Kirkpatrick (ed.), *The Doctrine of the Church* (1964), pp. 11-28, in particular p. 18.

8. To the very end, "I live and die a member of the Church of England" ("Farther Thoughts on Separation from the Church,"

written December 11, 1789 and published in the *Arminian Magazine*, April 1790).

9. See Williams, pp. 230f.

10. See F. Baker, *John Wesley and the Church of England* (1970), p. 311: "Dr Coke puts me in mind of a German proverb, which I may apply to himself and to myself. 'He skips like a flea; I creep like a louse.' He would tear all from top to bottom. I will not tear, but unstitch."

11. For Wesley's own death as the most precise date of Methodism's separation from the Church of England, see R. Kissack, *Church or No Church? The Development of the Concept of Church in British Methodism* (1964), p. 71.

12. J. M. Turner, "From Society to Church," in *London Quarterly and Holborn Review* 188 (1963), 110-15.

13. At the Conference of 1766 Wesley declared that Methodist preaching services were intended to *supplement* the public prayer of the Church and its celebration of the Lord's Supper (see Williams, p. 213). Note also Wesley's Sermon CIV, "On Attending the Church Service" (1788).

14. On Methodism's "self-confidence," see Kissack, pp. 68-95.

15. The Methodist reaction against the Oxford Movement and later Anglo-Catholicism may sometimes have been overemphasized by historians, but the anti-Puseyism of the 1840s was real enough (see J. Kent, *The Age of Disunity* [1966], pp. 56, 138). Nor should one ignore Methodism's difficulties with a resurgent (Calvinist) Evangelicalism in the Church of England.

16. C. J. Bertrand, "Le méthodisme, 'province' méconnue de la communion anglicane?" in *Aspects de l'Anglicanisme: Colloque de Strasbourg 14-16 juin 1972* (1974), pp. 103-22.

17. For hints that some Methodists, including Wesley himself, toyed with the idea that Wesley and perhaps others might be made "itinerant bishops," see F. Hunter, *John Wesley and the Coming Comprehensive Church* (1968), chaps. 7 and 8; see also Baker, pp. 279f.

18. See Bertrand's own remarks, pp. 119ff.

19. Admittedly, Stevens had a peculiar view of the apostolic age and of the "coming great Church," ignoring all the problems of "denominationalism": "Members of any denomination, or of none, can enter the spiritual Church which [Wesley] organized, provided they possess the necessary moral qualifications. 'One condition,' he continues, 'and one only, is required—a real desire to save their souls. Where this is, it is enough; they desire no more. They lay stress upon nothing else. They ask only, Is thy heart herein as my heart? If it be, give me thy hand.' Such was Wesley's 'United Society', such the Church of Methodism; and as such, is it not a reproduction of the Church of the Apostolic age, and a type of 'the Church of the future'?" (Abel Stevens, *History of Methodism*, II [1861], 353).

20. Workman's essay, under the title "The place of Methodism in the life and thought of the Christian Church," first appeared in W. J. Townsend, H. B. Workman, and G. Eayrs (eds.), *A New History of Methodism*, I (1909), 1-73. A revised edition, under the new title, was published separately in 1921. He wrote: "Unfortunately the dogmatism of certain theologians renders it necessary for us to claim that Methodism has a place in the development of the kingdom of God, and, so far as we can judge from existing phenomena, forms part of His divine plan. . . . No larger reunion is possible which either implicitly or explicitly ignores the *fact* of a [Methodist] Church which is today the largest Protestant Church in the world, with the possible exception of the Lutherans." Outdated triumphalism? Or a still necessary reminder?

21. The British union of 1932 brought together Wesleyan, Primitive, and United Methodists (the latter dating from a union of 1907). See Kent, pp. 1-43.

22. To be fair, the Bradford statement immediately continues: "It is their duty to make common cause in the search for the perfect expression of that unity and holiness which in Christ are already theirs."

23. H. A. Snyder, *The Radical Wesley and Patterns for Church Renewal* (1980), p. 151.

24. Wesley would certainly not have allowed a "spiritualizing" distinction between a "visible" and an "invisible" Church as a way of evading the concrete problems of disunity. In his confrontation with Calvinism, Wesley could admit a distinction between "the outward, visible church" and "the invisible church, which consists of holy believers" (*Predestination calmly considered* [1752], § 71). But his more characteristic usage (as in *An Earnest Appeal to Men of Reason and Religion* [1743], §§ 76-78) took the visibility and invisibility of the Church as referring respectively to its *assembled* and *scattered* existence. This needs to be borne in mind even in the "holy believers" definition he gives to Bishop Challoner: "Such is the Catholic Church, . . . the whole body of men, endued with faith working by love, dispersed over the whole earth, in Europe, Asia, Africa, and America." For Wesley, even the "spiritual" Church remains visible by word and sacraments; and his views on the gravity of "separation" reveal how evangelically intolerable for him was all disunity which could not fail to have an institutional manifestation. For further elaboration, see sections III and IV.

25. C. W. Williams and A. C. Outler appear to have popularized the "ecclesiola in Ecclesia" account of Methodism. They personally are to be absolved of all denominational complacency in its use.

26. Williams, p. 216.

27. N. P. Williams and C. Harris (eds.), in particular pp. 515-31.

28. A. C. Outler, *John Wesley* (1964), p. 306. That Wesley tended

to look on his traveling preachers as such an order is apparent from his address to the 1769 Conference (see Williams, pp. 214f.). It is a broadening of the idea to let it include all Methodists; but from the viewpoint of social organization, Michael Hill does in fact argue that early Methodism had "a status close to that of a religious order in the Church of England." See "Methodism as a Religious Order: A Question of Categories," in M. Hill (ed.), *A Sociological Yearbook of Religion in Britain,* VI (1973), 91-99.

29. As in note 7.

30. J. M. Todd, *John Wesley and the Catholic Church* (1958), in particular p. 12. This sounds like a "vestigia ecclesiae" understanding of non-Roman Christianity. While that view probably remains dominant even in Vatican II, A. Dulles has shown that the conciliar documents open up other approaches too: "The Church, the Churches, and the Catholic Church," in *Theological Studies* 33 (1972), 199-234.

31. F. Frost, "Méthodisme," in G. Jacquement (ed.), *Catholicisme, hier, aujourd'hui, demain* (1948ff.), Vol. IX, cols. 48-71.

32. This or a similar phrase occurs in several places, for example, the Minutes of the 1763 Conference.

33. Letter of March 20, 1739 to James Hervey.

34. Kissack, in particular pp. 89-95, 142-46.

35. E. G. Rupp, "The future of the Methodist tradition," in *London Quarterly and Holborn Review* 184 (1959), 264-74.

36. Sermon LXXV, "On Schism" (1786).

37. *A Farther Appeal to Men of Reason and Religion* (1744-45), III.4.6. The Catholic John Todd comments: "What seems so admirable about this passage is its serenity, from a man who certainly did believe that the Catholic Church was grossly in the wrong in his own time on fundamental points of doctrine" (pp. 180f.). In other places, Wesley allows that the Reformers were "thrust out" (see, e.g., Sermon CIV, "On Attending the Church Service").

38. A. C. Outler, *That the World may believe: A study of Christian unity and what it means for Methodists* (1966), in particular p. 64.

39. A. C. Outler, *The Christian Tradition and the Unity we seek* (1957). The distinctly theological motivation of ecumenism must be maintained in face of such a sociologically reductionist account of the reunion of British Methodism as R. Currie, *Methodism Divided: A Study in the Sociology of Ecumenicalism* (1968).

40. "The discovery of our total Christian past is the means of fuller initiation into the whole Christian family" (Outler, as in note 39, p. 41).

41. Belgium and Pakistan are voluntary, though small, exceptions.

42. Outler (as in note 39), p. 22.

43. Outler (as in note 28), pp. vii-xii.

44. Williams, pp. 5-10.

45. Todd, pp. 182f., 192.

46. Sermon XXXIV, "Catholic Spirit" (1749-50); over lesser matters, Wesley is prepared to "talk of them, if need be, at a more convenient season." See also the letter of July 3, 1756 to James Clark.

47. See Outler (as in note 28), p. 92. On "opinions" as distinguished from "essentials," see Williams, pp. 13-22; and J. Newton, "The Ecumenical Wesley," in *The Ecumenical Review* 24 (1972), 160-75.

48. Letter of July 18, 1749 (text in Outler, *John Wesley*, pp. 492-99).

49. See Outler (as in note 28), p. 92; see also letter of July 3, 1756 to James Clark.

50. Sermon LXXV, "On Schism" (1786).

51. *Journal*, February 19, 1761.

52. Letter of May 22, 1750 to Gilbert Boyce.

53. Ibid.

54. Under Non-Juror influence, the earlier Wesley favored the (re)baptism of Germans and Dissenters who had not received "episcopal" baptism. As late as October 21, 1738, an entry in Charles Wesley's *Journal* shows John to have taken up a stricter position than the Bishop of London on this point. See Hunter, chaps. 2 and 5.

55. On the "foreign reformed churches," see the Minutes of the 1747 Conference (Williams, p. 221).

56. To Bishop Challoner he countered: "*Whatever may be the case of some particular souls*, it must be said, if your own marks be true, the Roman Catholics in general, are not 'the people of God' " (letter of February 19, 1761). Yet Sermon LXXIV, "Of the Church" (1786), § 19, appears to consider the Church of Rome as "a part of the catholic Church"; see also above, at note 3.

57. Letter of May 22, 1750 to Gilbert Boyce.

58. See Sermon CIV, "On Attending the Church Service" (1788).

59. *Journal*, January 11, 1750.

60. Sermon CVI, "On Faith" (1788).

61. J. M. Todd shows that Wesley mistook the Roman Catholic doctrine of "intention" for one of "worthiness," but that Wesley then defended the *true* Roman (anti-Donatist) doctrine against his own misunderstanding of it (pp. 149, 175f.)!

62. The date is early and the context is autobiographical; but what Wesley thus wrote in a letter to his father on December 10, 1734 concerning the incumbency of Epworth, he undoubtedly held to throughout his ministry as universally applicable.

63. See Outler (as in note 28), pp. 177-80 for the Rules of the United Societies.

64. For "the congregation of English believers," see the Min-

utes of the 1744 Conference (Williams, p. 208); see also *An Earnest Appeal to Men of Reason and Religion* (1743), § 76.

65. See Sermon CXV, "The Ministerial Office" (1789). For further references to Constantine in Wesley, see Snyder, pp. 80-82, 95f.

66. Minutes of the 1747 Conference (Williams, p. 222).

67. On this, see Hunter, chap. 2.

68. See, for example, letter of July 3, 1756 to James Clark.

69. Letter of April 19, 1764 to "various clergymen."

70. Williams, pp. 154f.; see also pp. 16-20.

71. Letter of June 25, 1746 to "John Smith."

72. See R. E. Cushman, "Baptism and the Family of God," in D. Kirkpatrick (ed.), *The Doctrine of the Church* (1964), pp. 79-102; B. G. Holland, *Baptism in Early Methodism* (1970). Wesley might have done well to take with permanent theological seriousness the advice of Tomo-chacki, the American Indian in Georgia: "We would not be made Christians as the Spaniards make Christians: we would be taught before we are baptized" (Todd, p. 67).

73. Composite quotation from D. N. Power, "The basis for official ministry in the Church," in *The Jurist* 41 (1981), 314-42, and *Gifts that differ* (1980).

74. Sermon CXV, "The Ministerial Office" (1789).

75. See the Minutes of the 1747 Conference (Williams, p. 222).

76. "The uninterrupted succession I know to be a fable, which no man ever did or can prove" (letter of August 19, 1785 to Charles Wesley).

77. On "accidental variations" in church government, see the Minutes of the 1747 Conference (Williams, p. 222).

78. Faith and Order Paper No. 91, reprinted from *The Ecumenical Review* 31 (1979), 77-93.

79. For the ecumenical dimensions of authority, see the work of the British Methodist R. E. Davies, *Religious Authority in an Age of Doubt* (1968).

80. See Commission on Faith and Order Lima 1982, *Towards Visible Unity*, I (Faith and Order Paper No. 112 [1982]), 89-100; II (No. 113), 28-46.

81. A. D. Falconer, "Contemporary attitudes to the papacy," in *The Furrow* 27 (1976), 3-19.

82. G. E. Moede, in *Journal of Ecumenical Studies* 12 (1975), 367-88.

83. For the New Delhi definition, see, for example, L. Vischer (ed.), *A Documentary History of the Faith and Order Movement 1927-1963* (1963), pp. 144ff. On the complexities of "place," see the WCC publication *In Each Place: Towards a Fellowship of Local Churches Truly United* (1977).

84. See Frost, col. 70.

85. Frost, col. 70.

86. In the Preface to his *Notes on the Old Testament*, for ex-

ample, Wesley writes of "the analogy of faith, the connexion and harmony there is between those grand fundamental doctrines, original sin, justification by faith, the new birth, inward and outward holiness" (*Works*, XIV, 253).

87. Outler (as in note 28), pp. 3-33; see also his *Theology in the Wesleyan Spirit* (1975), and "The Place of Wesley in the Christian Tradition," in K. E. Rowe (ed.), *The Place of Wesley in the Christian Tradition* (1976), pp. 11-38.

88. Maximin Piette, *La réaction wesléyenne dans l'évolution protestante* (1925; ET *John Wesley in the Evolution of Protestantism* [1937; repr. 1979]).

89. Todd, p. 183.

90. T. Runyon (ed.), *Sanctification and Liberation* (1981).

91. H. Meyer, " 'Einheit in versöhnter Verschiedenheit'— 'konziliare Gemeinschaft'—'organische Union': Gemeinsamkeit und Differenz gegenwärtig diskutierter Einheitskonzeptionen," in *Oekumenische Rundschau* 27 (1978), 377-400.

92. Kissack, especially pp. 113f., 131-34, 148-59.

93. Kent, pp. 193-206.

94. Kissack, p. 130.

95. Bertrand, p. 121.

96. Outler (as in note 38), p. 54.

97. Outler (as in note 38), pp. 74f.

98. Outler (as in note 7), p. 28.

LIST OF SOURCES

Chapter I was written for this volume.

Chapter II was given under the title "The Holy Spirit in the Life of the Church" as a lecture at the celebration by the Greek Orthodox Archdiocese of North and South America of the sixteen-hundredth anniversary of the First Ecumenical Council of Constantinople, May 1981. It is here published for the first time.

Chapter III is based on a lecture to the international congress of Societas Liturgica at Canterbury, England, in August 1977. First published as "Christian Initiation in the Ecumenical Movement" in *Studia Liturgica* 12 (1977), 67-86, it has now been revised in light of the final text produced by the WCC Commission on Faith and Order at Lima, Peru, in January 1982: *Baptism, Eucharist, and Ministry* (Geneva: WCC, 1982).

Chapter IV was given in Rome during the celebration of the Holy Year of 1975. As "The Eucharist as an Ecumenical Sacrament of Reconciliation and Renewal," it appeared in *Studia Liturgica* 11 (1976), 1-18.

Chapter V was presented to a meeting of the Conference of European Churches in Sofia, Bulgaria, in October 1977 and was published as "Conciliarity and Eucharist" in *One in Christ* 14 (1978), 30-49, and in *Midstream* 17 (1978), 135-53.

Chapter VI is based on a lecture to the international congress of Societas Liturgica in Washington, D.C., in August 1979. The present text is a slightly revised version of "Theological Aspects of Ordination" from *Studia Liturgica* 13 (1979), 125-52.

Chapter VII was presented to the Society for the Study of Theology at York, England, in April 1979. It first appeared in *Queen's Essays*, the sesquicentennial volume of The Queen's College, Birmingham, England, 1980.

Chapter VIII figured as "Between God and World: The Worship and Mission of the Church" in K. Stevenson (ed.), *Liturgy Reshaped* (London: SPCK, 1982), pp. 94-108.

Chapter IX was published as "Revolution and Quietism: Two Political Attitudes in Theological Perspective" in *The Scottish Journal of Theology* 29 (1976), 535-55. It follows a presentation to a seminar on church and state relations at the School of Oriental and African Studies, University of London.

Chapter X modifies a lecture on "Mary in relation to the Doctrinal and Spiritual Emphases of Methodism" given to the Ecumenical Society of the Blessed Virgin Mary and published in *One in Christ* 11 (1975), 121-44.

Chapter XI is printed here for the first time. As "Methodism's Ecclesical Location and Ecumenical Vocation" it was delivered to the Oxford Institute of Methodist Theological Studies, Keble College, Oxford, August 1982.

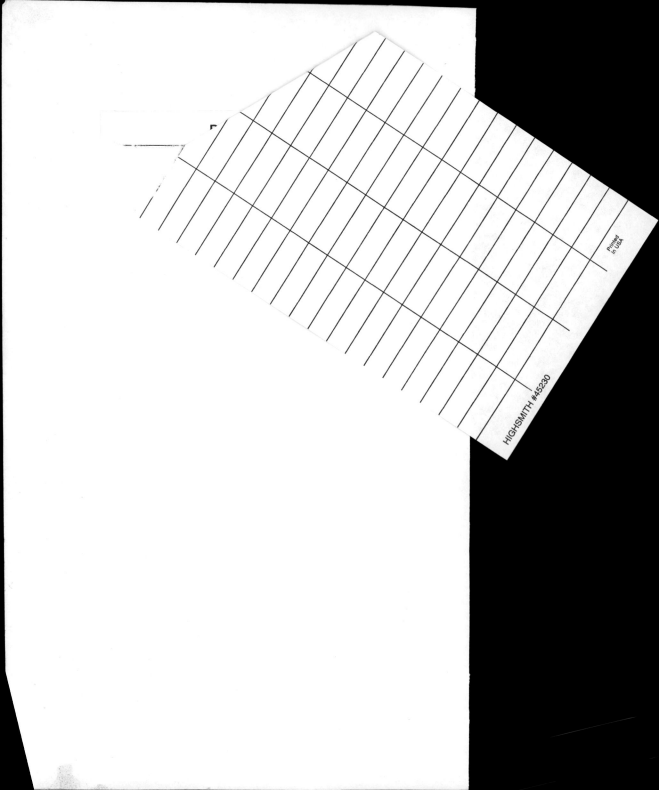